Semantics and Syntactic Regularity

SEMANTICS
AND SYNTACTIC
REGULARITY

GEORGIA M. GREEN

INDIANA UNIVERSITY PRESS

Bloomington & London

Published in Canada by Fitzhenry & Whiteside Limited, Don Mills, Ontario

Manufactured in the United States of America

Library of Congress Cataloging in Publication Data

Green, Georgia M
    Semantics and syntactic regularity.

    Bibliography: p. 230
    1. Grammar, Comparative and general—Verb.   2. Semantics.
3. Grammar, Comparative and general—Syntax.
I. Title.
P281.G68   1974   415   74-9947
ISBN 0-253-35160-X

Table of Contents

Tables

Acknowledgements

Although a public statement of gratitude is small thanks for the support and encouragement I have received in the writing of this thesis, I am glad for the opportunity to express my gratefulness to all of the people who helped me to get the ideas out of my head and onto paper in linear form. I shall always be grateful to Professor James D. McCawley, who supervised my work, for turning me on to syntax and to semantic arguments, and for his doubts of incomplete arguments in earlier drafts and his patience with them. I am also in debt to George and Robin Lakoff for their work on exceptions and governed rules which led to the raising of the central issue of this work. I am particularly grateful to George Lakoff for encouraging me in getting started, and for his thoughtful criticisms of this and earlier versions. They have permitted me to gain needed perspective and insight on several important issues. Part of this work, particularly in chapters 2 and 3, was supported by Grant GS-2939 from the National Science Foundation to the University of Michigan.

I must also thank Jerrold Sadock for the encouragement he gave me in all stages of the writing. Several other linguists deserve mention too. I am grateful to Alice Davison, Laurence Horn, Jerry L. Morgan, and Paul Neubauer, for the intellectual ferment which their perceptive comments and supporting and disconfirming data kept going.

This work is dedicated to the memory of my father, Lester V. Marks. He would have enjoyed linguistics.

Georgia M. Green

Urbana, Illinois
April 1972

Semantics and Syntactic Regularity

I Introduction

A Philosophical orientation
Why this is worth my writing and your reading even though I couldn't accomplish everything I set out to accomplish.

1 Classification and explanation
It is a tantalizing idea that one's own language – the very same language one uses to court his spouse, bawl out his children, and explain the nature of things to his parents – is a systematic structure, and that there are in general, for particular linguistic facts, explanations which follow in a natural way from other facts, both particular and general. The promise and challenge of explanation has converted skeptical mathematics and chemistry majors, and downright hostile language majors to the study of linguistics, even during times when the search for explanations was held to be off-limits, as "unscientific."

Many of us can remember a certain amount of awe at hearing that one reason for the difficulty an adult has in learning to speak without an "accent" in a foreign language is that he has to learn to make combinations of sounds which "cannot occur" in his native language, as well as learning new sounds and new conditions for alternations. Finding reason and order where we thought there was only chaos seemed like a pleasant enough way to spend one's time, and so, we thought, if we would just apply ourselves diligently enough, we could discover all the generalizations which characterize various languages, and which distinguish natural languages from artificial languages.

But, much more often than not, the generalizations proved to be as elusive as butterflies. It seemed that for every reasonably well-justified hypothesis there would always be some forms it failed to predict, or it would predict forms which never occurred, or both. This situation is as old as science. In linguistics, one response to it was to conclude that language is by nature arbitrary, that there is no generalization, and that it is wrong to insist on looking for one where none exists. Exemplifying this attitude is the following comment by Joos (1966:96) on Bloch's

1

"Phonemic Overlapping" (Bloch 1941), an article which describes one such situation in all of its gory detail:

An older term for the new trend in linguistics was "structural." It is not idle to consider how the term "descriptive" now came to replace it, even if not all the reasons can be identified. The Sapir way of doing things could be called structural, but the term was more often used for the stimulating new ideas that were coming out of Europe, specifically from the Cercle Linguistique de Prague. American linguistics owes a great debt to that stimulation; but in the long run those ideas were not found to add up to an adequate methodology. Trubetzkoy phonology tried to explain everything from articulatory acoustics and a minimum set of phonological laws taken as essentially valid for all languages alike, flatly contradicting the American (Boas) tradition that languages could differ from each other without limit and in unpredictable ways, and offering too much of a phonological *explanation* where a sober taxonomy would serve as well.

Children want explanations, and there is a child in each of us; descriptivism makes a virtue of not pampering that child.

Given this attitude, the task of the linguist is to discover and describe the "structure of the language on its own terms." To do this, he must keep his mind free of expectations regarding what sorts of relations may occur among the elements he is dealing with. "Linguistics," Hockett says, "is a classificatory science" (Hockett [1942:3]). The goal of the linguist was to classify all of the forms of the language – or in practice, all the forms of a given corpus, since it was not assumed that a description should predict the occurrence of forms the linguist happened not to hear. The only way the linguist could claim that his representation of the facts was correct was by claiming that he had followed the proper procedures for discovery, since it was assumed that the proper procedures guaranteed correct results – thus Joos' concern with adequate method.

Another response to apparent exceptions to a hypothesis was to assume that the generalization is there all right, but that the investigator has not been looking in the right places for it, or that there is more going on than meets the eye. From this point of view, the linguist's task is to find the generalization(s) by whatever means he can. Far from denying the relevance of his experience with other languages, and his intuitions about what might be natural in language, he cultivates his intuition, fertilizing it with as many correctly-stated, unfalsified generalizations as he can keep track of about as many languages as he can control, and he remains aware all the while that there may be types of conditioning factors of which he is not yet aware. He dares not put complete trust in his intuition, of course, for it may be skewed by systematic and asystematic gaps in the languages he knows well, but he lets it serve him as a sort of junior partner in the formulating and testing of precise hypotheses, which is his method of operating.

In this approach, the linguist's guiding principle is the *a priori* assumption that even where there appears to be only chaos, there are indeed generalizations lurking beneath the surface which make order of it. This may be characterized as an extreme position, and it is precisely in its extremism that its strength lies. In saying, "there are generalizations there; if you look hard enough, you will see them," it forces the investigator to work through the data forwards and backwards, inside-out, and upside-down, from various angles, and through various lenses until the generalizations are revealed.

It is sometimes objected that this position denies "what everybody knows to be a fact," that there are irregularities and suppletions in natural language, and that that is one of the characteristics which distinguish it from artificial languages. Certainly there are unique cases – morphology is full of them. But there is a real and sensible distinction between these fossils of formerly active regular alternations and other items which have been called irregularities. Children and other foreigners have difficulty learning the irregularities in inflectional paradigms – you can correct them, scold them, threaten and cajole them, and they still say *goed* for *went* and *seed* for *saw* – but no one ever has to be told that *have* does not have a passive.[1]

2 *Is it the language at fault, or the linguist?*

Real linguistic exceptions, as opposed to putative exceptions, can be characterized in linguistic terms. Real exceptions are a source of difficulty

---

[1] To my knowledge, a passive form of *have* appears in English in only two expressions. One, *a good time was had by all*, seems to be a facetious fixed phrase, not learned actively by children until they have been fluent speakers for five or ten years. The other, the idiom *to have been had*, occurs only as a passive, and apparently only in inflected forms:

    1a. I've been had.
    1b. You've been had.
    1c. He's been had.

    2a. *They had him.
    2b. *The con man had him.

    3a. *He expects to have been had.
    3b. *He is likely to have been had.
    3c. *He is known to have been had.
    3d. *He's going to be had.

It also is learned rather late.

to learners of a language, and *because* they are exceptions to the rules of that language. Real exceptions are subject to analogical regularization and, consequently, to dialectal variation and diachronic change. When new lexical items come into a language, exceptional syntactic properties will not be reflected in their syntactic behavior. Real exceptions are a subclass – the only linguistically significant subclass – of all putative exceptions. Putative exceptions are merely what cannot be reduced to consequences of generalizations motivated by other facts. They are characterized in negative terms, and in logical terms, not in linguistic terms.

From this point of view, every putative exception to a generalization is an admission of failure. The exceptions to a linguist's hypothesis or theory are explicitly what he has not been able to explain by it. If he cannot show that they are real exceptions or consequences of other phenomena, he must resort to merely entering them in a list which stands out as a monument to the vulnerability of his theory. This vulnerability is not to be confused with weakness, but the metaphor is apt: a vulnerable hypothesis is one that has precise form and substance. It can be attacked in specific places, and it stands or falls depending on whether the attacks strike vital or only superficial coverings. A list of putative exceptions is the blood of a wounded theory. But implicit in a list of real exceptions there are several sorts of claims: that the list embodies no generalization, that the items on it can be a source of difficulty in learning the language, that they are subject to dialectal variation and change through time, and that new lexical items coming into the language will not behave like them. Because lists of exceptions do imply claims of this nature, they are potentially just as vulnerable as the generalizations they are exceptions to. They make predictions, and those predictions can and should be tested with all the adequate tests we can devise.

This points up the crucial difference between explanatory grammar and classificatory grammar, because a classificatory grammar consists of an arrangement of lists. Suppose that someone should succeed in writing a classificatory grammar of English, consisting of lists of items which were completely homogeneous in terms of syntactic properties.[1] What claims would it make other than that the sets enumerated by the lists existed? What would it tell us about the nature of English as distinct from other languages, or about characteristics of natural language?

[1] I doubt that this is possible, but just suppose.

What would it predict about the ability of native speakers to create and pass judgment on wholly novel utterances, to tell whether a putative utterance belongs to their language? In short, what would save such a classificatory grammar from what a movie reviewer recently termed "the great 'so what?'"

3 First aid for flesh wounds

Suppose, on the other hand, that a linguist takes as a working hypothesis the perhaps quixotic position that the distribution of linguistic forms is governed by an exceptionless set of general rules.[1] What can he do when one of his specific hypotheses is confronted by the inevitable counter-examples? If the counterexamples are genuine,[2] he has no choice but to consider the hypothesis incorrect as it stands. If it is incapable of modification in a non-*ad hoc* way, it should be abandoned, buried, and left in peace. But if the theory seems basically correct in spite of the putative counterinstances,[3] and the linguist wishes to retain it, he is obliged to look elsewhere for regularities which will account for the exceptions to his rule.[4] This is, I think everyone will agree, a lifetime project, and one not very likely to succeed 100 per cent at that. Each hypothesis generates putative exceptions which generate more hypotheses which generate more putative exceptions, and so on. Eventually, it is hoped, principles will be discovered which will account for the apparent exceptions to several rules at once, and things will become easier, but in the meantime, what? If it is wrong for a linguist to publish research which fails to explain completely everything it was intended to explain, it will have to be considered wrong for him to publish whatever claims and results he has until he can exceptionlessly account for a portion of grammar or maybe even of human behavior in general which is likely to be several times larger than what his original plan called

---

[1] These might be of a grammatical nature, a psychological nature, a logical nature, a physiological nature, or possibly a mixture, or of some other nature. The point is that they be *general* (non-trivial *all*-statements) and *testable*.

[2] For example, if the counterexamples are classes of grammatical forms which his theory predicts are ungrammatical, or if they represent classes of ungrammatical forms which his theory predicts are well-formed, and which are not ruled out by any independently motivated principles.

[3] For example, if they are classes of grammatical forms which the theory fails to predict.

[4] This was, of course, just the attitude of the neo-grammarians, who proposed that 'every exception to the rules prevailing in language must have a cause' (Pedersen 1931:292).

for. And in the meantime, those of his colleagues with whom he is not in direct correspondence must remain ignorant of what partial progress he has made, and linguists will be bound to waste time looking down the same blind alleys as their colleagues and predecessors, simply because they won't know what has been tried and has failed.

On the other hand, if he makes public what he believes to be basically correct, and with it, not only the supporting evidence, but also a thorough discussion of what his theory fails to account for, he exposes the problem to his colleagues, one of whom may be able to provide just the fact to explain some or all of the exceptions, or just the fact which provides genuine counterevidence. If the former, then a positive advance has been made; and if the latter, and someone publishes the counterevidence, the hypothesis dies a relatively quick and painless death.[1] And in so far as understanding consists in knowing what will not work, as well as what might work, in either case our understanding of language is increased. Much time and energy is saved if we are able to avoid repeating all the mistaken analyses that have been put forth and destroyed, unknown to us.

From this point of view, when a linguist wishes to maintain a generalization which has exceptions, he is obliged to examine all of the putative exceptions, look for syntactic, semantic, or phonological regularities they might share, and classify and cross-classify them accordingly. If, after a reasonable amount of work, he cannot explain all of the cases which appear to be exceptions, he should present along with his generalization and the evidence supporting it, a discussion of the properties of the apparently exceptional cases, and of possible relations to other facts about language.

B   Linguistic orientation

I   Theoretical frame of reference
This work assumes a generative-transformational theory of grammar, and as background, some familiarity with the conclusions of Chomsky's *Aspects of the Theory of Syntax* (Chomsky 1965). Briefly, these are:

1. That every sentence of a language has a deep structure and a surface structure, and both may be represented as rooted, oriented trees

---

[1] Quick and painless relative to what it would have been if the author had worked for years until he thought he had a complete explanation.

with syntactic categories and grammatical/morphological forms labelling the nodes.

2. That sentences with different meanings[1] have different deep structures.
3. That a grammar contains four systems of rules:
   a. Base rules, which specify what deep structures are possible.
   b. Transformational rules, which convert deep structures, by way of intermediate structures, into corresponding surface structures.
   c. Semantic interpretation rules, which map deep structures into corresponding semantic representations.
   d. Phonological rules, which specify the phonetic representation of surface structures.
4. That the lexicon is part of the base rules. All transformations therefore operate on trees whose terminal nodes are labelled by lexical or grammatical formatives (morphemes).

It has been argued in recent work by G. Lakoff, McCawley, Perlmutter, Postal, Ross, and others, that

1. The distinction between deep structure and semantic representation should be rejected (McCawley 1967b, 1968a, b), making (3c) above unnecessary.
2. The lexicon should be seen as a body of essentially transformational rules which encode transformed semantic deep structures (McCawley 1968c).
3. Grammatical description requires, in addition to rules or conditions defining well-formed deep structures, constraints on derivations (Ross 1967, Postal 1968, G. Lakoff 1969b, 1970, 1971), and constraints on surface structure (Ross 1967, Perlmutter 1968).

These arguments have been accepted here, and will be recapitulated or cited explicitly where relevant. Some familiarity with G. Lakoff 1965 is also assumed.

2 Grammatical, acceptable, appropriate
Early transformational theory assumed that all putative utterances of a language, considered as labelled strings of formatives, could be classified

---

[1] For me, although not necessarily for Chomsky, the criterion of different meanings includes different topic and different focus. It does not include stylistic variation.

unambiguously as either grammatical or ungrammatical – the purpose of a grammar was to generate all and only the grammatical sentences of the language, with correct structural descriptions. Because of many cases where a sentence was well-formed and appropriate if one possible meaning was attributed to it, but word salad (the syntactic counterpart of the semantic ill-formedness of what is called nonsense) if some other meaning was attributed to it, the grammatical–ungrammatical dichotomy was soon found to be inadequate alone. For this reason, many linguists tended to reserve it for indisputable, unambiguous, syntactic well- (or ill-) formedness, or renounce it altogether, designating sentences as acceptable or unacceptable with respect to whatever phenomenon (transformational rule, co-occurrence restriction, selectional restriction, or meaning) they were concerned with. In discussing the theories of other linguists, I will try to use the terms they used. In discussing my own proposals, I will use the words *ungrammatical, unacceptable,* and *inappropriate (peculiar, strange,* etc.) more or less interchangeably, but I will almost always mean "syntactically ill-formed given the assumptions and/or intended meaning as designated." Forms which are ungrammatical, inappropriate, etc. will usually, but not always, be marked with an asterisk. Following Ross (1967), I will occasionally use the symbols [?], [??], and [?*] to indicate subjectively felt degrees of ungrammaticality.

3   Notational conventions

Italicization will distinguish words as lexical items (forms). Single quotes ('...') around ordinary type will mark off lexical items used to indicate meaning – English paraphrases or translations. SMALL CAPITALS will denote putative semantic entities (cf. chapter 2, sec. B.2.*c*) which may or may not be abbreviations for more complex structures of semantic entities. Therefore, not all items in small capitals are putative semantic primes. Small capitals surrounded by double quotes ("...") will indicate semantic units assumed not to be primes. A formal semantic representation will be in the form of a labelled tree, or labelled brackets. Except in numbered examples, informal semantic representations will be indicated by single quotes around items, some or all of which are in small capitals. Such representations may include various "meaningless" forms (e.g. complementizers such as *-ing,* the conjunction *that,* infinitival *to*) which render them more readable.

4 On the representation of meanings

The question of what a lexical item or a putative semantic entity means must remain an empirical (testable) question. I will therefore be as precise as seems necessary in saying which sense of a word I intend, when I am talking about the use of lexical items, and when I use them, capitalized, to represent putative semantic entities. Yet, as Gruber (1967) pointed out, a language may be wanting in lexical items to represent certain semantic structures, or it may have obligatory transformations which always obscure the underlying structure. Therefore, it may sometimes be necessary to propose semantic representations which can be "pronounced" only in a rather distorted English, or to explicitly restrict the meaning of a lexical item used to represent a semantic prime, in a way in which the lexical item is not restricted in its use as a lexical item.

The problem of appropriateness conditions on the use of lexical items, or felicity conditions,[1] is not so easily coped with. Some lexical items may be analyzed into a structure of presuppositions and assertions. These pose no new problem since the presuppositions and assertions can be considered separately. Other lexical items whose use requires the presence of certain presuppositions or assumptions are not so easily decomposable. The use of *try* in non-past tenses with an infinitive complement, for instance, involves an assumption by the speaker of some difficulty for the subject in accomplishing his endeavor. But it is not obvious what is left of *try* once this presupposition is skimmed off. For this reason, when I use lexical items to represent semantic units, it will appear that some semantic entities have felicity conditions. In the absence of statements to the contrary, it may be understood that I assume that semantic entities have the same felicity conditions as the lexical items which I use to represent them, but I do not see how to prove that this must be the case. Because of its second-order abstractness, I am not even certain whether it is an empirical question.

---

[1] Cf. Fillmore 1969. Felicity conditions are roughly conditions which the speaker of a sentence must believe are in effect in order for his speech act to be normal. For example, there is a condition on imperatives like *Open that door* that the door not be already open. More generally, there seems to be a felicity condition that the act requested be logically possible. To take another example, the use of the verb *know* is infelicitous if the speaker believes that the complement of *know* embodies a falsehood, even in such sentences as *John doesn't know that there were really six Beatles*.

2 The relevance of semantics to syntax

A Original goal and scope of this study

My purpose was originally to reanalyze several syntactic phenomena thought to be exceptional, in order to demonstrate the value of assuming that there are reasons for the behavior of most items believed to be exceptions. I expected to be able to present several cases of the syntactic properties of lexical items depending crucially and in regular ways on the meanings of those lexical items, and I believed I would be able to vindicate the traditional grammarians for dealing with syntactic phenomena in semantic terms.[1] Their fault, I felt, was only that they were imprecise, and I thought I had a way to remedy that.

B Why

1 The recent history of exceptions in syntax

When a linguist attempts to write a grammatical description with predictive powers, he soon runs aground against the problem of false predictions. Within transformational grammar, this problem was first encountered in the writing of phrase-structure rules. It takes but a moment's thought to realize that it is impossible, for instance, to introduce all verbs with the same single phrase-structure rule. There are some verbs which may not have complements, i.e. intransitive verbs such as *exist*:

    1. *Unicorns do not exist little boys.

and others, which must have complements, i.e. such transitive verbs as *like*:

    2. *Billy likes.

Still others, such as *pretend*, require sentential complements:

    3a. John pretended that he was in Paris.

    3b. *John pretended Paris.

    3c. *John has pretended.

---

[1] Statements like the following, from Gildersleeve and Lodge (1895), are typical of the traditional grammarians: "Verbs of Will and Desire take *ut* as well as the infinitive" (p. 277); "Verbs of Emotion, such as Rejoicing, Sorrowing, *etc.*, take *quod* with the Indic. or Subjunctive" (p. 329).

a Subcategorization. Writers of early transformational grammars such as Lees (1963) coped with this situation by hierarchically subcategorizing the category "Verb" into smaller, more homogeneous classes, e.g.:

$$Vb \rightarrow \begin{Bmatrix} V_{cop} + Pr \\ V \end{Bmatrix} \qquad V_{tr} \rightarrow \begin{Bmatrix} V_t \\ V_x + P \\ V_T + C \end{Bmatrix}$$

$$V \rightarrow \begin{Bmatrix} \begin{Bmatrix} V_{in} \\ V_{tr} \end{Bmatrix} + Nom \end{Bmatrix} (Man) \qquad V_t \rightarrow \begin{Bmatrix} V_A + Acc \\ V_B + Prt \\ V_{tn} \end{Bmatrix}$$
$$V_{mid} + Nom$$

$$V_{tn} \rightarrow \begin{Bmatrix} V_{t1} \\ V_{t2} \\ V_{t31} \\ V_{t32} \\ \vdots \\ V_{t44} \end{Bmatrix}$$

But when these writers started formalizing transformations which applied to various classes and subclasses of verbs, they found again that their rules made incorrect predictions. *Own, have,* and *possess,* for example, have similar if not identical co-occurrence and selectional restrictions. Yet *own* may be passivized and *possess* and *have* may not:

4a. A little old lady owns this car.
4b. This car is owned by a little old lady.

5a. Mrs Smith now $\begin{Bmatrix} has \\ possesses \end{Bmatrix}$ the Porsche we saw yesterday.

5b. *The Porsche we saw yesterday is now $\begin{Bmatrix} had \\ possessed \end{Bmatrix}$ by Mrs Smith.

Essentially two alternatives were available to the pre-*Aspects* transformational grammarian confronted with difficulties like this. He could assume that such items as *possess* and *have* were real exceptions, and reflected nothing more than the arbitrariness of human language. If he wanted to treat such items as exceptions, he had to write a condition on the application of the rule they were exceptions to. These conditions were usually of the form "does not apply if V = *have, possess, resemble,* etc." or "obligatory if 3 = *rumor, allege,* etc." Or the linguist could assume that grammatical categories and constituent types were defined by the syntactic rules. In this case, the difference in transformational properties of these items would have to be represented as a difference in category or in constituent structure. He would then rewrite his constituent-structure and transformational rules accordingly, so that the structural index of the transformation would not include the classes which contained items to which it would wrongly apply.

Neither of these solutions is really satisfactory. The first "solution" suffers from the inadequacies discussed earlier – it inherently makes the false claim that these items, as exceptions, are not rule-governed, but are learned individually and by correction. Furthermore, treating the exceptions as a part of the rule removes all possibility of universality from the rule, and predicts that it will be a marvelous coincidence if a counterpart to this rule in some other language (e.g. the passive in French or German) has exceptions with meanings corresponding to the meanings of the exceptions to this rule in English. Yet the verbs meaning 'have' and 'want, desire' are transitive in English, French, and German, and may not be passivized in any of these languages. One might want to say that this "coincidence" actually supports a claim of universality for the formulation of the rule which indicates a list of exceptions, since the exceptions in each language are translations of the exceptions in the others. But this means nothing since the exceptional items are individual *lexical* items, not semantic items, and there is nothing in the theory which says that we predict that, given two languages with a rule which in each language operates on the same structural description to produce the same structural change, the translations of the exceptions to that rule in one language will be exceptions in the other language as well. Such a principle would be in fact useless because, as anyone who has ever tried to translate knows, translation is an art, not a science; one cannot predict with any certainty that a word in one language will have a true equivalent in another language, appropriate under the same conditions to describe the same situations, even with closely related languages. A principle based on the notion of translation would be so vague, and its application so dependent on caprice, that it would be untestable, as well as useless.

The second alternative, further subcategorization, is unsatisfactory for a different reason. For one thing, subclassifying verbs by means of rewriting rules requires a hierarchically arranged subdivision of categories. If categories X and Y are subcategories of a class A which is mutually exclusive with a class B, then X and Y may not be rewritten as subcategories of class B. One would have to resort to two other names if two subclasses of B "happened" to have the same properties as X and Y. Yet syntactically relevant verb classes are typically cross-classified rather than hierarchically structured. Thus, to cite a case referred to by Chomsky (1965:79), nouns in English are either common (*boy, city*), or proper (*John, Cambridge*), and either human (*boy, John*) or non-human (*city, Cambridge*). The rule determining relative pronoun choice is sensitive to the human/non-human distinction, cross-cutting the common/proper distinction:

6a. John, who (*which) I visited yesterday, is still polluted.
6b. The red-haired boy, who (*which) I visited yesterday, is still polluted.
6c. Cambridge, which (*who) I visited last week, is still polluted.
6d. The smallest Eastern city, which (*who) I visited last week, is still polluted.

But the use of the definite article is sensitive to the common/proper distinction, and ignores the human/non-human distinction. For instance, proper nouns in English are capable of referring when they are names of specific spatio-temporal entities, but common nouns may be used to refer only by virtue of restrictive relative clauses (which may be reduced or ultimately deleted), which make them into definite descriptions:[1]

7a. John has red hair.
7b. Cambridge is polluted.

[1] Actually, in English, the use of the articles is more closely tied to assumptions about reference than to a purely grammatical property of proper-ness. So we have such expressions as (1):

1. This camera is a Pentax.

parallel to (2):

2. This device is a camera.

Such expressions with definite articles and proper nouns as (3–5):

3. The Cambridge which we have come to know and love is due for some changes.
4. The John I am talking about is not the same as the one you are talking about.
5. The John I am talking about has red hair.

treat the items *Cambridge* and *John* as common nouns. Such items refer only when they have restrictive relative clauses which make them into definite descriptions. Compare the following sentences, where *Cambridge* and *John* are not followed by relative clauses, are not descriptions, and do not refer:

6. The Cambridge is due for some changes.
7. The John has red hair.

7c. *Boy has red hair.

7d. *City is polluted.

8a.   The boy who we were discussing has red hair.

8b.   The boy in question has red hair.

8c.   The boy has red hair.

This is a fact about the use of proper and common nouns in English. In other languages (e.g. Italian, Balkan languages), proper nouns used as names occur with definite articles in many of the same ways that common nouns do.

Another case, cited by Lees (1963:xl), involves the fact that the transitive/intransitive distinction among verbs cross-cuts requirements for animate and inanimate subjects and objects.[1] Some verbs requiring animate subjects are transitive, like *chase*, while others are intransitive, like *leap* and *swim*:

9a.   The cat chased the rabbit across the yard.

9b.   *Chaos chased General Patton across Europe.

9c.   The horse leaped over the fence.

9d.   *The tone arm leaped over a whole band.

9e.   The bird swam after the snake.

9f.   *The tug swam after the freighter.

The same holds for verbs requiring inanimate subjects, such as *entail* (transitive), and *elapse* (intransitive), for verbs which require animate objects such as *cage*, and ones which require inanimate objects such as *prove*. To quote Lees (1963:xl):

Suppose the grammar must distinguish transitive and intransitive verbs, among each of these those with animate subjects and those with inanimate subjects, and finally among the two transitive subtypes those with animate objects and those with inanimate objects. Representing all categories on a tree:

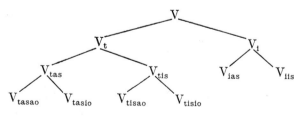

---

[1] Cf. p. 24, n. 1, but the ultimate nature of these requirements does not affect the problem considered here.

The expansion rules required would be:

(1) $V \rightarrow \left\{ \begin{matrix} V_t + NOM \\ V_i \end{matrix} \right\}$

(4) $V_{tas} \rightarrow \left\{ \begin{matrix} V_{tasao} \\ V_{tasio} \end{matrix} \right\}$

(2) $V_t \rightarrow \left\{ \begin{matrix} V_{tas} \\ V_{tis} \end{matrix} \right\}$

(5) $V_{tis} \rightarrow \left\{ \begin{matrix} V_{tisao} \\ V_{tisio} \end{matrix} \right\}$

(3) $V_i \rightarrow \left\{ \begin{matrix} V_{ias} \\ V_{iis} \end{matrix} \right\}$

But clearly rules (2) and (3) specify the same generalization, as do also rules (4) and (5)...

There is no way here to refer to a *class* of verbs requiring animate subjects; one must resort to a conjunction of classes, namely V_{tas} and V_{ias}.

A third example of cross-classification of categories concerns complement types. Whatever the rules are which determine whether a verb has as complement a *that*-clause, an infinitive phrase or clause, or a gerund, they apply to classes of verbs which intersect with the class which is relevant in the determination of *some/any* suppletion in the complement. The "negative" verbs which condition the *some/any* alternation include verbs like *deny* which take *that*-clauses, verbs like *fail* which take infinitive phrases, and verbs like *dislike* which take infinitive clauses or gerunds:

10. John denied (*said) that he had hurt anyone's feelings.

11. John failed (*tried) to impress anyone.

12a. The committee dislikes (*likes) for me to mention any names.

12b. The committee dislikes (*likes) my mentioning any names.

12c. The committee dislikes (*likes) mentioning any names.

b Syntactic features. Chomsky proposed to deal with the problem of cross-classification "and, at the same time [contribute] to the general unity of grammatical theory" (1965:82) by recognizing syntactic features associated with particular lexical formatives which would be similar to the phonological features which are associated with phonological segments ("phonemes"). To do this, he had to introduce into grammatical theory rules such as:

$$N \rightarrow [+N, \pm \text{Animate}, \pm \text{Common}]$$

$$[+\text{Common}] \rightarrow [\pm \text{Count}]$$

$$[-\text{Count}] \rightarrow \begin{bmatrix} \pm \text{Abstract} \\ -\text{Animate} \end{bmatrix}$$

$$[+\text{Animate}] \rightarrow [\pm \text{Human}]$$

which analyzed lexical categories such as Noun into complex symbols consisting each of a set of syntactic features. This was adequate to deal with the simple cross-classification of nouns; one could refer to the class of common nouns by the use of the single feature [+Common] in the complex symbol [+N, +Common], and similarly to the intersecting class of human nouns by the single feature [+Human]. Insertion of lexical items was accomplished by matching lexical formatives to complex symbols whose feature sets were not distinct from the feature sets of the lexical item.

However, a further refinement of the notion Complex Symbol was necessary to deal adequately with the case of selectional restrictions on subjects and objects as sketched above. Whereas the features of nouns were inherent features, selectional restrictions on verbs, it will be recalled, refer to features of nouns in the context in which the verb occurs, so the notion syntactic feature had to be extended from inherent features to include as well contextual features such as [+[+Animate]-Subject] or [+[+N, +Animate] Aux ___].

In addition, feature-rewriting rules of the sort below, parallel to the ones used for features of nouns, would fail to express important generalizations:[1]

(33) (i)
(ii) $V \rightarrow \left[+V, \begin{cases} +\text{Transitive}]/\underline{\quad} \text{NP} \\ -\text{Transitive}]/\underline{\quad}\# \end{cases} \right]$

(34) (i)
(ii)
(iii) $[+V] \rightarrow$
(iv)
$\begin{cases} [+[+\text{Abstract}]\text{-Subject}]/ \\ \qquad [+N, +\text{Abstract}] \text{ Aux} \underline{\quad} \\ [+[+\text{Abstract}]\text{-Subject}]/ \\ \qquad [+N, -\text{Abstract}] \text{ Aux} \underline{\quad} \\ [+[+\text{Animate}]\text{-Object}]/ \\ \qquad \underline{\quad} \text{Det} [+N, +\text{Animate}] \\ [+[-\text{Animate}]\text{-Object}]/ \\ \qquad \underline{\quad} \text{Det} [+N, -\text{Animate}] \end{cases}$

---

[1] Chomsky's numbering (1965:91).

For instance, in addition to distinguishing those verb classes defined just above, one would have to distinguish verbs which simultaneously require [+Animate] subjects and [+Human] objects, such as *murder*, from verbs which merely require [+Animate] subjects, like *leap* (intransitive) and *see* (transitive). This means that the following additional rules would be necessary:

$$[+V] \rightarrow [+[+\text{Animate}]\text{-Subject}, +[+\text{Human}]\text{-Object}]/$$
$$[+N, +\text{Animate}] \text{ Aux} \underline{\qquad} \text{Det } [+N, +\text{Human}]$$
$$[+V] \rightarrow [+[+\text{Animate}]\text{-Subject}]/[+N, +\text{Animate}] \text{ Aux} \underline{\qquad}$$

This complex apparatus misses the point that the requirement of an animate subject is independent of other selectional restrictions which a verb might have; nowhere is this requirement expressed as a generalization about the verbs which have it. Because of the obvious clumsiness of feature-rewriting rules here, Chomsky proposed (1965:90–106) conventions for *automatically* rewriting verbs as complex symbols which included the coding of specified features of their subjects and objects.

One effect of Chomsky's treatment of noun and verb subcategorization was that the base component, which formerly could be seen as an unordered set of sequentially applied context-free rewriting rules,[1] now had to be seen as a sequentially ordered set containing both context-free rewriting rules and quasi-transformational rules which referred to syntactic features of categories in the context or environment of various nodes (Chomsky 1965:88–90). This should not be considered an advantage; the implications of the *Aspects* conception of the base component are discussed in detail in McCawley 1968b. Chomsky's introduction into grammatical theory of syntactic features has an apparent advantage in that it permits a formal "solution" to the problem of cross-classifying syntactic properties of verb classes. Chomsky mentions this only briefly, saying (1965:87):

it is now unnecessary to use rewriting rules to classify Transitive Verbs into those that do and those that do not normally permit Object deletion. Instead, the lexical entries for *read*, *eat*, on the one hand, and *frighten*, *keep*, on the other, will differ in specification for the particular syntactic feature of Object deletion, which is not mentioned in the rewriting rules at all. The transformational rule that deletes Objects will now be applicable only to those words positively specified with respect to this feature, this information now being contained in the Phrase-marker of the strings in which these words appear.

[1] Cf. Chomsky 1965:64–8, 88. In Chomsky 1957, it is assumed that they are ordered (cf. pp. 26, 111), but no justification is given for this assumption.

This sort of solution permits one to deal with the cross-classification of "negative" verbs and types of complements permitted by simply assigning an arbitrary syntactic feature [+*some* → *any* Rule] or [+Affective] (cf. Klima 1964) to the "negative" verbs, and assigning other arbitrary syntactic features for each of the complement properties, as was done by Rosenbaum (1967).

Unfortunately this sort of solution involves having arbitrary syntactic features (e.g. [±Object deletion Rule]) for every rule of syntax to which certain verbs are "exceptions."[1] The use of these rule features (as they were called by G. Lakoff [1965:sec. 2], following Chomsky and Halle [1968:374ff.]) entails in addition that every lexical item be subcategorized for all of these rules, and that each terminal (lexical) node of a phrase-marker carry around with it, throughout the course of a derivation, a list of all these features and the values each has for the particular lexical item. Such a treatment, however, totally fails to characterize the notion "exception to a rule."[2] In particular, it does not distinguish cases where a rule does not apply to any of the members of a class which is definable semantically, but not in any non-*ad hoc* structural terms, from cases where the same rule fails for no apparent reason to apply to only one or two members of such a class. The rule of negative-transportation, or negative-raising,[3] offers a clear illustration of the difference between the two cases, and the consequences of failing to distinguish between them. This is an important distinction, so I will consider this rule in some detail.

The rule of negative-transportation moves a negative out of a complement clause to in front of the verb introducing the clause. It has been pointed out by Dwight Bolinger that sentences with "raised" negatives are not used under exactly the same circumstances as their counterparts with unraised negatives, unraised negatives being characteristic of

[1] For some highly perceptive remarks on the use of syntactic features, and also on the general problem of the predictability of syntactic properties, see Zwicky 1968.

[2] Apparently the arbitrary syntactic features of Chomsky 1965 have nothing to do with exceptions directly. For rules like Object deletion, there are apparently no exceptions, only [+Object deletion] verbs, and [−Object deletion] verbs. But in footnote 21 to chap. IV (p. 231) Chomsky speaks of *say* (with infinitive) and *shear* (e.g. of dignity) as exceptions to his redundancy rule (p. 166) that "every Verb in English that can occur with a Direct-Object and a following Manner Adverbial can occur just as well with just a Direct-Object, though not conversely," saying (p. 231) that such exceptions "require separate statement."

[3] For discussion, see Fillmore 1963, Klima 1964, G. Lakoff 1965, R. Lakoff 1968, 1969, and Lindholm 1969.

stronger feelings or convictions about the matter in question. Thus, when a person says (13):

13. I think John won't come.

he is more certain that John won't come, than when he says (14):

14. I don't think John will come.

Still, the normal use of (14) is to report a negative thought, not to report the lack of a thought. Likewise (15):

15. I don't want to hurt myself.

is a weaker statement than (16):

16. I want not to hurt myself.

In the latter, the possibility of being hurt seems to be set off as more likely and requiring more precautions. Still (15), with ordinary intonation and normal stress, is a statement about a desire for a negatively characterized circumstance, not a denial of a desire. The difference between raised and unraised negatives is even more obvious with some of the verbs which take gerund complements, such as *plan on*, and *feel like*, as in:

17a. I'm not planning on cooking dinner until later.
17b. I'm planning on not cooking dinner until later.

18a. I don't feel like cooking dinner until later.
18b. I feel like not cooking dinner until later.

Still, as the *until*-phrases make clear, these sentences are not ordinarily denials of plans or intentions to engage in "cooking dinner until later," but statements of intentions to refrain until later from beginning to cook dinner. (Naturally, these sentences *could* be used the other way, but ordinarily they are not.) Regardless of what assumptions by the speaker may be required for the raising of negatives, it is a syntactic fact about the verbs of opinion and intention that a negative which is logically lower may appear either before or after them, since this property is not inherent in all verbs. Thus, negative-transportation applies to verbs which mean roughly 'hold the opinion that...,' e.g. such surface transitives as *believe, think, predict, suppose,* performative *suggest, expect, see, imagine, anticipate,*[1] etc. but not, e.g. *claim,* and certainly not *know, realize, decide,* or *say*:

19a.   I didn't think John would leave until noon.
19b. = I thought John wouldn't leave until noon.

20a.   I didn't expect John to leave until noon.
20b. = I expected that John wouldn't leave until noon.

21a.   I don't suggest that you leave until noon.
21b. = I suggest that you not leave until noon.

22a.   I don't imagine John will leave until noon.
22b. = I imagine John won't leave until noon.

23a.   I don't see John as leaving until noon.
23b. = I see John as not leaving until noon.

24a.   I didn't claim that John would leave until noon.
24b. ≠ I claimed that John wouldn't leave until noon.

25a.   I didn't know that John would leave until noon.
25b. ≠ I knew that John wouldn't leave until noon.

26a.   I didn't decide that John would leave until noon.
26b. ≠ I decided that John wouldn't leave until noon.

and to such surface intransitives as *seem (to one), appear (to one), be likely,* but not to *leak out, be obvious,* or *be strange*:

27a.   John doesn't seem (to me) to have died until noon.
27b. = John seems (to me) not to have died until noon.

28a.   It isn't likely that John died until noon.
28b. = It is likely that John didn't die until noon.

29a.   It didn't leak out that John died until noon.
29b. ≠ It leaked out that John didn't die until noon.

30a.   *It isn't obvious that John died until noon.
30b. ≠ It is obvious that John didn't die until noon.

---

[1] Negative-raising applies to *believe, see, imagine,* and *anticipate* only when they have this sense. Thus it does not apply to *believe* when it means 'accept the claim that' (cf. Lindholm 1969), nor to *imagine* when it means 'form a mental image' as in *I am imagining myself not bound by the laws of nature,* nor to *see* when it means 'perceive visually' as in *I saw him not looking at me,* nor to *anticipate* when it means 'foresee,' but only when it means 'expect.'

Negative-transportation also applies to a class of verbs indicating intent, but this class is unfortunately at present more difficult to characterize precisely. This class includes *want, intend, plan, choose, contemplate, feel like, be supposed to, be meant to,* and perhaps others.[1] But it does not seem to include *hope,* and for no apparent reason:

31a. They didn't want to get here until tomorrow.
31b. = They wanted not to get here until tomorrow.

32a. I didn't intend for John to die until tomorrow.
32b. = I intended for John not to die until tomorrow.

33a. These goodies aren't meant to be eaten until tonight.
33b. = These goodies are meant not to be eaten until tonight.

34a. *I didn't hope that John would get here until tomorrow.
34b. ≠ I hoped that John wouldn't get here until tomorrow.

Intuitively these two groups of verbs (the "opinion verbs" and the "intent verbs") are coherent classes, and surely it is no coincidence that in other languages which have a negative-transportation rule (e.g. Latin), it applies to classes of verbs with similar meanings (e.g. to *puto* 'think,' *credo* 'believe,' *videor* 'seem,' *volo* 'want'). Notice that the Chomskian use of arbitrarily assigned rule features does not distinguish the fact that *hope* in English does not undergo negative-transportation from the fact that in no language that has negative-transportation does a word meaning 'regret' undergo it. It not only predicts that there might be (in the present, past, or future) a dialect of English in which, for example, *know* was a negative-transportation verb, so that (35a) and (35b) were paraphrases:

35a. I didn't know John left.
35b. I knew John didn't leave.

but it also predicts that it is an incredible coincidence that the Latin negative-raising verbs correspond semantically to the verbs that permit negative-transportation in English.

Yet we do not perceive this as a coincidence, but rather as something quite natural, and I think we would be quite surprised to discover a dialect of English in which *know* permitted negative-transportation.

---

[1] Negative-raising applies to *choose, contemplate,* and *feel like* only when they express intention, so it does not apply to *choose* when it means 'decide,' nor to *contemplate* when it means 'ponder,' nor to *feel like* when it means 'perceive oneself as similar to.'

My point here is that the arbitrary assignment of rule features as suggested in Chomsky 1965 does not permit, or even prevents characterization of these facts as "natural" or "unnatural."

Lakoff 1965 was concerned precisely with characterizing the notion "exception to a rule of grammar," and among the major contributions of this work was the characterization of the notions of naturalness and markedness in syntax. Lakoff was concerned, for instance, with the fact that it is "natural" or "normal" in English for stative predicates to be surface adjectives (*tall, similar*) and for active ones to be surface verbs (*crush, run*), although there are stative verbs (*wonder, resemble*) and active adjectives (*careful, noisy*). He proposed (in his Appendix C) to deal with this fact by using redundancy rules to predict that for unmarked cases the surface form of stative predicates would be adjectival, and the surface form of non-statives would be non-adjectival (i.e. "verbal" in his system – cf. his Appendix A). Stative verbs would be considered marked statives, and active adjectives would be considered marked non-statives. Thus Lakoff had rules of the form:

$$[\text{U Adjectival}] \supset \begin{cases} [+\text{Adjectival}]/[\underline{\quad}, +\text{Stative}] \\ [-\text{Adjectival}]/[\underline{\quad}, +\text{Stative}] \end{cases}$$

$$[\text{M Adjectival}] \supset \begin{cases} [-\text{Adjectival}]/[\underline{\quad}, +\text{Stative}] \\ [+\text{Adjectival}]/[\underline{\quad}, -\text{Stative}] \end{cases}$$

which treated the feature [± Stative] as an inherent feature of the lexical item (in his terms, a feature of the "lexical base" – cf. his sec. 8), that is, as part of, or as determined directly by, the meaning. These rules treated the feature [± Adjectival] as a purely syntactic feature whose plus or minus value was predictable to a certain extent from the value Marked or Unmarked for some inherent feature. In addition, the notion of exception to a rule could in general be identified with the notion "marked" for a given property or feature.[1]

George Lakoff did not, of course, invent redundancy rules, nor even extend their use from phonology; Chomsky had already done that in using them in lexical representations to predict values for the higher-

---

[1] This is strictly true only for what Lakoff termed major rules. For minor rules (rules which applied only to exceptions – cf. his sec. 4), the notion of exception was not defined. That is, Unmarked for a minor rule R_i was interpreted as $[-R_i]$ and Marked as $[+R_i]$, so an item which *unexpectedly* failed to undergo rule R_i would be considered Unmarked, and in no way exceptional.

level features among those that are hierarchically structured (Chomsky 1965:164–6), for example, in such rules as:

$$[\pm \text{Human}] \rightarrow [+ \text{Animate}]$$

and to deal with such trivial (my description, not Chomsky's) language-specific (Chomsky's claim, not mine) lexical redundancies of English as the following (from Chomsky 1965:166–8): "If a verb can occur with a Manner Adverb, it can occur without one." Lakoff did, however, suggest that syntactic redundancies were not merely a formal property or defect of the grammatical system and/or its notation, and suggested the resurrection of the hypothesis (common among "traditional" grammarians) that grammatical properties and syntactic distribution are determined (at least partially) by meaning (his secs. 8.3, 10).

The idea that syntactic properties could be predicted from semantic properties was not refined or elaborated until 1967, when separate works by Robin Lakoff and James McCawley took a fresh look at the relation between syntax and semantics.

2   *The courtship of syntax and semantics*

a   Selectional restrictions. McCawley (1968a) argued that the account of selectional restrictions given in *Aspects*, which held that selectional restrictions were syntactic in nature and applied between lexical items (e.g. between a verb and the head nouns of its subject and object noun phrases), was inadequate and should be discarded in favor of the approach proposed earlier by Katz and Fodor (1963), in which selectional restrictions were treated as semantic in nature, and as operating between a lexical item and an entire syntactic constituent (e.g. a verb and its entire subject or object noun phrase). McCawley first showed that selectional restrictions had to operate between lexical items and entire syntactic constituents and not just their head nouns or verbs by showing that there were sentences where the violation of a selectional restriction originated in a modifier in a noun phrase rather than in the head noun. Such a sentence is (36):

36. *My pregnant neighbor is the father of two girls.

which violates the same selectional restriction as (37):

37. *My rich sister is the father of two girls.

In the first case the violation must be traced to the modifying adjective *pregnant* which requires a [+ Female] head noun,[1] whereas in the second case it comes from the head noun *sister* which is a [+ Female] head noun. The violation cannot be traced to the head noun *neighbor* in the first sentence because the sentence (38):

38. My rich neighbor is the father of two girls.

contains no violations, and sentences like (39):

39. My rich neighbor likes pastrami.

neither refer exclusively to a female neighbor, nor are ambiguous regarding the sex of the neighbor.

McCawley then proposed (1968a:134) that

any piece of information which may figure in the semantic representation of an item may figure in a selectional restriction and secondly that no other information ever figures in selectional restrictions. As evidence for the former assertion, I will point out that on any page of a large dictionary one finds words with incredibly specific selectional restrictions, involving an apparently unlimited range of semantic properties; for example, the verb *diagonalize* requires as its object a noun phrase denoting a matrix (in the mathematical sense), the adjective *benign* in the sense "noncancerous" requires a subject denoting a tumor, and the verb *devein* as used in cookery requires an object denoting a shrimp or prawn.

He went on to argue that "the various nonsemantic features attached to nouns, for example, proper versus common, grammatical gender, grammatical number, and so on, play no role in selection" (1968a:134) except insofar as they are semantically motivated:[2]

For example, the verb *name* might at first glance seem to have a selectional restriction involving the feature [proper]:

28. They named their son John.
29. *They named their son that boy.

---

[1] George Lakoff (1969a) has argued that the violation of selectional restrictions is not strictly a matter of semantic properties of lexical items, since judgments of such violations depend partly on the speaker's beliefs about the world and his pre-suppositions regarding various properties of the objects he refers to (for example, relative chronology, sentience, co-reference, entailment, logical possibility, etc.). This view of the nature of selectional restrictions is wholly consistent with the arguments advanced by McCawley.

[2] Example numbers are McCawley's.

However, there are in fact perfectly good sentences with something other than a proper noun in the place in question:

30. They named their son something outlandish.

The selectional restriction is thus that the second object denote a name rather than that it have a proper noun as its head. Regarding grammatical number, verbs such as *count* might seem to demand a plural object:

31. I counted the boys.
32. *I counted the boy.

However, there are also sentences with grammatically singular objects:

33. I counted the crowd.

The selectional restriction on *count* is not that the object be plural but that it denote a set of things rather than an individual. Similarly, there is no verb in English which allows for its subject just those noun phrases which may pronominalize to *she*, namely noun phrases denoting women, ships, and countries. I accordingly conclude that selectional restrictions are definable solely in terms of properties of semantic representations and that to determine whether a constituent meets or violates a selectional restriction it is necessary to examine its semantic representation and nothing else. Since if the base component were then to contain any machinery to exclude structures which violate selectional restrictions, that machinery would have to duplicate what already must be done by the semantic projection rules, I conclude that the matter of selectional restrictions should be totally separate from the base component and that the base component thus be a device which generates a class of deep structures without regard to whether the items in them violate any selectional restrictions.

b   Syntactic features and meaning classes. Robin Lakoff's contribution was to show that a great number and variety of syntactic phenomena in Latin were predictable from semantic properties of complement-taking verbs. This involved: (1) providing an explicit definition for the notion "meaning-class," a notion that had been taken for granted by traditional grammarians, and (2) extending the use of redundancy rules to predict plus and minus values for rule features from markedness relative to a given meaning-class. Robin Lakoff gave an operational definition for meaning-class as follows (1968:165): "We define a meaning-class in terms of both syntax and semantics, as a set of semantic markers that can function in syntactic rules," and went on to explain (1968:165):

Not all semantic markers function in syntactic rules. For example, the semantic markers that define verbs of ordering will function syntactically in a redundancy rule specifying that, for this semantic class, one or more of the complementizer-changing rules must apply. On the other hand, for verbs of eating there is no semantic marker that functions syntactically or that distinguishes a rule that applies to verbs of eating from one that can apply only to verbs of drinking or verbs of digesting.

By "function in syntactic rules," she was referring to the concept of rule government. Rule government is, roughly, the notion that among the syntactic rules of a language are some whose application is determined (i.e. forced, permitted, or prohibited) by the presence of a particular verb or adjective in the environment of the rule's application. The term "government" was not well-defined when G. Lakoff re-introduced it into formal grammar from its use in traditional grammar (Lakoff 1965, sec. III), and it remained so here. Nonetheless, its meaning was relatively clear, and if a linguist was told to compile a list of verbs which governed a particular rule, he could understand what was wanted well enough to attempt to do so. Indeed, such lists were actually compiled (Alexander and Kunz 1964; Householder 1965).

Rule government had been identified with the notion "possible exception to a rule" (G. Lakoff 1965:III-2; R. Lakoff 1968:22–3), but these lists made it abundantly clear to anyone who read them that the lexical items which governed various rules were not a random or arbitrary collection of verbs or adjectives (all the lists were of verbs and adjectives), as one would be led to predict if syntactic properties were considered to be arbitrary, formal properties of lexical items. Instead the lists consisted of small numbers of coherent semantic classes. Aware of the fact that certain syntactic phenomena were normal for certain semantic classes, and abnormal or impossible for others, Robin Lakoff (1968) extended the use of redundancy rules to relate rule features to semantic properties by defining and interpreting markedness separately for different semantic classes. Her purpose was to predict for all lexical items, the plus or minus value for particular rule features, given only the meaning-classes the lexical item belonged to, and its markedness (i.e. whether it was normal or abnormal) with respect to the rule feature in question. For instance, if it is claimed that in English it is normal for "verbs of communication" (taking this to be the designation for a meaning-class in accordance with the criteria mentioned above) to have *that*-clause complements, and abnormal for them to have Poss-*ing* complements, but abnormal for "verbs of affective attitude" to have *that*-clause complements, and normal for them to have Poss-*ing* complements, a syntactic description of English would express this in redundancy rules which interpret these definitions of markedness as follows:

$V_{\text{communication}}$ (e.g. *say, tell, write, whisper*...)
[U *that*-finite] $\supset$ [+*that*-finite]
[U Poss-*ing*] $\supset$ [−Poss-*ing*]

$V_{\text{affective attitude}}$ (e.g. *like, love, hate, prefer*...)
[U *that*-finite] $\supset$ [−*that*-finite]
[U Poss-*ing*] $\supset$ [+Poss-*ing*]

McCawley (1968a) showed that the "grammatical" features of lexical items necessary for subcategorization and selectional restrictions were inherent in one aspect or another of their semantic representation; he argued that since they were required for semantic representation, separate, homologous syntactic features were superfluous, and unnecessary. Robin Lakoff (1968) argued for viewing a number of transformational properties of verbs, which had previously been seen as erratic and idiosyncratic properties, as at least partially determined by certain aspects of meaning. In the meantime, a fresh look was being given to semantic representation, the semantic structure of lexical items, and the place of lexical insertion in a transformational grammar.

c Removal of the boundary between syntax and semantics. McCawley had previously (McCawley 1967a) argued that (1) semantic and syntactic representations were of the same formal nature, both requiring propositional connectives, representation of individuals as constants,[1] predicates denoting properties and relationships among individuals and propositions, set symbols and quantifiers, and descriptions of individuals and sets; and that (2) the insertion of lexical items does not occur all at one time, defining a level of deep syntactic structure, as proposed by Chomsky (1965).[2] Rather, he argued, the use of such anaphoric

---

[1] A possible linguistic analogue of the distinction in logic between constant and variable is discussed in Morgan 1970.
[2] Cf., for example, p. 136 of that work: "the lexicon characterizes the individual properties of particular lexical items that are inserted in specified positions in base Phrase-markers. Thus when we define 'deep structures' as 'structures generated by the base component,' we are, in effect, assuming that the semantic interpretation of a sentence depends only on its lexical items and the grammatical functions and relations represented in the underlying structures in which they appear[9]" (Chomsky's

lexical items as *former, latter, respectively* (cf. McCawley 1967b) depends
on the prior application of well-known transformational rules which re-
order and combine constituents. But since other transformational rules
such as gender-agreement rules and clitic placement rules depend on
grammatical properties of particular *lexical* items, McCawley concluded
that the insertion of lexical items must be intermingled among the
transformational rules.

Drawing on these conclusions, McCawley (1968c) proposed that
semantic representation be considered the underlying level of linguistic
structure, to be related to surface structure by means of a single system
of transformational rules. He showed that this system would include
all the familiar cyclic and post-cyclic rules which had been discussed in
the works of Rosenbaum (1967), G. Lakoff (1965), and Ross (1967)
(among others), and, in addition, the body of lexical insertion transformations, which were to be seen as substituting lexical items for constituent portions of derived semantic-syntactic representations.

McCawley's concern in that paper was to determine where among the
body of transformations the lexical insertion transformations applied.
He devoted the bulk of his paper to showing that lexical items could
not be inserted at the beginning of a derivation which began with semantic structure as underlying structure. He argued (1968a:72) that:

the complex of semantic material which a lexical item corresponds to need
not be a constituent of the semantic representation *per se* but may be a
constituent which arises through a transformation, i.e. I will argue that
lexical items can be correlated correctly with their meanings only by recognizing prelexical transformations, which apply to trees that terminate in
semantic material rather than in lexical material, and stating the conditions
for inserting lexical items in terms of the results of these prelexical transformations rather than in terms of the ultimate semantic representation.

McCawley went on to demonstrate his argument that the meaning of
certain lexical items (typically predicative words – verbs and adjectives,
and nominalizations of them) could be represented adequately only

footnote 9 inconclusively discusses possible counterevidence revolving about quantifier order) and p. 84: "The system of rewriting rules will now generate derivations
terminating with strings that consist of grammatical formatives and complex symbols.
Such a string we call a *preterminal string*. A terminal string is formed from a preterminal string by insertion of a lexical formative in accordance with the following
lexical rule: 'If Q is a complex symbol of a preterminal string and (D, C) is a lexical
entry, where C is not distinct from Q, then Q can be replaced by D.'"

by decomposing the lexical items into smaller semantic components which bore particular definable structural relations to each other and to the arguments they related. The example he chose was the English verb *kill*. The lexical item *kill* relates a constant x, a constant y, and an event prior to which y is alive, in which y ceases to be alive, and to which x bears some causal relation. These relations are diagrammed most naturally as below:

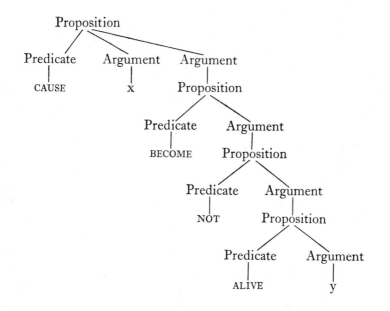

Notice that this representation assumes a verb–subject–object (VSO) order of underlying elements. Syntactic arguments for assuming that this underlying order is correct for English are presented in McCawley 1970b. Nothing that is presented here crucially depends on this ordering, but it is adopted here where convenient in discussing pre-lexical representations and transformations. Assuming underlying VSO order entails having a subject-creating rule which permutes an initial verb and the first following NP. This rule will not be discussed here, and no systematic significance should be attached to SVO representations which will occasionally be used for the reader's convenience.

Additional, syntactic motivation for such semantic decomposition is to be found in some facts pointed out by Morgan (1969a), McCawley (1968c), and Binnick (1968a), which concern ambiguity in the scope of adverbial expressions. The adverb *almost*, for instance, in the following sentence can be taken as modifying the entire verb phrase, or as modifying only the quantified object noun phrase:

40. I almost drank all my milk.

Only the second possibility may be paraphrased as (41):

41. I drank almost all my milk.

This suggests that ALMOST may appear in either position in underlying structure, and that an optional rule moves it higher up in the syntactic representation. What is interesting to us about this is that a similar ambiguity of scope occurs on a sublexical level with *kill*. Thus sentence (42):

42. I almost killed the fly.

has at least three readings:

43a. I almost did something which would have killed the fly [but I missed my chance].
43b. I did something which almost killed the fly [but my aim was bad and I missed it].
43c. I did something to the fly which caused it to become almost dead [but it recovered and flew away].

These readings correspond to semantic structures with ALMOST just above CAUSE, BECOME, and NOT, respectively, and suggest that the rule which promotes such quantifiers applies before lexical insertion. The absence of a reading for ALMOST just above ALIVE may be attributed to independently required constraints on possible quantifier-negative relations as discussed in Morgan 1969a and G. Lakoff 1969b and 1971.

Morgan produced similar evidence from ambiguities found with the adverb *again*. Sentences like (44):

44. John knocked Harry down again.

may refer to the repetition of an event, in which John knocked Harry down, or to the repetition of a state, in which Harry was down. Whether

one finds the same ambiguity in sentences with *kill* is limited only by
the fact that sentences like (45):

45. Ruby killed Oswald again.

are "ungrammatical" for people who don't believe in the possibility
of reincarnation.

Binnick, in independent work, showed that time and place adverbials,
such as *for four years*, and *in Reading*, had the same ambiguity with
complex expressions, where the scopes were discrete phrases present
in surface structure, as they had with simple transitive verbs. Thus
sentences like (46a,b):

46a. The Sheriff of Nottingham jailed Robin Hood for four years.
46b. The Sheriff of Nottingham jailed Robin Hood in Reading.

have the same ambiguities as (47a,b):

47a. The Sheriff of Nottingham put Robin Hood in jail for four
years.
47b. The Sheriff of Nottingham put Robin Hood in jail in Reading.

respectively. The (a) sentences in either case may mean either, 'the
Sheriff of Nottingham caused Robin Hood to be in jail for four years'
(the usual reading), or 'the Sheriff of Nottingham spent four years
putting Robin Hood in jail'; and the (b) sentences may mean either,
'the Sheriff of Nottingham caused Robin Hood to be in the Reading
jail,' or 'the Sheriff of Nottingham was in Reading when he caused
Robin Hood to be in jail.' These facts imply that *jail* is a derived causative verb, and that in the semantic representation of sentences with
such adverbs as these, the adverb may be either above or below the
causative predicate.

It is evident from the semantic representation proposed above for
sentences containing the lexical item *kill*, that the semantic components
representing *kill* do not form a single continuous constituent; there
are non-predicative elements in their midst. But since McCawley's
view of syntax required that lexical items be inserted only for constituents, it was necessary for him to assume that there existed processes
which group the predicative elements together into a single constituent.
He described one such process, which he called predicate-raising, and
argued that it would have to be optional and cyclic. This transformation
would take a predicate (V) and attach it to the predicate of the next

higher proposition (sentence, S). It would thus be able to encode a structure such as (48):

48.

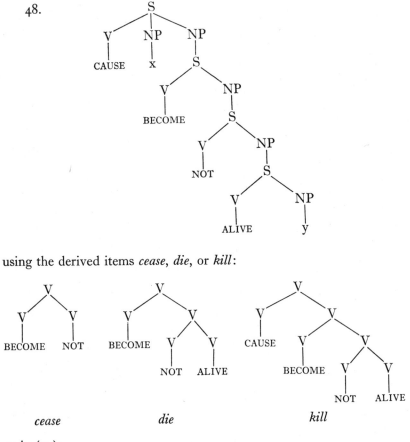

using the derived items *cease*, *die*, or *kill*:

cease   *die*   *kill*

as in (49):

49a. x caused y to cease to be alive.
49b. x caused y to die.
49c. x killed y.

C How; an immodest proposal

It follows as an important consequence of accepting a conception of grammar in which the rules of syntax operate on semantic representations rather than lexical representations (i.e. structures consisting only of morphemes and grammatical category labels), that various aspects of the semantic structure of lexical items may be referred to in a much more precise way than was previously possible. This means that it is no longer necessary to define semantic classes as R. Lakoff did, in functional, operational terms, as classes of lexical items which share a set of semantic features which are relevant (i.e. function) in syntactic rules. Instead, one can define semantic classes in semantic and structural terms, referring directly to the structural position of the specific relevant semantic units in derived semantic constituents. What follows here is an illustration of this slightly different approach to the correspondence of syntactic and semantic classes. The utility and adequacy of the approach do not depend on the specific analyses I propose here being absolutely correct, and I present no rigorous justification for them.

As an illustration, suppose that we want to talk about the syntactic properties of "verbs of communication," and that we are interested in such properties as what kinds of complements they can have (sentential *that*-clauses, infinitival *to*-phrases, *ing*-phrases, etc.), whether they require an indirect object, whether an indirect object can or must be preceded by a preposition, and so forth. If we take a number of verbs which we agree are in some intuitive sense "verbs of communication," say: *deny, inform, say, shout, teach, tell,* and *write*, one of the first things we notice is that they are not really a very homogeneous group in terms of syntactic properties (see Table 1, below). All may have sentential complements; *say, shout, teach, tell,* and *write* may have infinitival complements; *deny* and *teach* may have *ing*-phrase complements; *inform, teach,* and *tell* must have an indirect object (at least understood, if not overtly present on the surface); all may have an indirect object overtly present; *deny, say,* and *shout* require the preposition *to* before a pre-complement indirect object; *write* permits a preposition there; *inform, teach,* and *tell* do not permit a preposition there.

TABLE 1 *Some properties of seven "communication verbs"*

	Complement types			Presence of IO		Form of IO	
	that S	*to* VP	V-*ing*	Obligatory	Possible	*to* NP	NP
Deny	×		×		×	×	
Inform	×			×	×		×
Say	×	×			×	×	
Shout	×	×			×	×	
Teach	×	×	×	×	×		×
Tell	×	×		×	×		×
Write	×	×			×	×	×

If we consider all of these verbs as belonging to a single class, how can we define markedness for the rule which determines whether or not a preposition precedes a pre-complement indirect object, in such a way that a preposition is obligatory for *deny*, *say*, and *shout*, optional for *write*, and impossible for *inform*, *teach*, and *tell*? If we study sentences with these words:

50a. A denied to B that the air was polluted.
50b. A said to B that the air was polluted.
50c. A shouted to B that the air was polluted.
50d. A wrote (to) B that the air was polluted.
50e. A informed B that the air was polluted.
50f. A taught B that the air was polluted.
50g. A told B that the air was polluted.

we may observe that (50a–d) describe actions which are of a slightly different nature from the actions described in (50e–g). Sentences (50b) and (50g) both involve linguistic communication, ordinarily verbal, but somehow the use of *tell*, as opposed to *say*, indicates that the indirect object was affected by the communication, changed somehow, in a way that the subject intended – although not necessarily in all the ways that the subject might have desired. That is, it seems to me that when we use (50e–g) we indicate that we perceive the event as A having an effect on B, whereas when we use (50a–d) we perceive the event as something that involves B as a recipient rather than a "receptacle." In (50e–g), A directly and intentionally affects B; in (50a–d), A presents B with something which B is free to accept or reject.

It seems to be the case that all verbs like *deny*, *say*, and *shout*, which denote communicative events in which A "gives" something to B, may occur with a preposition before the indirect object. A small set of these verbs, which denote direct communication at a distance (e.g. *write*, *cable*, *radio*, etc.), may apparently optionally delete the preposition with no change in meaning. With one apparent exception that I know of, all verbs denoting communicative events in which the subject causes a change in the indirect object (e.g. *teach*, *inform*, *tell*) require there to be no preposition before the indirect object.[1] It appears that the syntac-

---

[1] At first glance, *prove* seems to be an "effect" verb rather than a "presentation" verb; after all, if it is appropriate to assert that you proved something to someone, it cannot also be appropriate to assert that he refused to admit the proof. But I think that this is a consequence of the ordinary meaning of *prove*, namely 'show to be a fact (or

tic property of permitting a preposition before the indirect object is correlated in a nearly one-to-one fashion with a certain aspect of meaning.

Given these conclusions, we may suppose that there is a rule which inserts or deletes or in some way alters the structural relations of an element realized in some cases as *to*, and that this rule is sensitive to the semantic difference between these classes. How, exactly, this difference is represented in semantic representation, what it consists of, and whether it is a difference in assertion or presupposition, are empirical questions. Analyses must be formulated and tested for each "verb of communication" which occurs in either syntactic environment. I have not succeeded in justifying even the relevant parts of the semantic analyses of all of these verbs, but let us suppose for ease of illustration that the semantic difference which corresponds to the syntactic difference is in assertion. Then it should be possible to refer to the class of verbs which triggers the *to*-rule by means of a notation which contains a representation of the predicate-structure which is common to all of the verbs which the rule applies to, and a variable representing the remainder of the semantic constituent which each of the lexical items encodes. If we abbreviate the predicate-structure common to the verbs which permit *to*, probably derived by predicate-raising from something like (51) or (52) below (cf. chapter 3, sec. c.6.*d*):

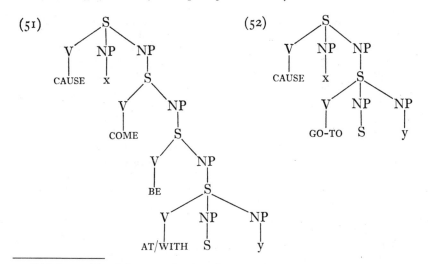

---

valid inference),' and that *prove* is otherwise semantically and structurally similar or identical to *show* or *demonstrate*, which are more clearly "presentation" verbs. This is an empirical question, of course, but substantiating my speculation would take me far afield of present concerns.

as "SEND"[1] using "SEND" in the sense that an operator of a signal-transmitting device (e.g. a radio-wave transmitter) sends,[2] we can refer to this class of verbs with the notation ["SEND" X]$_V$[3] since *deny* would be 'send that not,' *shout* would be 'send with a shout/by shouting,' and *say* would be 'send in words' or something of the sort.

The verbs for which the indirect object type is optional might be characterized as ["SEND" "WITH THE USE OF" X]$_V$, assuming that one can justify an analysis of *radio* as used here as 'send with the use of radio,' of *write* as 'send with the use of a literal encoding system,' and so forth.[4] Presumably we would be able to refer to the other class of verbs

[1] This is explicitly not a claim that SEND is an atomic predicate, although for expository purposes I am referring to it as if it were one. The only predicate of whose atomicity I am convinced is NOT.

[2] I am sorry if this usage seems a little strained. I have searched in vain for a better term in English which would include auditory, visual, tactile, and perhaps extra-sensory communication as well.

[3] Such an analysis is in fact attempted in more detail in chapter 3, sec. C.6.*d*. The use of *write* considered there is, however, a slightly different one, as the discussions in chapter 3, secs. C.2 and C.6.*d* should make clear. The use presently under consideration implies or asserts the sending of the message; the other use, as in *I wrote my brother a check*, does not assert or imply any such sending.

　　The illustration given here involves meaning-class definitions with variables to the right of specified predicate structures, but variables are not in principle restricted to the right of the specified predicate structure. For instance, it has been argued (Green 1969a) that the class of negative elements which triggers *too-either* suppletion (for example, *not, never, hardly, seldom, doubt, deny, cease*...) can be specified as [X NOT]$_V$. That is, they are analyzed as 'not,' 'always not,' 'almost not,' 'almost always not,' 'believe that not,' 'say that not,' 'come to not,' etc. These words differ in this syntactic property of triggering *too-either* suppletion from other "negative words" such as *impossible, unfortunate,* and *refuse,* which can be shown on independent grounds to contain a negative element in a non-rightmost position. The fact that there are two senses of the "negative word" *unlikely,* one of which occurs with *too,* the other with *either,* supports this class-description; the usage which occurs with *either,* as in:

　　1. Bill hasn't written a novel, and it's unlikely Harry has written one either.

means 'likely that not,' and the other usage, which occurs with *too,* and is found in:

　　2. I have no reason to believe that Bill has written a novel, and it's unlikely Harry has written one too.

means 'not likely that.'

[4] An alternative analysis of these data is conceivable, in which *write, radio, cable,* etc. do not permit prepositional and prepositionless indirect objects as stylistic variants, but have slightly different meanings correlated with each of the indirect object types. In addition to requiring separate but related lexical entries for each of the verbs involved (cf. chapter 2, sec. D.1), this analysis entails the claim that examples (1) and (2) below

　　1. We wrote Santa Claus that we wanted him to stop the war.

　　2. We wrote to Santa Claus that we wanted him to stop the war.

in an analogous fashion, perhaps as [[CAUSE[RECEIVE]] X]$_V$,[1] if we analyzed *inform* and *tell* as 'cause to receive a message...' and *teach* as
'cause to receive by instructing' or something like that (cf. chapter 4,
sec. B).

D Implications of this proposal

1 How many lexical items?
It follows from the discussion above that if a verb's syntactic properties
are related in precise ways to its semantic characteristics, there might be
homophonous verbs for which one syntactic property is associated with
only one meaning, and other syntactic properties with other meanings.
And, of course, this is the case. For example, when *run* occurs as an
intransitive verb, with or without a directional prepositional phrase,
it refers to a sort of locomotion, as in (53):

> 53a. John ran fast.
> 53b. John ran into the room.

But when *run* occurs before *for* and a noun denoting an elective office,
it refers to a certain sanctioned, goal-oriented activity which doesn't
particularly involve any locomotion, as in (54):

> 54. Lenore ran for senator.

The first use of *run* is paralleled by the use of other locomotion verbs
such as *walk, skip, tip-toe*, etc., but these others can never be used the
way *run* is used in (54). Sentences like (55):

> 55a. Lenore walked for senator.
> 55b. Paul skipped for alderman.

are simply ungrammatical. It seems clear that the two syntactic usages
correspond in a precise manner to two semantic uses, but it is another
question altogether whether there are two lexical items involved. After
all, they both form their past tense and past participle in the same
"irregular" way. The question of how many lexical items is a very

---

are non-synonymous, and would not always be interchangeable. Unfortunately, I
have been unable to obtain firm judgments from either myself or other speakers
regarding the synonymy of such sentences, so I can neither substantiate nor disprove
this claim.

[1] RECEIVE is intended to denote a cognitive process analogous to *reception* as applied to
signal-receiving devices such as radios, televisions, etc. (cf. "SEND").

complex one, and it has been discussed at some length – in Green 1969b, for instance,[1] where it was suggested that a single lexical item (e.g. *write*, *run*) could encode any of a number of related lexical entries (derived semantic representations). The notion "related lexical entry" was left undefined, however, since research on the question was only very sketchy, and published discussions (e.g. McCawley 1968a) primarily anecdotal. Other proposals have been made, of course, to deal with the phenomenon of two different uses of the same lexical item. McCawley (1968a) considered such cases as (56):

56. This coat is warm.

which is ambiguous between the readings, 'this coat has a relatively high temperature,' and 'this coat makes its wearer feel warm.' Since in many languages words denoting temperature ranges have exactly this ambiguity (range of internal or surface temperature of object *v.* range of temperature sensation produced by object), McCawley did not want to consider this an accidental fact about English. But, he claimed (1968a: 130):

> while the derived lexical item involves the notion of causation, it is not derivable by the usual causative transformation because that transformation would not give rise to the restriction of the derived item to articles of clothing and because the causative transformation yields sentences in which the underlying subject of the "basic" lexical item is present as the object of the "derived" item (as in "John opened the door," which is a causative in which the structure underlying "The door opened" is embedded), whereas the derived adjective *warm* does not allow the overt presence of a noun phrase corresponding to the person or thing which is made warm.

and, therefore, felt obliged to rule out a syntactic treatment of this ambiguity. Apparently McCawley wanted to claim that there were two lexical items *warm*, but that it wasn't or shouldn't be necessary to list both of them in the lexicon of a language. He proposed to deal with this dilemma by saying (1968a:130) that "probably all languages have implicational relationships among their lexical items, whereby the exist-

---

[1] Cf. also McCawley 1968a and Makkai 1969. Makkai argues that a separate level or component of morphological paradigms is necessary for a natural and economical treatment of the fact that inflectional morphology, regular and irregular, is remarkably stable throughout sets of words and idioms which are morphologically and historically related, even when there is little or no systematic synchronic correspondence between morphology and meaning. I suspect that something like what Makkai proposes may be necessary for the treatment of cases like *run*, and for the reasons she gives, *in addition to* the notion "related lexical entry" as discussed below.

ence of one lexical item implies the existence of another lexical item, which then need not be listed in the lexicon." He cited reification as another example of such implicational relationships – reification being the relationship which holds between the two senses of nouns denoting persons and works of art and scholarship, where one sense refers to the entity as an abstract work of art or scholarship (to the person as a carnate animus), the other to the physical embodiment of the work (the body of the person). This relationship is exemplified in (57a) and (57b):

57a. John's dissertation mentions Fermat's last theorem.
57b. John's dissertation weighs five pounds.

For other examples, cf. (61–2) below.

McCawley's proposal is rather attractive, since it expresses both language-specific and cross-linguistic generalizations about the use of lexical items *as* generalizations, and not as item-specific details which have to be learned separately for each lexical item. However, it appears to be too strong a statement. For example, his claim (1968a:130–1) that

English has two lexical items *warm*, of which only one appears in the lexicon, the other being predictable on the basis of a principle that for each lexical item which is an adjective denoting a temperature range there is a lexical item identical to it save for the fact that it is restricted to articles of clothing and means "producing the sensation corresponding to the temperature range denoted by the original adjective."

is false in that the words *hot* and *cold*, which are certainly used to denote temperature ranges of objects, are not used to refer to articles of clothing producing these sensations. One would not say of a thin, loose jacket:

58. This jacket is cold.

if he meant 'this jacket makes me feel cold.' *A cold jacket* and *a hot coat* are highly unlikely, or even impossible English phrases, although sentences like (59):

59a. This jacket makes me feel cold.
59b. This coat makes me feel hot.

and even (60)

60. This coat is too hot.

in the sense 'this coat keeps me feeling too hot' are perfectly ordinary utterances. Whether this reflects systematic linguistic facts, idiosyncratic linguistic facts, or pragmatic facts is not at all clear.

In addition, this "derived" use of *warm, cool,* and *hot* is not restricted to articles of clothing, but refers also to fabrics intended for clothing, blankets, behavior, colors, and music (e.g. jazz), to name a few.

Nonetheless, I am sympathetic to a desire to avoid having to list as separate entities several senses of what is intuitively "the same word." Yet, as McCawley was aware, different senses of a word have different syntactic properties. This is exactly what was illustrated for *run,* and below are further examples:

61a.   *James Bond$_{[person]}$ broke the window with himself$_{[body]}$.
61b.   James Bond$_{[person]}$ húrled himsĕlf$_{[person]}$ through the window.
61c.   *James Bond$_{[person]}$ hŭrled himsélf$_{[body]}$ through the window.
61d.   James Bond$_{[person]}$ hurled his body through the window.

The grammaticality of (61c) and (61d) is constant, even when one assumes that James Bond is capable of detaching his body from the animate forces which usually occupy it. Likewise in:

62a.   James Bond kissed Olga$_{[person]}$ on the foot.
62b.   *James Bond kissed Olga$_{[person]}$'s body on the foot.
62c.   James Bond kissed Olga$_{[person]}$'s mother on the foot.

62d.   James Bond kissed Olga$_{[person]}$'s foot.
62e.   *James Bond kissed Olga$_{[person]}$'s body's foot.
62f.   James Bond kissed Olga$_{[person]}$'s mother's foot.

This correspondence of syntactic and semantic differences of separate senses of a single lexical item seems to make it imperative that all of the semantic representations of a lexical item be available somewhere in the grammar, rather than being merely constructible or reconstructible. Can we reconcile the two goals of a small lexicon with implicational rules for universally derived senses, and the prediction of syntactic properties from semantic properties; or are they mutually exclusive? Gaps in the lexicon and in the syntactic distributions of individual lexical items which are apparently accidental seem to indicate that the implicational rules approach as proposed is too strong. It fails to explain why there is no *cold* meaning 'producing the sensation of being cold,' and why only *cool*, *hot*, and *warm* have parallel metaphorical extensions as classes of colors as in *hot colors*, *warm colors*, and only *warm*, *cool*, and *cold* may refer to personality characteristics. That is, we say that someone has a warm personality, and that he is warm to people, but not that he has a hot personality, or that he is hot to people.

However, it would be possible to think of rules that imply the possibility of specific kinds of "derived" uses (implicational possibility rules) as defining the notion "related lexical entry." These would bind together as one lexical item lexical entries which have semantic relationships related by these rules. This way, the non-existence of a usage would not have to be seen as an exception to a rule, which has to be learned in addition to the rule. Rather, it may be seen simply as the existence of a gap in the lexicon; if a word or usage should be added to the lexicon to fill that gap, it would be seen as an addition to the lexicon, not as a change in a rule of grammar.

Notice that a syntactic treatment of the ambiguity of *warm*, etc. is more plausible than it originally appeared if looked at in the light of recent advances in syntactic and semantic theory. The causative transformation (described by G. Lakoff [1965: IV, 14–18]) turns out to be a subcase of the independently motivated rule of predicate-raising in the conception of syntax proposed in McCawley 1968c. If the semantic representation of the sensation-producing sense of *This coat is warm* can be represented roughly as in (63):

63.

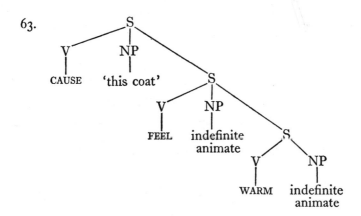

then predicate-raising, equi-NP-deletion, and the long-assumed rule which deletes unspecified noun phrases[1] will reduce this to something like (64):

64.

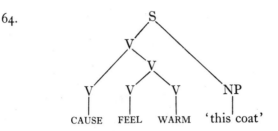

CAUSE   FEEL   WARM   'this coat'

If a definite NP occurred in place of the unspecified or indefinite NP, the additional constructions and uses of *warm* in (65):

65a. This coat makes NP feel warm.
65b. This coat makes NP warm.
65c. This coat warms NP.

could be derived from the above semantic representation or one very similar to it. The causative subject is not restricted to articles of clothing, as McCawley assumed, but to artifacts, materials, etc. which volitional agents intentionally use to produce or maintain body sensations. The fact that the adjective *warm* – in contrast to the derived causative verb *warm* as in (65c) – does not have an overt object may be seen as reflecting the systematic surface fact that English adjectives (in contrast to Latin adjectives, for example, and English prepositions) do not in general have surface objects.

2   *Types of classes*

The treatment of selectional restriction which McCawley proposed in "The Role of Semantics in a Grammar" was to treat it as a derived notion, and say that selectional restrictions are a function of semantics, not of grammar – or in a more sophisticated version, that they are a function of the speaker's presuppositions about the objects and events

---

[1] Equi-NP-deletion is described in detail in Postal 1970 and Morgan 1970. I am not aware of any systematic treatment of unspecified-NP-deletion in the literature. It should be sufficient to note, however, that such a rule is required in the derivations of both of the celebrated examples:
    John is easy to please.
    John is eager to please.

he refers to (cf. G. Lakoff 1969a). What I am attempting to do here is to show that other syntactic properties are not inherent in the lexical items *per se*, but in the meanings that those lexical items encode, and in the presuppositions which permit those lexical items to be used. The purpose of this section is to counter the objection that the kinds of classes which my approach leads one to propose are *ad hoc*, and therefore not worthy of being taken seriously.

It might indeed be objected that the syntactic-semantic classes which this approach leads one to delineate are *ad hoc*. For instance, one might claim that the three-way classification of communication verbs outlined above in section C of this chapter, is *ad hoc* since it cannot be used to predict the other facts about the syntax of these verbs which were pointed out at the beginning of that section. That is, the group of verbs which takes infinitive complements is not a subclass of or a superclass of any of the indirect object classes, but cross-cuts the classification which indirect object-type distribution imposes. As is clear from Table 1, *deny* belongs to one class, *inform* to the other, and neither occurs with infinitive complements. But, in fact, when *say, shout, teach, tell,* and *write* are used with infinitives, they express the idea of the subject's 'sending' that the addressee ought to conform to certain expressed desires or expectations of his. These verbs may also be used to express this meaning with *that*-clauses, provided that the *that*-clause contains as its main verb the modal *should*, expressing the indirect object's obligation or subject's suggestion (but not subject's expectation). Thus:

66a.   I said (to them) to respect their peers.
66b. = I said (to them) that they should respect their peers.

67a.   I shouted to them to respect their peers.
67b. = I shouted to them that they should respect their peers.

68a.   I taught them to respect their peers.
68b. = I taught them that they should respect their peers.

69a.   I told them to respect their peers.
69b. = I told them that they should respect their peers.

70a.   I wrote to them to respect their peers.
70b. = I wrote to them that they should respect their peers.

But *deny* and *inform* have neither of these uses:

71a. *I denied ((to) them) to leave.
71b. *I denied ((to) them) that they should leave.[1]

72a. *I informed them to leave.
72b. *I informed them that they should leave.

I maintain that the property of permitting infinitive complements is a function of the meaning of *say*, *shout*, *teach*, *tell*, and *write*, not by virtue of their expressing the communicative activity between subject and indirect object, but by virtue of their describing an action by the subject of the main verb toward the subject of the complement verb, regarding possible behavior of the latter. How this meaning is represented is an empirical question, and it would take me far afield to attempt to answer it here. For a start, however, I can suggest a representation which indicated the subject's opinion that the standard to which the complement subject is asked or supposed to be obliged to conform is the "proper" one under the circumstances. Such a representation would account for the fact that other "verbs of communication," such as *report, state, announce, proclaim, declare, predict*, etc., which do not take infinitive complements, cannot be semantically characterized this way. That is, these verbs do not describe any activity of the subject of the main verb towards the subject of the complement regarding the bringing about of the situation described in the complement, and correct use of them does not require belief in the existence of any attitude of the subject toward the situation described by the complement.

My point is that while these classes are *ad hoc* to the extent that they may be delineated in order to account for the distribution of a single syntactic property, they are not arbitrary; they are defined in semantic terms, which are from a formal point of view, and from an *a priori* point of view, totally independent of syntactic properties. Furthermore, they must be empirically justified on independent, semantic grounds. It is a mistake to think merely because I am looking for semantic correlates of a single syntactic property, that I am setting up *ad hoc* classes. The assumption of early transformational grammarians like Lees, that shared sets of syntactic properties would define a reasonably small number of hierarchically arranged verb classes turned out to be

---

[1] Recall that only the obligation or suggestion sense of *should* is intended here. That sense is ungrammatical with *deny* and *inform*.

unwarranted; it was seen that syntactic properties cut across almost every conceivable verb classification. Chomsky (1965) recognized this, and used it as a justification for introducing arbitrary syntactic features to control rule application (cf. sec. B.1 of this chapter, above).[1]

3 Types of rules

The above discussion has assumed that the application of particular transformational rules may be correlated in a one-to-one fashion with structural properties of semantic representations, and has hypothesized that, in particular, the systematic absence of a preposition with the indirect object of "verbs of communication" is related to whether or not the semantic representations of clauses containing them include something which indicates or implies successful persuasion. However, no way of formally expressing correspondences of this sort was put forth. It is the purpose of this section to consider ways in which this might be done.

It would be possible, for instance, if there were only two syntactically relevant classes of communication verbs, those sentential complement verbs which always had *to* before their indirect object, and those which never did, to express the correspondence between meaning and surface syntactic form by means of a precisely formulated redundancy rule such as (73):

73. ["SEND" X]$_V$ implies [+ *To*-Rule]

The rule given as (73) should not be interpreted as making any claims about the analysis of the syntax of communication verbs. I have at present no evidence on which to decide which class is subject to the rule, nor to decide what exactly the rule would have to do which accounts for the difference in surface distributions which distinguishes the classes of communication verbs.[2] This rule is intended solely as an illustration

---

[1] I think the only way to interpret his statement (1965:87): "Any attempt to construct a careful grammar will quickly reveal that many formatives have unique or almost unique grammatical characteristics, so that the simplification of the grammar that can be effected in these ways will certainly be substantial," is by assuming that by "unique or almost unique grammatical characteristics" he was referring to sets of grammatical properties. There are very few formatives which have any properties which are shared by no other formatives. To put it another way, there are very few, if there are any, grammatical properties which are unique to a single formative.

[2] It is entirely conceivable (and consistent with my assumptions about the form of a grammar) that the presence of *to* with one class of communication verbs, and its absence from the other would follow naturally as a consequence of the specific

of the kind of redundancy rule I wish to discuss, namely one which states that if a verb has a lexical representation (derived semantic representation) with the predicate-structure "SEND" as its leftmost member, regardless of what else the lexical representation contains, then the *to*-rule must apply.

Redundancy rules which refer to derived configurations of semantic constituents such as ["SEND" X]$_V$ make the implicit claim that it must be the semantic sub-tree derived by predicate-raising and other rules which combine predicates, rather than the underlying semantic predicates or structures themselves which is relevant in determining the applicability of semantically-controlled rules. This claim predicts that the structural relations (including order) of predicates in the derived structures which lexical items encode are important as well as the presence or absence of particular predicates, and, in fact, we saw in chapter 2, p. 36, n. 3, that this was true in the case of [LIKELY NOT]$_V$ and [NOT LIKELY]$_V$. Of course, if it could be shown that *unlikely* only encoded [NOT LIKELY]$_V$, which could be derived by predicate-raising, or by negative-raising, and then predicate-raising, then another example would have to be used.

Redundancy rules like (73) do not require a notation for markedness; implicit in them is the claim that the implication has no exceptions. They state that all verbs which may be characterized in such-and-such a way must undergo such-and-such a rule. Since this is the case, the redundancy rule is superfluous in a sense, and the meaning-class specification could as well be built into the rule, as in (74), again an arbitrary illustration:

74.   Y["SEND" X]$_V$ NP [[AT]$_V$ NP S]$_S$ Z
    SD: 1   2   3   4   5 6 7
    SC: Chomsky-adjoin[1] 4 to 5.

Rules of this type are formally distinct from redundancy rules like (73) in that they are transformations, and from transformational rules as

predicates or configurations of their underlying structures, without the need for any special preposition insertion (or deletion, or adjunction) rule to differentiate their surface syntax. However, if the indirect object type with *write, radio*, etc. is truly optional, then to describe their syntax, it will presumably be necessary to have either a transformational rule or an optional base component 'rule'.

[1] *Chomsky-adjunction* is the term used to refer to the adjoining of a node A as a sister of a node B, by the formation of a new node above B, with the same label as B. For further discussion, see Ross 1967, footnote 12 to chapter IV.

usually conceived, in that they refer to semantic constituents and variables, as well as syntactic category labels and syntactic variables. Of course, when one takes into consideration the class of communication verbs which permits either indirect object type, and which is semantically distinct from both of the other classes, it is necessary either to have two redundancy rules, or to have a disjunctive rule which says that the structural change of (74) is optional if term 2 is ["SEND" "WITH THE USE OF" X]$_V$, but obligatory if term 2 is ["SEND" Y]$_V$, where Y does not include ["WITH THE USE OF" X].

The choice between two rules or a single disjunctive rule is not merely an aesthetic one, however. To see this clearly, consider the rule of subject-raising as presently understood. This rule promotes the subject of a complement clause into a position in the same clause as the verb introducing the complement. It operates on a number of intransitive subject-complement verbs, including *begin, continue, cease, happen,* and *tend,*[1] as in:

75a. [Pornography bore John] began.
75b. Pornography began to bore John.

76a. [Paperbound books be inexpensive] tends.
76b. Paperbound books tend to be inexpensive.

and on a number of transitive object-complement verbs denoting mental states and activities, e.g. *believe, know, expect, want, like:*

77a. Agnew believes that he is persecuted.
77b. Agnew believes himself to be persecuted.

78a. We know that he is the vice-president.
78b. We know him to be the vice-president.

79a. We expect that he will attack us again.
79b. We expect him to attack us again.

80a. We want [that he grow up].
80b. We want him to grow up.

81a. We do not like [that our classes be disrupted].
81b. We do not like our classes to be disrupted.

We know from the fact that the derived object in (77b) is reflexive (i.e.

---

[1] Justification for the claim that these verbs have subject complements is presented in G. Lakoff 1966, R. Lakoff 1968, and Perlmutter 1968.

himself, and not *him* or *he*) that the underlying subject has moved into a different clause, and from the fact that in (77b–80b) it is non-nominative (i.e. *him* or *himself*, and not *he*) that it bears different structural relations to other clause elements than it originally bore. These two classes of verbs which govern subject-raising seem to have nothing in common semantically. If this is indeed so, and the set of all non-subject-raising verbs is also a disjunction of classes, as seems probable, then it would be impossible to write a disjunctionless rule for subject-raising. But notice that it is impossible to provide a disjunctionless rule regardless of how or where we represent the classes of verbs it applies to; the structural description of this rule must permit an NP before the complement (to allow it to account for the transitive verbs), but it must not require one (or the intransitive verbs will not meet the structural description). This means that the rule must be written with parentheses to denote an "optional" or "semi-obligatory" NP:

$$X \text{ [whatever verb class or classes]}_V \quad (NP) \ [V \ NP \ Y]_S$$

These parentheses are an abbreviation for the disjunction:

"(i) $X \text{ [whatever verb class}_i \dots]_V \quad NP \ [V \ NP \ Y]_S$

or

(ii) $X \text{ [whatever verb class}_j \dots]_V \quad [V \ NP \ Y]_S$"

that is, "(i), unless it doesn't apply, in which case, (ii)"; or "if not (i), then (ii)." Furthermore, since version (i) applies to one class, and version (ii) to a semantically totally distinct class, the "generalization" that would be "captured" by writing subject-raising as a single rule would seem to be a spurious one. This would not be the case if the additional NP were truly optional for even only some of the verbs in one or both classes. If this were the case, then and only then could the rule be accurately said to contain an optional element.

Still, there is a third class of subject-raising verbs which puts us right back where we started. These are transitive verbs like *cause, force, make*, and *permit, allow, authorize*, and *let*:

82a. The rain caused [NASA cancel the moonshot].
82b. The rain caused NASA to cancel the moonshot.

83a. My tooth fairy allows [I oversleep].
83b. My tooth fairy allows me to oversleep.

In the event that it is impossible to characterize both groups of transitive verbs (the mental activity and state verbs and the causation and permission verbs) by means of the same derived semantic or lexical schema, independent justification such as different ordering still will have to be found for considering them parts of different rules, "abbreviated" or not. Since the semantic classes they would refer to would be distinct from each other, it is difficult to see how either rule could be shown to be extrinsically ordered[1] before the other. And to show that they were intrinsically ordered, one would have to show that some other rule was intrinsically ordered before the application of subject-raising to one class, but after its application to the other. In such a case, subject-raising would have to be considered two separate rules, and because a third rule intervened between them they could not be "abbreviated" as a single rule. At any rate, it is an empirical question whether there are as many different rules which perform analogous changes on analogous inputs as there are distinct semantic classes which trigger that change. Given the principle that a single rule may not refer to a disjunction of semantic classes, the question of whether to specify the single relevant semantic class by redundancy rule, or in the transformational rule itself, is a notational question, without empirical consequences.

Negative-transportation is another rule which it is interesting to consider in regard to the question of how many semantic classes control a rule. This rule, as described above (sec. B.1.*b* of this chapter) seems to apply to non-factive[2] verbs of mental state. The factivity requirement thus permits the rule to apply to verbs of opinion (*think, seem, expect, imagine* in the sense 'expect'...) but not to verbs of knowing (*know, realize*...) or to *imagine* in the sense 'pretend'; to verbs of intending (*want, intend, mean, desire* in the sense 'want') but not to verbs of attitude (*like, love, hate*...) or to wishes (*wish, desire* in the sense 'wish').

---

[1] Transformational rules are said to be "extrinsically ordered" when their application in the "wrong order" produces incorrect output; two transformational rules are said to be "intrinsically ordered" when the structural description of the second cannot be met unless the first has applied.

[2] Roughly speaking, non-factive verbs are complement-taking verbs which are neither factive nor counter-factive. That is, the content of the complement is neither presupposed by the referent of the subject of the next higher "world-creating" verb (*want, claim, dream*...) to be true (e.g. *know, regret, like*... [factives]), nor presupposed by that individual to be false (e.g. *pretend, dream, claim, wish*... [counter-factives]). For an early discussion of factive verbs, see Kiparsky and Kiparsky 1970 (written in 1968). For a more recent treatment, and discussion of the relevance of world-creating verbs, see Morgan 1969b.

Specification of the state as mental accounts for the fact that the rule applies to verbs describing opinions and wants but not to perception verbs (*see, hear...*), which somehow denote neural rather than mental or psychic states. The specification of the condition as a state rather than an activity provides for the rule's applying to *think that*, but not *think about* in the sense 'ponder'; the sentences of (84):

84a. I'm not thinking about going to Canada.
84b. I'm thinking about not going to Canada.

are not synonymous. We could attempt to find the appropriate represen-tation for "non-factive verbs of mental state" and write the rule in terms of a single meaning class. But there is a hitch; *hope* is a non-factive verb of mental state, but under ordinary circumstances (i.e. with *not*) it does not permit negative-raising. The following (a) sentences are never synonymous with the (b) sentences:

85a. I don't hope I see you tomorrow.
85b. I hope I don't see you tomorrow.

86a. I don't hope to see you until tomorrow.
86b. I hope to not see you until tomorrow.

On the other hand, *hope* does permit negative-raising if the negative is *never*. There is a reading for each of the sentences of (87):

87a. I never hope I have to live in Boston.
87b. I never hope to see you again.

which is synonymous with the corresponding sentence of (88):

88a. I hope I never have to live in Boston.
88b. I hope to never see you again.

Furthermore, the meaning of *hope* in some sense provides a bridge between the two classes of negative-raising verbs, since *hope* expresses a desire which the subject believes can be fulfilled through ordinary channels (expectation). Consider the difference between (89a) and (89b):

89a.   I want to get a breath of fresh air, but I doubt I'll be able to.
89b. ??I hope to get a breath of fresh air, but I doubt I'll be able to.

In (89a) it is asserted that getting a breath of fresh air is a desire of the subject, but that the subject believes that it is unlikely that this desire will be fulfilled. In my speech, the presupposition required for the use of *hope*, that the desire can reasonably be expected to be fulfilled, is contradicted in (89b) by the assertion of doubt in the second cause. Likewise in (90), given the assumption that without diet or exercise losing weight will not be possible:

> 90a.   I want to lose weight but I can't diet or exercise.
> 90b.   ??I hope to lose weight but I can't diet or exercise.

In a converse way, *plan* and *contemplate* also provide a bridge between the "intent" verbs and the "opinion" verbs. In the sense in which they permit negative-transportation, *plan* and *contemplate* express expectations that an intention will be carried out:

> 91a.   I don't plan to sleep until I've finished this paper.
> 91b.   = I plan not to sleep until I've finished this paper.

> 92a.   I'm not contemplating leaving town until after Easter.
> 92b.   = I'm contemplating not leaving town until after Easter.

In my speech, at least, it appears that there is a possibility of defining the set of negative-transportation verbs as a single semantic class, with a single partial exception, *hope*. For other idiolects, however, there are words (e.g. *anticipate, guess, recommend*) which are semantically of the negative-transportation class, but do not undergo the rule. In some cases, these differences may be systematic; that is, whole semantic subclasses may be excluded from negative-transportation. Thus one informant does not have negative-raising for any of the suggestion verbs (*suggest, recommend, propose*). In other cases, there appears to be no semantic correlation. The exceptions may be idiosyncratically limited to one or two words; several speakers claim that they cannot use *anticipate* or *guess* or both as negative-raising verbs.[1] In such cases, if the meaning of these words is not systematically distinct from that of the negative-raising verbs, these verbs must be treated as exceptions. The treatment of exceptions required by a theory of semantic and syntactic interaction such as I have suggested will be taken up below (sec. D.4 of this chapter).

---

[1] Typically the inventory of such exceptions varies from speaker to speaker, and is subject to change through time. In my own case, I remember nudging *guess* into the class of negative-transportation verbs about eighteen years ago, long before I even heard of negative-transportation as such, on analogy with *think* in such expressions as *I don't think so*.

4 Exceptions

It appears that a grammatical description of English will have to treat the lexical item *hope* as exceptional in some way, no matter what theory of syntactic description is being used – regardless of whether it uses marked and unmarked rule features, subcategorization, or a semantic base. The exact conditions under which negative-transportation moves which negative adverbs over which verbs are not clear, and there is a certain amount of idiolect variation in them. For me, negative adverbs which quantify non-universally like *seldom* and *hardly*, and adverbs expressing negative affect, such as *unluckily* and *inappropriately*, are never raised. *Not* may be moved over any negative-transportation verb (except *hope*). *Never* may be moved over some verbs in each of the *not*-transporting classes (e.g. *seem, expect*; *want, hope, be supposed*), but not all (e.g. not *likely, think*; *mean*). Since it appears that there must be, in addition to a NOT-raising rule, and maybe a "NEVER"-raising rule,[1] a rule which raises "EVER" over negative-raising and non-negative-raising verbs alike, the exceptionality of *hope* is apparently best treated as a derivational constraint (cf. G. Lakoff 1969b, 1971) on the insertion of the lexical item *hope*. That is, it is necessary to postulate an "EVER"-raising rule to account for such paraphrases as:

93a. Can you ever remember not hearing a few played at every social event?

93b. Can you remember ever not hearing a few played at every social event?

94a. Do you ever want me to come back?

94b. Do you want me to come back ever?

95a. I don't ever want you to come back again.

95b. I don't want you to ever come back again.

---

[1] This would refer not to the lexical item *never*, but to the semantic content of *never*, since *hope* behaves the same way with *not ever* and *no-* . . . *ever* as it does with *never*, as illustrated below. Likewise, NOT-raising would refer to a semantic representation, and include *no* and *no-* as well as *not*.

    1a.   Nobody hopes to see him tomorrow.
    1b. ≠Everybody hopes to not see him tomorrow.
    2a.   Nobody ever hopes to see him again.
    2b. =Everybody hopes to never see him again.
    3a.   I don't ever hope to see him again.
    3b. =I hope to never see him again.
    3c. =I never hope to see him again.
    3d. *I don't hope to ever see him again.

95c. I don't want you to come back ever again.

95d. I don't want you ever to come back again.

The (a) sentences may be ambiguous, but they all have natural readings which paraphrase the (b) (and [c]) sentences. Since there is independent evidence for an "EVER"-raising rule (which may be related to the raising of other adverbs, such as *almost* and *always*, as in (96):

96a.   I hope you will always love me.

96b. = I hope you always will love me.

but which is certainly not a subcase of negative-raising), the simplest description of the behavior of *hope* is that if negative-raising has applied, it may not be inserted for the semantic configuration it encodes unless "EVER"-raising has also applied. To put it another way:

The lexical item *hope* (however it is to be represented) may encode the derived semantic configuration ["HOPE"] (however it is to be represented) unless the latter is preceded in the same clause by a negative which originated in a lower clause and which is not accompanied by a universal temporal quantifier (i.e. ["EVER"]) which also originated in a lower clause.

Because many (probably all) cyclic rules will be applying before lexical insertion on a given cycle, it is necessary to say that the prior application of rules determines the possibility of inserting certain items, rather than saying that the presence of a given lexical item determines the possibility of certain rules applying, as we would if we considered exceptional properties to be arbitrary properties of lexical items that unpredictably prevent or force application of a rule. In some respects, constraints on insertion are mirror images of constraints on rule application, but there are differences. For instance, treating *hope* as an exception in the traditional sense requires not one, but several rules which raise negatives (a *never*-raising rule, a *not*-raising rule, *not ever-*, *no-. . . ever*, and *no*-raising rules, and probably a host of others as well) since *hope* would be an exception to some but not all of these rules.

It is trivially easy to extend this sort of treatment to "exceptions" such as *anticipate* and *guess*, if this is necessary. The derivational constraint on the insertion of *anticipate* would be something like:

The lexical item *anticipate* may encode the derived semantic configuration ["EXPECT"] (or whatever), unless the latter is preceded in the same clause by a negative which originated in a lower clause.

The only drawback to such a treatment of exceptions is that it is too easy, and inhibits the search for explanations of apparently exceptional behavior. Because of this, it is all the more important to establish and use empirical criteria such as dialect variation, difficulty in learning, and historical change for determining whether an item is to be considered an exception or a counterexample.

Regardless of whether this is the correct treatment of *hope* and other apparent exceptions to syntactic rules, conditions on lexical entries will probably have to be included in an adequate theory of grammatical description. For instance, the lexical item *attempt*, which in its contemporary use is synonymous, or nearly so, with similar uses of *try*, may not occur without a complement unless a token (i.e. a pronoun) or a trace (i.e. infinitival *to*) remains in the sentence. Thus *try* and *attempt* may both have infinitive complements:

> 97a. John tried to touch his toes.
> 97b. John attempted to touch his toes.

and action nominalization complements:

> 98a. John tried a flight to Cuba.
> 98b. John attempted a flight to Cuba.

Both have elliptical uses which permit an ordinary referential noun phrase as surface complement:

> 99a. John tried the lock.
> 99b. John attempted the lock.

and in fact (98a,b) are both ambiguous between action nominalization and elliptical readings. They may describe an attempt by John to make a flight to Cuba, or to sell, stall, board, hijack, describe, etc. one. *Try*, however, permits a broader range of ellipses than *attempt*, and may end up, for example, with an animate noun phrase as the surface complement, as in (100a). *Attempt* can not have such surface complements, as (100b,c) demonstrates:

> 100a. I'll attempt to persuade the chairman, and you can try the dean.
> 100b. *I'll attempt to persuade the chairman, and you can attempt the dean.

100c. *I'll try to persuade the chairman, and you can attempt the dean.

100d. I'll try to persuade the chairman, and you can try the dean.

The complement of *attempt* may not be deleted without a trace, whether by infinitive verb-phrase deletion:

101a. You'll never know if you can write, unless you try.

101b. *You'll never know if you can write, unless you attempt.

by unspecified-object deletion:

102a. One thing about John, he always tries.

102b. *One thing about John, he always attempts.

or by a discourse rule of verb-phrase suppression:

103a. Can you do it? I can try.

103b. Can you do it? *I can attempt.

but if a pronoun or infinitive marker remains, deletion and suppression are permitted:

104a. We'll never know if we can write, if we don't try it.

104b. We'll never know if we can write, if we don't attempt it.

105a. Can you do it? I can try it.

105b. Can you do it? I can attempt it.

106a. Can you do it? I can try to.

106b. Can you do it? I can attempt to.

It is conceivable that the differences in syntax between *try* and *attempt* follow naturally from subtle differences in their meanings. The assumptions I have adopted would in fact lead one to expect this. But I have not been able to detect such subtle differences, much less discover semantic representations from which the syntactic properties would follow.

The restrictions illustrated in (101–6) on the use of *attempt* involve the application of at least two rules. If we were to claim that these restrictions were not the result of a single limitation on the syntactic environments in which the lexical item *attempt* may occur at a given level or levels, and claim instead that *attempt* is an exception to both or all of these rules, we would have to say that both or all of the rules are governed in Lakoff's sense, requiring description in terms of rule features, one for each rule to which *attempt* is an exception.[1] Furthermore, if the surface structure distribution of *attempt* is determined by these two or three rules, rather than by a single restriction on possible surface structure environments, then we would predict that there would be speakers of English for whom one rule was blocked for *attempt*, but not the other. This is an empirical question; it predicts, for instance, that there could be a speaker of English for whom (101b) would be grammatical, but (102b) would not. I find this unlikely, but, as I say, it is an empirical question. Moreover, we would predict that children would often make mistakes in the use of *attempt*, and have to be corrected by adults, since they wouldn't know which rules it was an exception to.

If, on the other hand, we consider the non-occurrence of *attempt* in certain surface-structure positions to be determined by a single specific condition on the syntactic environments in which it may occur, rather than by its being an exception to a number of syntactic rules, then we predict that speakers of English can indeed differ in their use of *attempt*, but that the occurrence or non-occurrence of certain constructions (such as [101b]) will imply the occurrence or non-occurrence of other constructions (such as [102b]).[2] Furthermore, it is much more plausible to assume that, in learning the syntax of a verb which is relatively restricted, a child extrapolates from adult speech to formulate an idea of what a well-formed environment is for the item in surface structure, or at some well-defined stage before surface structure, than it is to assume that he tries to assign rule features or lists of exceptions.

At any rate, I think it is quite natural to consider constraints like the one described above on *attempt* (p. 55), as output conditions[3] on the use

---

[1] Cf. Lakoff 1965, and discussion in chapter 3, sec. B, of the present work.

[2] For Shakespeare, object deletion was permissible for *attempt*, as evidenced by the line: "Our doubts are traitors, And make us lose the good we oft might win By fearing to attempt" (*Measure for Measure*, I, iv, 79–81). Infinitive verb-phrase deletion was apparently also possible for Shakespeare, as in: "You are to know, That prosperously I have attempted, and With bloody passage led your wars even To the gates of Rome" (*Coriolanus*, v, vi, 74–7). It is, of course, conceivable that at one time the restrictions on *attempt* reflected its being an exception and that the present constraint results from a reinterpretation of its restricted environments in surface structure.

[3] The term is self-explanatory. The notion 'output condition' was introduced in Ross 1967 (chapter III) and discussed in considerable detail in Perlmutter 1968.

of lexical items. Such output conditions on lexical items are in a sense constraints on the derivation of sentences containing those items, although not all of them need to refer to more than one stage in a derivation; the condition on *attempt* apparently needs to refer to only one level of structure, but the condition on *hope* (p. 53) has to refer to semantic representation as well as surface structure.[1]

5   Government

To the extent that these lexical output conditions are constraints on derivations, they bear a certain resemblance to the notion of rule violation as defined in Lakoff 1965. Lakoff defined syntactic rule violation as an incompatibility or contradiction (1965: sec. 0.52) between the inherent possibilities for a lexical item (the rule-feature markings and structural-description markings in the lexical member of a lexical item's complex symbol) and the actual derivational history of that item (the rule-feature and structural-description markings in the grammatical member) (1965: sec. 2). He used the notion of 'exception' (embodied as 'rule feature') to define 'violation,' and to approach a definition of 'rule government,' saying that the notion of 'government' in his sense corresponded to the notion of possible exception: a rule which could have exceptions would be in his sense of 'government' a governed rule. Infinitive verb-phrase deletion, unspecified-object deletion, and verb-phrase suppression produce violations when applied to clauses with *attempt*, but not when applied to clauses with *try*. If *attempt* as just discussed is an exception, then these rules would have to be considered to be governed in Lakoff's sense. Lakoff's use of *governed* does not correspond to the use of *govern* in the preceding sections, and the two notions should not be confused with each other.

The notion of government as used here corresponds much more closely to the traditional notion. In traditional usage words (usually verbs, adjectives, and prepositions) were said to govern the inflections of other words (typically nouns or verbs) when they required those other words to be in a certain case or mood. Thus:

> We speak of both verbs and prepositions as governing in the objective the word that is their object. (1877)[2]

---

[1] Other global derivational constraints on lexical items are discussed in G. Lakoff 1970.

[2] All dated citations are from the *Oxford English Dictionary*.

The genitive is also governed by certain adjectives. (1892)

In our language evermore Words that govern go before. (Seventeenth century)

The use of *govern* in grammar thus had quite a bit in common semantically with other uses of the word, where it meant 'control,' 'determine,' 'rule,' 'regulate,' 'influence,' 'guide,' and even 'administer' or 'manage.'[1] Use of the word *govern* by traditional grammarians to refer to the control by a verb or adjective over the case or mood of a following noun or verb led naturally to extension by transformational grammarians, who spontaneously and independently of each other spoke of the application of some transformational rules as being governed by a certain verb or adjective in the domain of the rule. This is the sense in which *govern* is used here. A rule will be said to be governed when its application depends on its domain being commanded by a particular type of predicate, regardless of whether the type of predicate is specified in the structural description of the rule itself, or has to be specified by redundancy rule. The term *command* is a technical one, but the metaphor is particularly apt here. A node X is said to command a node Y if X does not dominate Y and if the nearest S-node dominating X also dominates Y. Thus in the tree below, A commands B, C, D, and E, and B commands A, but C, D, and E do not command A, although C, D, and E command each other, and P commands everything in the tree except the highest S.

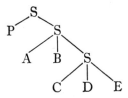

The domain of a rule is defined as the structural description of that rule, excluding any end variables which mark the boundaries of the domain.

A predicate will be said to govern the application of a governed rule if statement of that rule requires that its node be mentioned in the structural description in a position which commands the domain of the rule. *Predicate* is used to refer to an underlying- or intermediate-

---

[1] For example, in such uses as: "'Tis not folly, But good discretion, governs our main fortunes" (1625). "Whiles I goe tell my Lord...How I have govern'd our determined iest" (1588).

structure notion, 'node labelled V,' and not directly to any surface-structure notion. The usual surface-structure counterpart of predicate is verb, but predicates which are encoded as adjectives (cf. Lakoff 1965: Appendix A) govern many of the same rules as verbs do (e.g. negative-transportation, subject-raising); predicates encoded as prepositions (cf. Becker and Arms 1969) govern at least case-assignment rules; pre-dicates encoded as nouns (cf. Bach 1968, McCawley 1968c) govern at least one NP-movement rule, namely the rule or rules variously called Pronoun Replacement (Rosenbaum 1967), Tough-Movement (Postal 1968), and Irving (Morgan 1968), which is involved in the derivation of such sentences as:

> 107a. John is hard (*stupid, *advisable) to talk to.
> 107b. John is a bitch (*an illuminating experience) to talk to.

from something like:

> 108a. It is hard (stupid, advisable) to talk to John.
> 108b. It is a bitch (an illuminating experience) to talk to John.

Predicates are encoded as conjunctions (cf. Green 1969a), adverbs, and quantifiers (cf. Lakoff 1965: Appendix F) as well. A lexical item may be said to govern a rule when the statement of that rule requires reference (either overtly or by redundancy rule) to a semantic class which contains that lexical item.

The motivation for this definition of governed rule is simply to distinguish rules which mention semantically-defined units as well as syntactic categories (governed rules) from rules which mention ex-clusively syntactic categories (ungoverned rules). Governed rules may then be seen as defining the semantic classes which are relevant in the grammar of a language,[1] just as ungoverned rules have been implicitly assumed to define the (surface) syntactic categories of a language.

Lakoff's conception of rule government was a notion derivative of the notion 'exception to a rule.' Governed rules were rules with exceptions, and no distinction was made between exceptions to rules explicitly inferred by linguists (putative exceptions), and exceptions to rules presumably implicitly inferred by speakers – exceptions learned only by discovery and correction of errors. In contrast to this, the notion of rule government proposed here is based on syntactic regularities of semantic classes. It exposes putative exceptions to severe scrutiny in regard to its

---

[1] R. Lakoff's redundancy rules operating on meaning-classes did this indirectly.

assumption that exceptions are characterized by cross-dialectal and developmental variation and change, and by a lack of cross-linguistic regularity. The two conceptions of exception and government differ from each other in definition and framework, and so are probably not strictly comparable. The consequence of differences in basic definitions is a different distribution of labels resulting from the application of these definitions, and definitions derived from them. Since what something is called is not usually considered an empirical matter, there may be no empirical difference between the two conceptions of exception and government. So be it. The proposals I have made are intended as a revision and an improvement, in order to provide for an untortured description of certain regularities, and to force the search for regularities, by demanding that exceptions be viewed with suspicion.

6   *Implications for a theory of syntactic change*

Robin Lakoff (1968) presented persuasive arguments that the differences between Latin and Spanish in the syntax of verb complements arise from changes in the redundancy rules which define the input to the governed rules, rather than arising in the addition, deletion, re-ordering, or change in form of rules. She distinguished two types of redundancy-rule change. In the first type, the domain of the rule changes: the redundancy rule applies to more or fewer classes of verbs. In the other sort of change, the domain of the redundancy rule remains the same, but the markedness properties are interpreted differently. For example, the interpretation of *unmarked* may change from *optional* for a given rule, to *obligatory* for that rule, or to *negative* for that rule. Both of these types of change affect entire meaning-classes. When a change in markedness interpretation occurs, it

takes place throughout a whole meaning-class, rather than in individual verbs. When *dico* becomes able to take *quod*, for instance, *aio* and *puto* presumably can also do so, as can all the other verbs of this class. It is not that any verb becomes irregular, but rather that the regular situation for a meaning-class shifts (1968:229).

Likewise, when a change in domain takes place, it affects a whole meaning-class in involving the addition or subtraction of a meaning-class in the domain of a redundancy rule. Both of these types of change represent extended or reduced applicability of the governed rules involved, but when described in terms of redundancy rules which interpret irregularity markings, they are formally very different from each other. One is a change in the input of a rule, and one is a change in the output of a rule. Furthermore, change in governed rules appears as formally very different from change in ungoverned rules, since redundancy rules which assign rule features are defined only for governed rules. Despite rather strong evidence for locating governed-rule change in the redundancy rules, even R. Lakoff herself was skeptical of the unique status thereby accorded to governed-rule change.

If rule-specific irregularity features (i.e. markedness for a rule defined separately for each lexical item) are eliminated from the vocabulary of primitives available for syntactic description, as I have suggested they be, and if a rule which is optional for one semantic class and obligatory for another is treated as two rules, then it is no longer necessary to distinguish two types of governed-rule change which both have the same sorts of effects. An increase or decrease in the applicability of a rule over time may be seen as one phenomenon, namely, the re-definition of the semantic class which triggers the rule, so that it includes more or fewer lexical items. If governed rules differ from ungoverned formally only in that the structural descriptions of the former contain precise references to meaning, as I have suggested, then change in governed rules of the sort R. Lakoff discusses, extension and reduction in scope, would be typologically no different from other changes in the structural descriptions of rules, governed or ungoverned. The change would, however, still be located in the specification of the relevant meaning-class, as Lakoff intended, and this is, after all, what makes governed rules governed.

If governed rules are rules which apply to semantically defined classes of verbs, one would expect change in governed rules to interact with semantic change (change in the set of meanings which a lexical item may encode). I can imagine at least five apparently different sorts of effects which such interaction might produce. First of all, there might be no semantic change among the lexical items which constitute the governing semantic class in the older stage, but a new semantic class might be defined in the later stage which would contain most but not all of the lexical items of the old one (that is, it might contain the phonological descendants of those lexical items), and they might retain their previous meanings.

Second, there might be some semantic drift, and while the new semantic class contained the historical descendants of the lexical items which were the members of the old one, they might not all have their previous meanings. This is a very different sort of situation, and the retention of these lexical items must be considered a coincidence, unless one assumes, contrary to what both Robin Lakoff and I have suggested, that lexical items rather than semantic classes govern rules. I have not been able to find examples of this sort of change on a large scale, and the isolated instances which I have been able to find (e.g. Latin *amare* with the sense 'be wont to' taking a subjectless infinitive complement as a "verb of habit," and its French descendant *aimer* with the sense 'like' taking a subjectless infinitive as a "verb of enjoying") suggest that it is indeed a coincidental and non-systematic occurrence.

Third, the new definition for the semantic class governing the rule and the semantic changes might work in contrary directions, and no lexical items of the new semantic class would be historical descendants of members of the old class, although the new semantic class might still include some or all of the meanings included in the old one. The development of French provides an example of this on a small scale. In both Latin and French, verbs meaning 'begin' have infinitive complements. But none of the French words (*commencer à, se mettre à, se prendre à*) is historically derived from any of the Latin verbs (*incipere, coepi, exordiri, adoriri, adgredi, ingredi*).

Fourth, semantic drift and semantic class re-definition could conspire to leave a governed rule operating on lexical items that are not related either semantically or historically to the lexical items which the governed rule operated on in an earlier stage of the language. At least in theory, in extreme cases successive re-definitions of the relevant semantic class could also produce this result.

Finally, it is quite natural to think of the disappearance of a governed rule (e.g. the imminent disappearance of infinitive complements in some Rumanian dialects) as coming about through successive reductions in the number and scope of the semantic classes governing a given rule. Whether all of these situations do in fact occur awaits detailed research, which I think cannot fail to be interesting and illuminating, whatever conclusions are to be drawn from it.

One would expect changes in lexical insertion conditions such as that described for the verb *attempt* to be related to semantic change as well as to governed-rule change. The verb *endeavor*, for instance, in present-day English, as in (109):

109. Bill endeavored to answer the question.

encodes a meaning essentially identical to 'exert oneself' and is construed obligatorily with an infinitive complement which appears to represent an underlying purpose clause.[1] Unlike *try* and *attempt*, *endeavor* may not have a nominalization as object, nor may it be used

---

[1] It is necessary to emphasize that I mean purpose clause, as distinct from reason clause. Reason clauses may be questioned with *why*, but strict purpose clauses and infinitives may not. Thus:

    1.   Why did you rob the bank?

    2a.   Because I wanted to get arrested.
    2b.   Because I wanted money to pay tuition.
    2c.   ?For the purpose of financing my education.
    2d.   ?In order to finance my education.

The complement of *endeavor* may not be questioned with *why*, although it can, of course, be questioned:

    3a.   *Why were you endeavoring?
    3b.   What were you endeavoring to do?

Reason clauses may be referred to anaphorically by *for the same reason* and *for that reason*, while purpose clauses may not:

    4a.   Bill is holding his breath because he thinks it will annoy his mother, and Sam is holding his { for the same reason. / for that reason too. }
    4b.   *Bill is holding his breath to stop his hiccups, and Sam is holding his { for the same reason. / for that reason too. }
    4c.   *John looked under the bed to find my shoes, and Bill looked under the chair for that reason.

Of course, purpose infinitives may be referred to by *for that purpose*:

    5a.   Bill is holding his breath to stop the hiccups, and Sam is holding his { for the same purpose. / for that purpose too. }
    5b.   John looked under the bed to find my shoes, and Bill looked under the chair for that purpose.

The complement of *endeavor* has a distribution similar to that of purpose infinitives:

    6a.   *John is endeavoring to stop his hiccups, and Bill is acting like he is { for that reason too. / for the same reason. }
    6b.   *John endeavored to find my shoes, and Bill exerted himself { for that reason too. / for the same reason. }
    6c.   John is endeavoring to stop his hiccups, and Bill is acting like he is { for that purpose too. / for the same purpose. }
    6d.   John endeavored to find my shoes, and Bill exerted himself { for that purpose too. / for the same purpose. }

elliptically with the concrete object of an "understood" verb, and it may not occur without a complement. These properties are illustrated in (110–12):

110.   *John endeavored the seduction of Sabina.

111a.   *John endeavored the lock.
111b.   *John endeavored the Dean.

112.   *John couldn't convince the Dean, although he endeavored.

If *endeavor* is analyzed as obligatorily incorporating an object co-referential to its subject,[1] the fact that it cannot have a surface direct object follows naturally; it already has a direct object. In earlier stages of English, however, *endeavor* meant something more like merely 'exert' and could have animate direct objects co-referential to the subject, as well as abstract objects denoting power or potential, as in (113) and (114):

113.   Endevoir youre self and put to your hand and spare no cost. (1491)

114a.   Marcus Aurelius...endeuoured his power to persecute the Christians. (1574)
114b.   Every man endeuored his thoughts how to make his duty, love [etc.] encrese to him. (1606)

The verb of a purpose infinitive may not be deleted leaving a dangling *to*, and neither may the complement of *endeavor*:

7a.   *Bill is holding his breath to stop his hiccups, and Sam is holding his to, too.
7b.   *John looked under the bed to find my shoes, and Sam looked under the chair to.
7c.   *Bill was endeavoring to convince the Dean, and Janet was also endeavoring to.
7d.   *I was instructed to persuade the senators, and I endeavored to.
7e.   *Bill was exerting himself to convince the Dean, and Janet was exerting herself to.
7f.   *I was instructed to persuade the senators, and I exerted myself to.

[1] Optional incorporation of such an object occurs with *surrender*. Thus *surrender* in (1) means 'give oneself up,' while *surrender* in (2) and (3) means merely 'give up.'

1. John surrendered to the Indians.
2. John surrendered himself to the Indians.
3. John surrendered his gun to the Indians.

It could also optionally encode in addition to 'exert,' an object co-referential to the subject, and occur "intransitively" as in (115):

> 115. The pardon of his Holines, giuen to all...that...indeuor in this quarrel. (1588)

At the same time, it could also optionally encode the notion 'for the purpose of' and occur with abstract nouns as object as in (116):

> 116a. It is nought but a learned ministry which their champion Martin endeuors. (1589)
> 116b. We shall...endeavour the extirpation of Popery. (1647)
> 116c. He was stimulated to endeavour the restoration. (1818)

At some time in the recent past, the insertion of *endeavor* was deprived of these options, and was restricted to the meaning 'exert oneself.' At about the same time, the restriction must have developed that some token of the complement remain in surface structure, resulting in the difference in grammaticality between present-day (112) and sixteenth-century (115), on the one hand, and present-day (117), on the other:

> 117a. I couldn't open the door, although I exerted myself.
> 117b. I was instructed to persuade two senators, and I endeavored to do so.

Compare these last to (118):

> 118a. ?I was instructed to persuade two senators, and I endeavored to.
> 118b. *Bill was endeavoring to convince the Dean, and Janet was also endeavoring to.

The history of *attempt* provides another example of surface syntax changing along with meaning. In the past, *attempt* could be used with a wider range of ellipses than at present, so that sentences like (119), with animate surface objects, were grammatical:

> 119a. I have attempted, one by one, the lords...With supplication prone and father's tears, To accept of ransom for my son. (1671)
> 119b. They attempt us, as the Devil did Adam. (1691)
> 119c. How I should escape from them, if they attempted me. (1719)

although at present these sentences, like (100b), are ungrammatical.

Attempt could also take animate direct objects by virtue of its meaning 'tempt,' which required an animate direct object:

120a. Sore attempted by his gostly enemy. (1513)
120b. His Highness should not be attempted to recede from the Religion. (*c.* 1670)
120c. Nothing will be found, I fear, to attempt a man to be a thief. (1773)

One may plausibly speculate that the decrease in permitted ellipses and the loss of the sense 'tempt' reinforced each other in making animate surface objects impossible for *attempt*.

E   A summary and defense of the hypotheses adopted in this chapter

I have proposed that syntactic rules which appear to be "irregular" (exceptional, idiosyncratic, etc.) should instead be thought of as operating as regularly as other rules, but on nodes which are characterized in terms of semantic composition rather than in terms of syntactic category. This proposal invites the criticism that it is quixotic, and doomed to failure, since it takes the position that all differences in syntactic properties between two lexical items must be assumed to be based on semantic properties, and contradicts the widely-held belief that language, especially lexicon, is arbitrary, that exceptions are characteristic of natural language, opposing it to artificial languages. I take the position that *I* don't "know" that language is arbitrary and full of exceptions, since I hold that it is in principle impossible to prove by strictly linguistic arguments that any item is by nature an exception to all conceivable significant generalizations about a phenomenon. It is, on the other hand, in principle possible to prove that an item is not an exception – namely by providing an independently motivated generalization which accounts for the "exceptional" character of that item. I do not see how anyone can expect to make progress in finding basic principles which determine syntactic distributions except by assuming that there are basic and general principles which may not be overridden at the caprice of individual lexical items, but which may only be superseded or constrained by other equally general principles. The specific proposal I have put forth here is that in general syntactic properties and distributions are determined by semantic properties (e.g. the unacceptability of *∗It is viscous to please John*); semantically possible but non-occurring distributions may apparently result from grammatical conditions on the well-formedness of surface structures (e.g. the present unacceptability of *John endeavored the lock*), from pragmatic conditions (the unacceptability of *John died until Friday* in the sense 'John spent all the time until Friday dying' – cf. *I washed dishes until midnight*), and from cultural conditions (e.g. the fact that *John died until Friday* in the sense 'John died, and was/is dead, not to return to life again until Friday – cf. *John left until Friday* meaning 'John left and was/is gone, not to return until Friday' – is unacceptable to speakers who don't believe in reincarnation). Conceivably there are others; conceivably these last two principles are derived from the general principle that semantics determines syntax, in that they reflect the speaker's assumptions about what words mean, and about what is possible in the real world and what is conceivable in any world.

The general position I have taken, that linguistic phenomena are characteristically overwhelmingly regular, is also subject to criticism – namely to the criticism that it is not falsifiable, and therefore not scientific. After all, if I fail to find a generalization which I am looking for, I will say that that is a result of my nearsightedness, or lack of adequate tools, or even laziness or wrongheadedness, and not that it is because language is arbitrary. But I take this general position as my methodology, not as a thesis, and methodologies are not by nature falsifiable, although they may be sterile or otherwise hinder progress. As a methodology, it is nothing new; it is only applying to linguistics the scientific aphorism "always look for a generalization – and always distrust it." Pedersen, in introducing his discussion of the *Junggrammatiker*, writes (1931:290):

After all the discoveries that had taken place in the course of the seventies, the view which met the eye of the scholar in the study of the old Indo-European languages was very different from the earlier one. Where before there was mere irregularity, there was now the most striking regularity. The material now induced scholars to postulate complete adherence to laws in the development of sounds, and to seek an explanation for every deviation from the usual.

These scholars were concerned with historical phonology, but there is no reason to believe, and we have no right to assume, that the principle of exceptionlessness of linguistic rules is any less valid for syntax than it is for phonology. In espousing this principle I am putting myself in the company of men who may have been imprudent (cf. Pedersen 1931:293–

4), and who probably were insufferably self-righteous and patronizing, but I have had my nose rubbed in the data often enough to have a good deal of respect for the complexity and depth of linguistic phenomena, and to have, I hope, some humility in investigating it.

Pedersen says (1931:283) of Verner's explanation of exceptions to the first Germanic consonant shift, that it "suggested how exhaustively one must study the phenomena, and how accurately one must discriminate, to understand the development of sounds. It was, in fact, an emphatic warning not to regard any such development as a mere whim of language." Syntax, I am saying, is no different. Quite a bit of work had been done on the syntax of many languages before Robin Lakoff noticed that many of the governed rules of Latin were essentially the same rules as the governed rules of English (e.g. Equi-NP-Deletion, negative-transportation, subject-raising), that these rules applied not to a list of exceptional verbs, but to classes of verbs that were semantically defined, and that furthermore, the rules applied to approximately – but not exactly – the same semantic classes in each language. If the governed rules of English and Latin applied to semantically similar lists of exceptions, it would have to be considered a fantastic coincidence. That the lexical items involved are *not* exceptions is predicted by one of the working principles which follows from the assumptions that the items which govern syntactic rules form classes which are defined by their semantic structure, and that true syntactic exceptions are diachronically and geographically unstable. This is the principle that an item of some language cannot be considered even provisionally or tentatively exceptional with respect to a syntactic phenomenon if words with (roughly) the same meaning show the same "exceptional" behavior in languages with which it has no particularly close genetic or social affinities (e.g. English and Papago, even English and Greek).

The other working principle derived from my hypothesis about the nature of rule government is that if a lexical item has two meanings, it may have different syntactic properties associated with each of those meanings, and vice versa: if a lexical item appears to undergo a rule only sometimes, it may have different meanings associated with whether it undergoes the rule or not. This was a methodological principle of linguists even when they were called grammarians, and it was not questioned until the advent of structuralism. Its validity is demonstrated by the fact that *think, believe, imagine,* and *see* (. . . *as*), and *desire* and *choose* govern negative-raising only when they mean, roughly speaking, 'hold the opinion' or 'intend,' and never when they mean 'ponder,' 'accept the claim,' 'form a mental image,' 'perceive visually,' 'wish,' or 'decide,' since verbs with these meanings, e.g. *ponder, be convinced, dream, behold, wish,* and *decide,* never undergo negative-transportation. It is demonstrated by the fact that an inference of success is associated with *teach* and perhaps also with *write* when they occur without prepositions before their indirect objects, but not when their indirect objects are preceded by *to* (cf. sec. C in this chapter, above and chapter 4, sec. B, below). These facts, and those demonstrated by Robin Lakoff, provide evidence of the strongest sort that these principles are useful in investigating the character of syntactic rules.

Denials of the relevance of semantic information for syntactic rules have persisted since the development of the structural tradition in linguistics, apparently because the semantics of the lexical items presumed to govern particular rules have not been investigated closely, systematically, and rigorously enough, and because in most cases attempts have not even been made to determine and characterize, or even suggest the range of cases over which particular rules presumed to be governed applied. Chapters 3 and 4 of this work are the result of an effort to deprive these denials of their plausibility by using the approach to linguistic investigation described in this chapter and the previous one to determine the status of a putative rule of English syntax, and to explore the implications of the resultant analysis.

3 *Dative movement*

Among the syntactic phenomena I had originally planned to investigate is the alternation known as dative movement, or indirect object movement. Such an alternation is presumed in order to account for the intuitively obvious relationship between sentences like (1a) and (1b), and (2a) and (2b):

    1a. I gave a book to John.
    1b. I gave John a book.

    2a. I bought a book for John.
    2b. I bought John a book.

In this chapter, I will discuss aspects of this relationship which prevent its description as a single straightforward movement rule.

A The passive problem

1 Fillmore's treatment
The earliest generative treatment of dative movement is to my knowledge Fillmore 1965. This work, a version of which first appeared in 1962, was concerned with, among other things, the fact that *to*-datives like (1) have three passive forms:[1]

    3a. A book was given to John.
    3b. John was given a book.
    3c. A book was given him.

corresponding to external and internal dative phrases as in (1a) and (1b), respectively, while *for*-datives like (2) have only one passive form, which corresponds to the active form with an external dative:

    4a. A book was bought for John.
    4b. *John was bought a book.
    4c. *A book was bought him.

---

[1] Judgments of unacceptability in sec. A, as marked by asterisks, are Fillmore's.

It appeared that the acceptable passives were formed from sentences underlying (1a), (1b), and (2a), but not (2b), and Fillmore argued that for this reason, the rule relating sentences (1a) and (1b), whatever it was, had to precede the passive rule, while the rule which related (2a) to (2b) had to follow the passive, and that therefore the two rules must be distinct.

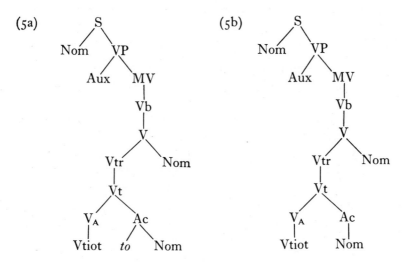

The two indirect object rules which Fillmore proposed were quite different from each other. The first related deep structures like (5a) to intermediate structures like (5b). The second related deep structures like (6a) to intermediate structures like (6b). Fillmore's passive rule

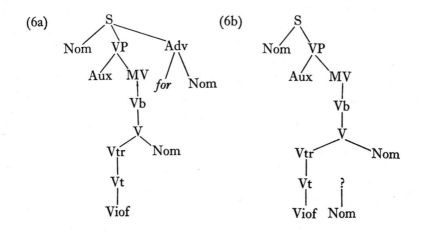

referred to a node labelled *either* Vtr or Vtiot, and the immediately following Nom, so it could apply to the object of Vtr in either (5a) or (6a), and to some object in (5) whether or not the first indirect object rule had applied. It could apply in either of two ways to structures like (5b), providing altogether for three passive versions of sentences with deep structures like (5a).

Fillmore's proposed treatment of dative movement requires an additional rule to extrapose an unreduced *to*-phrase (Ac node), that is, to correct the order in (7) to that in (1a):

7.   I gave to John a book.

1a.   I gave a book to John.

Thus the treatment he presents involves an optional *to*-deletion rule, an obligatory *to* *NP*-movement rule, and an optional rule which simultaneously deletes *for* and moves its object NP. Fillmore's treatment requires different deep structures for indirect object constructions corresponding to *to*-phrases and indirect object constructions corresponding to *for*-phrases. The fact of different deep structures makes two separate movement rules relating the (a) sentences of (1) and (2) to the (b) sentences more plausible, but no independent justification or defense was presented for these particular deep structures. It was in fact implied[1] that the choice was at least partly arbitrary.

2   *Order and prepositionality*

Before going further, it is important to make clear what the *crucial* difference is between the two indirect object constructions, since there are two differences. In (1a) and (2a), the direct object precedes the indirect object; in (1b) and (2b), it follows. In (1a) and (2a), the indirect object has a preposition; in (1b) and (2b), it has none. Is the order the crucial difference, or the presence of the preposition? The phenomenon of Complex NP Shift (Ross 1967: chap. III) will provide an answer,

---

[1] For example, on p. 11 (Fillmore 1965): "In treating these relationships among sentences, the grammarian has two choices. He may allow the strings [sic] underlying (3) and (5) [parallel to (1b) and (2b)] to be generated by the phrase-structure component of the grammar, providing the needed transpositions and the addition of the appropriate prepositions by means of transformational rules; or he may construct the phrase-structure grammar in such a way that the strings underlying (4) and (6) [parallel to (1a) and (2a)] are among the terminal strings of the phrase-structure component, with the transposition of the objects, where needed, and the deletion of the preposition to be taken care of by transformational rules. In the rules proposed here, the latter choice has been made."

since it extraposes "heavy" noun phrases to the end of the sentence, as in (8) and (9), producing sentences in which the indirect object precedes the direct object, but still has a preposition:

8a. ?John demonstrated the sixteen proofs for the existence of God which he found in a medieval manuscript over the weekend to me.

8b. John demonstrated to me the sixteen proofs for the existence of God which he found in a medieval manuscript over the weekend.

8c. *John demonstrated to me the proofs.

9a. ?*Arthur will try to obtain the recommendations which you say I need for me.

9b. Arthur will try to obtain for me the recommendations which you say I need.

9c. *Arthur will try to obtain for me the recommendations.

But verbs that may occur in sentences which have undergone Complex NP Shift (an ungoverned rule) cannot always occur in sentences with a prepositionless indirect object, as demonstrated in (10) and (11):

10a. John demonstrated the proofs to Herbert.

10b. *John demonstrated Herbert the proofs.

11a. Arthur will obtain the recommendations for Joan.

11b. *Arthur will obtain Joan the recommendations.

For apparently independent reasons,[1] prepositionless indirect objects

---

[1] These factors, whatever they are, may be responsible for the fact that intransitive verbs have only prepositional indirect objects, and no prepositionless indirect objects:

   1a. They surrendered to him.
   1b. *They surrendered him.

   2a. They marched for him.
   2b. *They marched him.

This fact may be related to the output condition on pronoun position discussed in chapter 5, sec. C.3, which apparently restricts dative movement when the direct object is co-referential to the subject. Thus, while we find such sentences as:

   3a. They gave themselves up to him.
   3b. They marched themselves for him.

we never find versions of them where the indirect object is prepositionless and internal, as in:

   4a. *They gave him up themselves.
   4b. *They marched him themselves.

may never directly follow the direct object, as illustrated in (12) and (13):

12a. *John gave the ideas Herbert.
12b. John gave Herbert the ideas.

13a. *Arthur will get the recommendations Joan.
13b. Arthur will get Joan the recommendations.

It is not the case that prepositionless indirect objects may *never* follow the direct objects, since they do exactly this in sentences with relative clauses, such as (14a,b):

14a. The book which they gave him was a novel.
14b. The book which they bought him was a novel.

For the same reason, it cannot be claimed that a prepositionless indirect object may never occur sentence-finally:

15a. He liked the book which they gave him.
15b. He liked the book which they bought him.

The sentences cited as (8–9) and (14–15) provide two independent demonstrations that prepositionality of the indirect object and direct object–indirect object order are independent of each other. These sentences appear to indicate that the crucial feature of sentences like (1b) and (2b) for indirect object movement is the prepositionlessness of the immediately post-verbal indirect object, not its position. I may occasionally refer to the prepositionless indirect object as "internal" as opposed to "external," but unless it is explicitly stated otherwise, I will mean a prepositionless indirect object, and be excluding such instances as (8b) and (9b).

B   The exception problem

A second problem encountered by anyone who wanted to account for all indirect object constructions was the fact that not all indirect object verbs occur with both indirect object constructions. Thus, verbs like *donate, transfer*, and *select*, seem not to occur with internal prepositionless indirect objects:

16a. We donated $10 to UNICEF.
16b. *We denoted UNICEF $10.

17a. We transferred some stock to Bill.
17b. *We transferred Bill some stock.

18a. The Maître d' selected a French wine for us.

18b. *The Maître d' selected us a French wine.

although such near synonyms as *give, send,* and *choose,* all permit both constructions.

19a. We gave $10 to UNICEF.

19b. We gave UNICEF $10.

20a. We sent some stock to Bill.

20b. We sent Bill some stock.

21a. The Maître d' chose a French wine for us.

21b. The Maître d' chose us a French wine.

Furthermore, there are verbs such as *allow,* and expressions such as *give someone a punch in the nose, a pain in the neck, impetigo,* etc., which under normal circumstances never occur with external prepositional phrase indirect objects:

22a. John allowed his sister a peek.

22b. *John allowed a peek to his sister.

23a. Measle germs give you measles.

23b. *Measle germs give measles to you.

24a. Bill gave Sue a little pinch.

24b. *Bill gave a little pinch to Sue.

George Lakoff (1965) set up an exception mechanism to deal with cases like this, where the applicability or inapplicability of a rule was unpredictable. As he pointed out (Lakoff 1965: sec. 7.2), his two kinds of exception features define only four of five logically possible cases for optional rules. This means that his system is inadequate to describe formally the whole range of dative constructions (let alone explain them), since, as I will show below, any grammar written within the framework of Chomsky 1965 or Lakoff 1965, with a single optional dative-movement rule for *to*-datives will have to account for one normal case and five kinds of exceptions, regardless of whether the rule intraposes a noun phrase, or extraposes a prepositional phrase.

First, I would like to sketch a description of the relevant aspects of G. Lakoff's exception mechanism. This mechanism was based on two kinds of marked exception features: rule features, and structural-description features (SD features). For obligatory rules, the interpretation of the exception features of lexical entries was very straightforward. The notation [+ Rule$_i$] was the unmarked case, and meant Rule$_i$ had to apply to the clause containing the lexical item so marked; [− Rule$_i$] was the marked case, and meant that the rule was not to apply to it. As for the SD features, the marking [+ SD$_i$] on a lexical item meant that the clause containing the lexical item must meet the structural description of Rule$_i$, and [− SD$_i$] meant that it must not meet the structural description of Rule$_i$. Both were marked features, interpreted as plus or minus by an ordered set of metarules, some of which were context-sensitive (Lakoff 1965: secs. 2.3 and 5.31–2).

For optional rules, the situation is a little more complicated. G. Lakoff (1965: Ex. 7–7) defined five logically possible cases as follows:

1. Normal case: the item may or may not meet the SD of the rule, and if it does, the rule may or may not apply.

2. Obligatory exception: the item may or may not meet the SD of the rule, but if it does, it must undergo the rule.

3. Negative exception: the item may or may not meet the SD, but if it does, it must not undergo the rule.

4. Positive absolute exception: the item must meet the SD, and must undergo the rule.

5. Negative absolute exception: the item must not meet the SD of the rule.

It seems to me that there is a sixth logical possibility, namely, an item which must meet the SD, but must not undergo the rule, and a seventh, namely, an item which must meet the SD, but need not undergo the rule, but G. Lakoff doesn't mention them. A two-feature system will define only four cases, but that appeared sufficient to G. Lakoff, since there were only two kinds of exceptions for which he had found empirical evidence: obligatory exceptions and positive absolute exceptions (Lakoff 1965: sec. 7.2).

Unfortunately, a system of rules with a single optional *to*-dative-movement rule has to deal with at least five kinds of exceptions in addition to the normal case, and G. Lakoff's two exception features are inadequate to distinguish all of these cases, which are sketched in Table 2. Thus here are five kinds of exceptions to a *to*-dative-movement rule formulated as an extraposing and preposition-inserting rule, and five kinds of exceptions to a *to*-dative-movement rule formulated as an

TABLE 2 *Kinds of exceptions to dative-movement rules*

Type of expression	Extraposition of NP, insertion of preposition		Intraposition of NP, deletion of preposition	
	To	*For*	*To*	*For*
Normal case	Give	Buy	Give	Buy
Obligatory exception	Transfer Delegate	Obtain Give one's life	Allow Spare	
Negative exception	Allow Spare		Transfer Delegate	Obtain Give one's life
Positive absolute exception			Give a pain, punch, cold, etc.	
Negative absolute exception	Give a damn; a cry, a yell; one's life		Give a damn; a cry, a yell; one's life	
No. 6: must meet SD, and must not undergo rule	Give a pain, punch, etc.			
No. 7: must meet SD, and may optionally undergo rule	Feed Entrust Bequeath		Feed Entrust Bequeath	

intraposing and preposition-deleting rule. The fact that I have found only one kind of exception to each possible kind of *for*-dative-movement rule does not mean that there couldn't be more.[1]

In any case, the mere fact of the rather large number of different kinds of exceptions to either form of a *to*-dative-movement rule justifies a closer look at the phenomena, to see if some of these "exceptions" are not predictable from other grammatical facts.

C Dative-movement verbs

1 Phonology

It is often observed that there seems to be a phonological difference between verbs (not constructions) which permit both internal and

---

[1] As with the *to*-datives, a *for*-dative verb that had to have an internal indirect object, if it had an indirect object, would simultaneously be an obligatory exception to an intraposing rule, and a negative exception to an extraposing rule; a *for*-dative verb which had to have an indirect object that had to be internal would simultaneously be a positive absolute exception to an intraposing rule, and a sixth kind of exception to an extraposing rule. A *for*-dative verb that could not have a surface indirect object of either kind would be a negative absolute exception to either kind of rule, and so on.

external dative constructions, and their near-synonyms which permit only one (cf. examples [16–21]). The obvious observation is that the verbs which permit both are shorter, while the verbs which permit only an external dative are longer. But this sort of statement is too imprecise to have enough predictive power to be testable (i.e. falsifiable). It will be necessary, therefore, to examine some hypotheses which are more precise in attempting to delimit the relevant boundaries of "shorter" and "longer."

Hypothesis I: There is a constraint on surface structures to the effect that only one-syllable words may have internal indirect objects. Objection: *carry, cable, promise,* and several other words permit both external and internal indirect objects:

    25a. I carried Bill a six-pound ashtray.
    25b. I carried a six-pound ashtray to Bill.

    26a. I cabled Bill the news.
    26b. I cabled the news to Bill.

    27a. I promised Bill an apple.
    27b. I promised an apple to Bill.

Hypothesis II: There is a constraint on surface structures to the effect that only initial-stressed words containing less than three syllables may have internal indirect objects. Objections: (1) There exist final-stressed bi-syllabic words which permit internal indirect objects, and thereby prove Hypothesis II false:

    28a. I allowed Cyndy an ice-cream cone before dinner.
    28b. I advanced Sam $10.

(2) There are some initial-stressed bi-syllabics which do not permit internal indirect objects – cf. (16b, 17b). Hypothesis II fails to exclude these. (3) Some words with three syllables permit internal datives:

    29a. Sears delivered them the wrong sofa.
    29b. They had guaranteed them prompt delivery.
    29c. But they telephoned them an apology.

Hypothesis II would wrongly exclude these. (4) Bi-syllabic stems have more than two syllables when they are inflected in the progressive form, but they still permit internal indirect objects:

    30a. We'll be promising the children new coats.
    30b. We'll be forwarding the Smiths their mail.

Hypothesis II would predict that such tri-syllabic forms would not permit internal datives.

Hypothesis III: This stress and syllable business is a red herring – a fortuitous consequence of the real surface-structure restriction which requires that only [+ Anglo-Saxon] words may have an internal indirect object. Objections: (1) Native speakers know the restrictions on occurrence for these verbs regardless of whether they even know that other languages than English exist. (2) Some words of Anglo-Saxon (or at least native English) origin do not permit internal indirect objects:

31a. *The USIA broadcast the Russians the news.
31b. *Bill muttered Sue sweet nothings.

(3) Some verbs of Romance origin permit internal indirect objects, e.g. *permit, promise, offer*, etc.

Hypothesis IV: The restriction is phonological, but it is a restriction on the operation of the dative-movement rule, not on surface structure; the rule applies only to words with initially-stressed stems of two syllables or fewer. Reference to stems rather than words eliminates objection II 4, and reference to the operation of the rule rather than the output structure it creates eliminates, for solutions which purport to be exceptionless, all putative counterexamples which occur with only external or only internal datives, since it may be claimed that the word orders which occur are not the result of any movement transformation, but rather come from base structures with that order. However, this hypothesis still fails to account for final-stressed bi-syllabics which occur in both constructions, such as *advance*, and variously stressed tri-syllabics which permit both forms, such as *deliver, guarantee*, and *telephone*.

Phonological constraints may well be relevant in dative-movement derivations, but for the present, they seem to have led only to a dead end. In addition, they can never account for the fact that *give* generally permits both kinds of indirect object, but with certain kinds of direct objects permits only an internal indirect object. For this reason, I will devote the next four sections (c.2–5) to an examination of the semantics of dative-movement verbs (verbs which permit both kinds of datives), and semantic constraints on the free substitution of dative forms. I will attempt to determine whether the occurrence of a particular indirect object form is predictable from the semantics of the verb and the semantics of the utterance it occurs in.

2 *Kinds of* to-*dative verbs*

In this section, I will attempt an informal semantic characterization of the verbs which participate in *to*-dative alternations – verbs which may have direct objects of the type Noun ± modifiers,[1] and internal indirect objects which may be paraphrased as *to NP*. *To*-dative verbs may be divided into five major classes on the basis of the semantic relationships they encode. These classes and their subclasses have a remarkable, though admittedly incomplete, syntactic coherence in terms of whether they permit indirect object passives, and deletion of direct and indirect objects, as charted in Appendix I.

a To-*class 1*. Class I is composed of verbs denoting the direct and accompanied physical transfer of an object from an agent to the individual denoted by the indirect object expression. The members of this class thus describe situations where an agent comes or goes to the individual described by the indirect object, with some object which he intends for that individual to have. Class I may be characterized as encoding the notions 'bring' and 'take,' and instrumentals of the form 'bring (take) by means of V-ing.' Obviously no claim is being made that these notions (and those below) are semantic primes. This class includes such verbs as *bring, take, carry, drag, hand, haul, pass, pull, push*, and will for convenience sometimes be referred to as the *bring*-class.[2] The semantic characterization suggested also includes at least one verb, *tug*, which for me requires a prepositional dative phrase.

b To-*class 2*. *To*-class 2 is composed of verbs denoting the direct and unaccompanied transfer of an object to an individual denoted by the indirect object phrase. Neither the transfer, nor the transferred object, is necessarily physical. Class 2 includes *give, advance, award, cede, concede, entrust,[3] feed, lease, lend, loan, sell, serve*, etc. It may be characterized as encoding the notion 'give' with or without presuppositions

---

[1] I am not sure at what level, if any, this is a proper characterization. I wish to include abstract as well as concrete nouns, and nominalizations, with their objects, but not gerunds, infinitives, or clauses, with or without head nouns.

[2] The name has only mnemonic significance; it should be understood as meaning '*to*-class I, of which *bring* is a member.' The mnemonic terms for the other classes are intended to be understood in a parallel fashion.

[3] With *entrust*, and possibly a few other verbs, if the indirect object is internal and prepositionless, the direct object is preceded by *with*. Thus:

      1a. I entrusted my ray gun to your son.
      1b. I entrusted your son with my ray gun.

I take this to be a lexical property of these verbs. *With* seems to occur with the

regarding (1) the nature of the transferred object (*feed, serve, cede, concede, advance, rent*), and (2) the limitations or conditions on the transfer (*lease, lend, loan, sell, advance, rent, pay*). This characterization thus excludes at least three verbs, *distribute, contribute,* and *donate,* which do not permit both dative constructions, since the presuppositions they involve have to do with the nature of the indirect object (that it be a set or a sanctioned and trustworthy object of charity, or whatever). Notice that *give away* and *give out,* expressions more or less synonymous with *donate* and *distribute,* respectively, likewise permit only an external dative construction:

32a. I donated an old coat to the Salvation Army.
32b. I gave away an old coat to the Salvation Army.
32c. *I donated the Salvation Army an old coat.
32d. *I gave away the Salvation Army an old coat.

33a. I distributed apples to the children.
33b. I gave out apples to the children.
33c. *I distributed the children apples.
33d. *I gave out the children apples.

even though they are composed of a particle (*away, out*), and a verb (*give*) which ordinarily permits, and in fact often demands (cf. sec. c.2.c of this chapter, below) an internal dative. This supports a distinction in terms of presuppositions among 'giving' verbs, since *give away* and *give out* require approximately the same presuppositions about the nature of their indirect objects as do *donate* and *distribute* respectively,

---

direct object of *award* when *award* is used, perhaps metaphorically, like *reward* to describe a spontaneous and non-institutionalized gift, as in (2a) as opposed to (2b):

2a. I awarded him with a bowl of hot chicken soup.
2b. I awarded him the A. E. Newman Bowl of Chicken Soup for Tranquility.

Contrary to what has occasionally been suggested, it cannot be claimed that *attribute* (NP$_d$ to NP$_i$) and *credit* (NP$_i$ with NP$_d$) as in (3):

3a. UPI attributed the recovery of the bomb to the Navy.
3b. UPI credited the Navy with the recovery of the bomb.

are syntactically suppletive variants of a single dative-movement verb meaning 'give credit (to NP$_i$ for NP$_d$),' as in (4):

4a. UPI gave the Navy credit for the recovery of the bomb.
4b. UPI gave credit to the Navy for the recovery of the bomb.

since *credit* (noun and verb) requires a presupposition that the 'direct object' (the noun referred to by NP$_d$) is a "good" thing (cf. Fillmore 1969), and thus differs from *attribute,* which is neutral in this respect.

and, *a priori*, one would expect particle-expressions with *give* to have the same syntactic properties as naked *give*, unless restricted by independent syntactic constraints.

One might suppose that such a constraint was operating here, and that these particle verbs do not permit internal indirect objects because they have particles that "get in the way." However, other particle verbs permit prepositionless indirect objects, as in (34):

34a. I will send off a letter to them in the morning.
34b. I will send them off a letter in the morning.
34c. Pick out a coat for me.
34d. Pick me out a coat.

Nor is it the case that *give away* and *give out* fail to occur with internal indirect objects because their particles cannot be separated from the verb – their particles can be separated from the verb by the direct object, as in (35):

35a. I gave your coat away to the Salvation Army.
35b. I gave them out to the children.

but putting an internal prepositionless indirect object before the particle does not make it any more acceptable, as (36a,b) demonstrate:

36a. *I gave them away an old coat.
36b. *I gave them out the apples.

c   Restricted expressions with give. A large number of expressions with *give* normally[1] permit only prepositionless datives. These fall into productive classes which are characterized in semantic terms. The first represents expressions which describe the source of some physical or psychic condition:

37a.   Mary gave John the measles.
37b.   Mary gave John an inferiority complex.
37c.   Mary gave John a cold.
37d.   Mary gave John pneumonia.
37e.   Mary gave John a broken arm.
37f.   Mary gave John a hickey.
37g.   Mary gave John a black eye.
37h.   Mary gave John a pain in the neck.
37i.   Mary gave John a sense of well-being.

[1] For what I mean by non-normally, see chapter 5, sec. A.

38a. *Mary gave the measles to John.
38b. *Mary gave an inferiority complex to John.
38c. *Mary gave a cold to John.
38d. *Mary gave pneumonia to John.
38e. *Mary gave a broken arm to John.
38f. *Mary gave a hickey to John.
38g. *Mary gave a black eye to John.
38h. *Mary gave a pain in the neck to John.
38i. ?*Mary gave a sense of well-being to John.

Give here is sometimes stative, sometimes not, depending on whether the subject is assumed to be able to create the condition at will.

A second class is composed of non-stative expressions, most of which involve physical contact, and have paraphrases in single lexical items:

39a. Mary gave John a bath.
39b. Mary gave John a kiss.
39c. Mary gave John a punch in the nose.
39d. Mary gave John a handshake.
39e. Mary gave John a shove.
39f. Mary gave John a beating/thrashing/whipping.

40a. *Mary gave a bath to John.
40b. *Mary gave a kiss to John.
40c. *Mary gave a punch in the nose to John.
40d. *Mary gave a handshake to John.
40e. ?*Mary gave a shove to John.
40f. ?*Mary gave a beating/thrashing/whipping to John.

41a. Mary bathed John.
41b. Mary kissed John.
41c. Mary punched John in the nose.
41d. Mary shook John's hand.
41e. Mary shoved John.
41f. Mary beat/thrashed/whipped John.

A third class of restricted *give*-expressions describes non-physical interpersonal behavior, often of a communicative nature, as in (42):

42a. Mary gave John a piece of her mind.
42b. Mary gave John her best wishes.
42c. Mary gave John some flak.

42d.   Mary gave John a call.
42e.   Mary gave John a nod.
42f.   Mary gave John a talking-to.
42g.   Mary gave John a rough time.
42h.   Mary gave John a dirty look.
42i.   Mary gave John the finger.

43a.   *Mary gave a piece of her mind to John.
43b.   ?*Mary gave her best wishes to John.
43c.   *Mary gave some flak to John.
43d.   ?*Mary gave a call to John.
43e.   ?*Mary gave a nod to John.
43f.   *Mary gave a talking-to to John.
43g.   ?*Mary gave a rough time to John.
43h.   ?*Mary gave a dirty look to John.
43i.   *Mary gave the finger to John.

When *give* means 'provide with' as opposed to 'present as a gift,' the indirect object is restricted to a prepositionless form, and the action in many cases (e.g. [44a,c]) can be conceived of as non-volitional. Thus *give* in (44) is ambiguous between these two senses, and in the 'provide with' sense may have an abstract subject as in (45), while *give* in (46) means only 'present as a gift,' and is ungrammatical with an abstract, non-volitional subject, as (47) shows.

44a.   Mary gave John an idea.
44b.   Mary gave John a devastating counterexample.
44c.   Mary gave John the clue to the Sphinx's riddle.

45a.   Mary's behavior gave John an idea.
45b.   Mary's behavior gave John a devastating counterexample.
45c.   Mary's behavior gave John the clue to the Sphinx's riddle.

46a.   Mary gave an idea to John.
46b.   Mary gave a devastating counterexample to John.
46c.   Mary gave the clue to the Sphinx's riddle to John.

47a.   *Mary's behavior gave an idea to John.
47b.   *Mary's behavior gave a devastating counterexample to John.
47c.   *Mary's behavior gave the clue to the Sphinx's riddle to John.

A fifth class is composed of partially implicative expressions (sufficient condition or *if*-verbs, to be precise[1]) which indicate that the subject (either by granting permission or by enabling) lets the indirect object engage in having, getting, taking, or suffering whatever action, behavior, etc. is denoted by the direct object noun phrase. It is illustrated by such examples as:

48a. John gave Mary a turn on his unicycle.
48b. John gave Mary a ride on his motorcycle.
48c. Mary gave John a ride in her XKE.
48d. Mary gave John a lift in her XKE.
48e. Mary gave John a shot at photographing the bears.
48f. Mary gave John a look at her etchings.
48g. Mary gave John a voice on the Central Committee.

d To-*class 3*. *To*-class 3 is composed of verbs denoting the unaccompanied physical transfer of a physical object from an agent to an individual denoted by the indirect object phrase. It includes such verbs as *send, float, fling, forward, hurl, lower, mail, pitch, push, relay, roll, ship, shove, slide, throw, toss*, and may be characterized as encoding the notion 'send' and means and manner notions of the type 'send by V-ing.' This characterization of the *send*-class does, however, include at least three verbs, *drive, lift,* and *raise*, which for me have only a *to*-phrase indirect object.

e To-*class 4*. Class 4 is in a sense a subclass of one of the "communication verb" classes discussed earlier. Class 4 is composed of those communication verbs which (a) permit a non-complex NP as object, and (b) permit the indirect object NP to go either before the direct object, with no preposition, or after it, preceded by *to*. More precisely, class 4

---

[1] Cf. Karttunen 1970a,b. Implicative verbs are verbs (such as *manage, bother, remember*) with the following properties. When they are asserted, the truth of their complements is implied. When they are negated, falsity of the complement is implied. Thus, *John managed to kiss me* implies that John kissed me, and *John didn't manage to kiss me* implies that John didn't kiss me. When sufficient condition verbs (such as *force, prevent, make, cause, have, dissuade*) are asserted, the truth of their complements is implied, but when they are negated, nothing is implied about the truth of the complements. Thus, *John forced Sam to kiss me* implies that Sam kissed me, but *John didn't force Sam to kiss me* does not imply that Sam didn't kiss me. Implicative verbs are distinct from factive verbs (cf. Kiparsky and Kiparsky 1970, and Morgan 1969b) in that with factives (such as *know, regret, realize*), the truth of the complement is implied regardless of whether the factive verb is asserted or negated. Thus, asserting *John knows that Sam is unhappy* implies a belief that Sam is unhappy, and asserting *John doesn't know that Sam is unhappy* implies the same belief.

is really two or three classes. Class 4a, the *radio*-class, consists of denominal instrumental communication verbs – verbs like *radio, wire, cable, telegraph, telephone,* and means of communication verbs like *shout, gesture, relay, mail,* etc. which denote 'send by means of N.' The objects of these verbs are typically nouns like *news, information, response,* which describe (rather than denote) the communicated information.[1] As an illustration of this, consider (49a–c):

49a.   He radioed us the news.
49b.   *He radioed us the eruption of Mt. Etna.
49c.   ?He radioed us the fact that Mt. Etna was erupting.

Class 4b, the *read*-class, consists of verbs encoding essentially the notion 'bring forth,'[2] with various rather severe presuppositions about the nature of the object: *tell, cite, preach, quote, read, write.* The objects of these verbs are typically nouns or noun phrases which respectively denote or describe narratives (*joke, story, anecdote; the one about the farmer's daughter*), evidence and arguments (*statistics, sermon, research; the 6,000,000 Jews, Velikovsky's theory*), and written messages and information (*letter, note, news*). Obviously, not all of the verbs can take all of the objects. *Tell* and *read* take nouns and noun phrases denoting and describing narratives, and nouns describing arguments and evidence, but not noun phrases denoting arguments and evidence:

50a.   I $\begin{Bmatrix} \text{read} \\ \text{told} \end{Bmatrix}$ them $\begin{Bmatrix} \text{a joke} \\ \text{the one about the farmer's daughter} \end{Bmatrix}$.

50b.   I $\begin{Bmatrix} \text{read} \\ \text{told} \end{Bmatrix}$ $\begin{Bmatrix} \text{a joke} \\ \text{the one about the farmer's daughter} \end{Bmatrix}$ to them.

50c.   I $\begin{Bmatrix} \text{read} \\ \text{told} \end{Bmatrix}$ them $\begin{Bmatrix} \text{the statistics.} \\ \text{*the 6,000,000 Jews} \end{Bmatrix}$.

50d.   I $\begin{Bmatrix} \text{read} \\ \text{told} \end{Bmatrix}$ $\begin{Bmatrix} \text{the statistics} \\ \text{*the 6,000,000 Jews} \end{Bmatrix}$ to them.

Cite and *quote*, however, can take both. *Read* can have as object a noun or noun phrase describing or denoting almost anything written (*news,*

---

[1] As of this writing, *wire* can also have noun phrases describing flowers or sums of money as its object.

[2] In the case of *tell, cite, preach, quote,* and *read,* I mean *bring forth* in the sense of 'offer' or 'adduce.' In the case of *write,* the intended meaning of *bring forth* is 'create.' These two meanings appear to differ primarily in assumptions about what is involved in bringing forth the particular direct object, that is, whether the direct object exists prior to the described activity, or not.

newspapers, advertisements, letters; the Rosetta stone, some Latin inscriptions, Cicero's letters to his wife), but *write* may have only nouns describing written messages:

51a. I wrote him a $\left\{ \begin{matrix} \text{check} \\ \text{note} \end{matrix} \right\}$.

51b. I wrote a $\left\{ \begin{matrix} \text{check} \\ \text{note} \end{matrix} \right\}$ to him.

51c. I wrote him the news (about Cousin Jake).

51d. *I wrote the news to him.

There is, in addition, a small group of "communication verbs" which are often confused with class 4 verbs. Their meanings, however, vary subtly depending on whether the indirect object NP is expressed by a prepositional phrase or not, and so, properly speaking, these verbs are not dative-movement verbs at all since they each represent two different meanings which occur with different complement types. Examples include *teach*, *show*, and *write*.[1] I mention them here because they superficially resemble true dative-movement verbs, but there are many cases where it is clear that the meanings are distinct. *Teach* and *show* are discussed in more detail in chapter 4, section B.

Expressions with *write* and *to*-NP prepositional phrases may be either three-argument *NP-V-NP-Directional Adverb* surface constructions, or two-argument *NP-V-N + Reduced Relative Clause* surface constructions. The three-argument construction is associated with an intent on the part of the subject to send the direct object to the indirect object, or at least to cause him to have it. The indirect object noun phrase must thus denote a being which the subject believes exists. The direct object noun phrase may be relativized, as may noun phrases in verb phrases with other, e.g. locative, adverbs:

52a. The letter which I wrote to my brother was never mailed.

52b. The letter which I wrote in Paris was never mailed.

---

[1] *Present*, which is semantically a *to*-class 2 (*give*-) verb, also has this property. When the indirect object NP of *present* precedes the direct object, the direct object is preceded by *with*:

  1. I presented the trophy to him.

  2. I presented him with the trophy.

When *present* NP_i *with* NP_d is used, it is asserted that the thing presented to the indirect object is intended for him; with *present* NP_d *to* NP_i, it is merely asserted that the direct object is put forth for the indirect object to receive.

The adverbial phrase may be preposed, like most other adverbial phrases:

53a. To my brother, I wrote a letter.
53b. In Paris, I wrote a letter.

It is this construction which has paraphrases with prepositionless pre-direct-object indirect objects. This is the sense of *write* in class 4b. The two-argument construction describes merely an act of creating an object which is addressed to the indirect object. The subject does not have to believe that the denotatum of the indirect object actually exists (cf. sec. c.5, below). The head noun in the direct object noun phrase cannot be relativized apart from its following modifiers, and this is generally true of head nouns with reduced relative clauses, as demonstrated by (54–6):

54a. Huxley wrote a warning to future generations.
54b. *The warning which Huxley wrote to future generations is terrifying.
54c. The warning to future generations which Huxley wrote is terrifying.

55a. I wrote the letter (which is) under the door.
55b. *The letter which I wrote under the door is sure to be removed.
55c. The letter under the door which I wrote is sure to be removed.

56a. I wrote a letter (which was) designed to infuriate the recipient.
56b. *The letter which I wrote designed to infuriate the recipient is still on the table.
56c. The letter designed to infuriate the recipient which I wrote is still on the table.

The modifier of the direct object noun cannot be preposed, as (57a–c) illustrate:

57a. *To future generations, Huxley wrote a warning.
57b. *Under the door, I wrote a letter.
57c. *Designed to infuriate the addressee, I wrote a letter.

Write in this construction does not have paraphrases with prepositionless internal indirect objects, as shown by (58):

58a. Huxley wrote a warning to future generations.
58b. *Huxley wrote future generations a warning.
58c. The Pope wrote a letter to Santa Claus.
58d. *The Pope wrote Santa Claus a letter.

There are quite a few "communication verbs" which permit only a prepositional indirect object. Most of these fall into none of the three subclasses described above. Some describe a manner rather than a means of communication (*mutter, mention, mumble*).[1] Others assert more than merely 'communicate' or 'utter' (*admit* and *confess* 'say [that oneself is] guilty of,' *repeat* 'say again'). Some, however, appear to be indistinguishable from *read*-verbs on the basis of my informal characterization of them (e.g. *narrate, recite, report*). Others such as *articulate, voice, utter, declare,* and *state* seem to be very unspecified semantically, yet are quite restricted in use. A few verbs (*describe, explain, recommend, recount*) appear to marginally permit internal pronominal indirect objects, as demonstrated by (59):

59a. She explained him her behavior.
59b. ?She explained Marion her behavior.

but it is not clear that such indirect objects are paraphrased by *to*-phrases and not *for*-phrases, since both occur with pronouns and full noun phrases alike:

60a. She explained her behavior to him.
60b. She explained her behavior for him.

61a. She explained her behavior to Marion.
61b. She explained her behavior for Marion.

---

[1] This analysis entails claiming that *whisper, shout,* and the like incorporate means adverbials rather than manner adverbials since they may occur with both internal and external datives.

    1a. He whispered a word of encouragement to her.
    1b. He whispered her a word of encouragement.

    2a. He shouted the instructions to her.
    2b. He shouted her the instructions.

Like means and instrumental verbs, these have paraphrases with *use*, as in (3):

    3a. Using a whisper, he gave her a word of encouragement.
    3b. Using a shout(ing voice), he told her the instructions.

while *mumble, mutter, mention,* etc. do not. For an interesting discussion of manner-of-communication verbs, see Zwicky 1971.

One might think that the fact that we find sentences like (62a) and (62b), but not (62c):

62a.   She explained her behavior to him for me.
62b.   She explained him her behavior for me.
62c.   *She explained me her behavior to him.

would indicate that internal indirect objects with these verbs paraphrase *to*-phrases rather than *for*-phrases. However, it appears to be the case that when a verb can take both a *to*-phrase complement and a *for*-phrase complement at the same time, the *to*-phrase always precedes the *for*-phrase, and only it may occur prepositionlessly before the direct object, as (62-3) indicate:

62d.   *She explained her behavior for me to him.

63a.   She brought a donut to him for me.
63b.   *She brought a donut for me to him.
        (≠ She brought a donut which was for mé to hím.)
63c.   She brought him a donut for me.
63d.   *She brought me a donut to him.

It is conceivable that constructions like (59a) paraphrase sentences which have co-referential *to*-phrases and *for*-phrases, such as (64):

64.   ?She explained her behavior (towards us) to him$_i$ for him$_i$.

but I do not presently see how one could justify such a claim. The verbs cited above (*explain, recommend*, etc.) do not seem to fit into any of the classes described above, nor to form a coherent semantic class of their own.

f To-*class 5*. The fifth class of *to*-datives is composed of verbs which refer to a situation in the future relative to the tense of the verb, in which the individual denoted by the indirect object expression will have the object described by the direct object. This class includes *promise, guarantee, owe* (money or other negotiable property), *permit, offer, grant, assign, bequeath, leave, allot*, and no doubt others. *Owe* as in (65):

65a.   He owes his present success to his father.
65b.   He owes his present success to good luck.

is not a verb of 'future having,' since the having is contemporaneous with the 'owing,' and is predicated of the subject, not the indirect object. *Owe* in this sense does not permit internal datives:

66a. *He owes his father his present success.
66b. *He owes good luck his present success.

Leave is a *to*-class 5 verb when it has the sense of 'bequeath.' In the sense of 'leave behind,' as in (67):

67. He left me some fruit for dinner.

it does not have a *to*-phrase paraphrase, but rather one with *for*:

68a. *He left some fruit to me for dinner.
68b. He left some fruit for me for dinner.

"Negative" verbs of 'future having,' such as *deny*, *refuse*, and *spare* occur ordinarily[1] with only internal indirect objects. There are one or two words which fit the characterization I have given for this class (*delegate*, and possibly *deed over*), but which occur normally only with external indirect objects, and one or two (e.g. *allow*) which normally have only an internal indirect object.

I should point out here that I am hesitant about the syntactic properties (especially possibility of both dative constructions) of several of the apparent exceptions to all of these classes. If these exceptions to my generalizations are lexical exceptions (that is, idiosyncratic syntactic restrictions on occurrence at some post-lexical level – surface structure, say, or the end of the cyclic rules – or derivational constraints across two levels [cf. chapter 2, secs. D.3–4]), as I suspect they are, then it should be the case that the list of particular exceptional items is subject to idiolectal and stylistic variation. I regret that I have not had the opportunity to investigate this question systematically, but in my own case, as I worked with dative-movement sentences, several verbs in my vocabulary ceased to be exceptional (for instance, *purchase*), and others fluctuated.

3 Kinds of for-*dative verbs*

A very large number of verbal expressions denoting actions undertaken by an agent for the appreciation of the individual described by the indirect object phrase may occur with the indirect object expressed as either a prepositional phrase of the form *for* + NP, or as

---

[1] For the extraordinary cases, see chapter 5, sec. A.

the post-verbal noun phrase. In terms of other syntactic properties, *for*-dative verbs are a more homogeneous set than the *to*-datives (cf. Appendices I and II). On semantic grounds, *for*-datives may be divided into five classes.

a For-*class I*. *For*-class I is composed of verbs denoting creative acts – acts in which an object is created or transformed to produce a certain effect: *make, cook, boil, roast, sew, knit, paint, draw*, etc. The notion of creativity here exists in the intention of the agent, not in some inherent property of the verb. Thus, verbs denoting destructive activity, such as *burn, smash, crush*, and so on, function like creation verbs when the activity or its result is understood as intended to be artistic in some sense. For this reason, (69a–c) are perfectly grammatical and acceptable, while (69d,e) give a feeling of *syntactic* ill-formedness:

69a. Mary burned John a steak because she thought he liked it that way.

69b. Mary burned John a steak because she realized he liked it that way.

69c. Mary burned John a steak because she didn't realize he didn't like it that way.

69d. *Mary burned John a steak because she didn't realize he liked it that way.

69e. *Mary burned John a steak because she realized he didn't like it that way.

Their counterparts in (70a–b), with *for*-phrases, are perfectly well-formed and meaningful, assuming a malicious Mary:

70a. Mary burned a steak for John because she didn't realize he liked it that way.

70b. Mary burned a steak for John because she realized he didn't like it that way.

The burning in (69a–c and 70a–b) is understood as intended creatively, as are the acts referred to in (71a–b):

71a. No one baked anyone anything.

71b. No one burned anyone anything.

Sentence (71b) is grammatical or ungrammatical depending on whether or not one supposes that a person might purposely burn something he intends for someone.

For-class I appears to be an open class, such that any verb which may be used to describe a creative act in the sense above will have the syntactic properties of *for*-class I verbs. Verbs which describe relatively unusual creative activities (unusual relative to the creative activities of the agent, that is) and verbs which have more than one or two syllables, or perhaps merely verbs which are unusual in the speaker's speech, are found with the prepositionless indirect object immediately after the verb much less frequently than is the case for shorter, more common verbs. When "unusual" verbs do have post-verbal indirect objects, they are much more likely to be pronouns than is the case with other *for*-dative verbs. Thus, I would be more comfortable saying (72a) than (72b), although the opposite preference might prevail for someone with other cooking habits than mine, and I would be more likely to say (72b) than (72c):

72a. If I roasted him a chicken, do you think he'd like it?
72b. If I fricasseed him a chicken, do you think he'd like it?
72c. If I fricasseed Jerry a chicken, do you think he'd like it?

I thought for some months that some creation verbs, including *create* itself, never had prepositionless indirect objects, but recently I read a sentence like (73) and it did not strike me as odd:

73. They had created me a monster!

b For-class 2. The second class of *for*-dative verbs is composed of verbs denoting activities involving selection, such as *buy, purchase, find, get, choose, pick out, gather, save,* and *leave,* in the sense 'leave behind.'[1] These verbs seem to express the notion 'get' with or without various presuppositions about what is involved in the getting, or 'save' with or without presuppositions. The verbs *select, collect,* and *abandon* sound to me a bit awkward with prepositionless indirect objects, but it

---

[1] It is not clear to me whether *spare* in the sense 'part with' is also a member of this class. If such sentences as

1. Can you spare a poor hippie a dime?
2. Can you spare a dime for a poor hippie?

are synonymous, then probably it is. My own reaction to such sentences is that they cannot be used in exactly the same situations; (1) is a request to give a dime to a particular hippie who, if he is not the speaker of (1), is at least present or indicated specifically by the speaker. Sentence (2), on the other hand, need not refer to a particular hippie, and may be a request that the hearer part with a dime which the speaker will (presumably) give to some poor hippie.

would be rash to say that they never have such indirect objects. *Obtain* sounds much worse, and I would not expect to find it with a preposition-less indirect object.

c   For-*class 3*. A third class of *for*-dative verbs is composed of verbs denoting performances considered artistic: *sing, chant, recite, play* (instruments and compositions), *dance*. It appears that verbs denoting particular kinds of dancing, playing, etc. which depend on the proper-ties of the object performed upon or the work performed cannot occur with prepositionless indirect objects, although they do occur with *for*-phrase datives. Thus the sentences of (74) are better than those of (75):

74a.   She played us her trombone.
74b.   She played us "Taps."

74c.   She danced us $\left\{\begin{array}{l}\text{the first act of an original ballet.}\\ \text{a waltz.}\\ \text{a few bars of "The Blue Danube."}\end{array}\right\}$

75a.   ?She blew us her trombone.
75b.   ?She blew us "Taps."
75c.   ?She waltzed us a few bars of "The Blue Danube."

Verbs denoting kinds of vocal productions which depend on the nature of the work performed, rather than on properties or actions of the performer do, however, occur with internal, as well as external datives:

76a.   She hummed us "Let It Be."
76b.   *She trilled us three bars of "God Bless America."
76c.   She recited us "The Charge of the Light Brigade."
76d.   She whistled us three bars of "Let It Be."
76e.   She chanted us three blessings.

The performance verbs of *for*-class 3 would appear to be semantically a subclass of *for*-class 1, the creation verbs, except that, as (75) shows, *for*-class 3 is more restricted.

d   For-*class 4*. Class 4 consists of a small group of verbs which unlike the other *for*-dative verbs may take inanimate subjects. These verbs express a kind of obtaining; *earn, gain*, and *win* are the most conspicuous members. The inanimate subjects permitted are various kinds of nominalizations with semantically reconstructible animate subjects:

77a.   Tolerance for your enemies will gain you no friends.
       (cf. Your tolerating your enemies will gain you no friends.)

77b. Selling cookies will earn John enough to buy a bike.
(cf. John's selling cookies will earn him enough to buy a bike.)

77c. The toleration of interruptions will win you no converts.
(cf. Your tolerating interruptions will win you no converts.)

77d. The publication of your article (in *Word*) will gain you a world-wide reputation.
(cf. Your publishing your article (in *Word*) will gain you a world-wide reputation.)

77e. *Word's publishing your article will gain you a world-wide reputation.

and concrete nouns understood as such nominalizations:

78a. Stunts like that will earn John a bad reputation.
(cf. John will earn himself a bad reputation with stunts like that.)

78b. Those stones will earn their discoverers $5 a piece.
(cf. The sale of those stones$_i$ by their discoverers$_j$ will earn them$_j$ $5 a piece.)

From the difference between (77d) and (77e), it appears that it must be possible to reconstruct underlying animate subjects for sentences of this sort with inanimate surface subjects.

e For-class 5. For-dative movement also occurs in the so-called "benefactive" construction:

79a. They're going to kill a hippie for Reagan.
79b. They're going to kill Reagan a hippie.

but the expressions involved don't seem to be characterized as a set of verbs so much as expressions which can be used to denote acts intended to be symbolic of the subject's devotion to the indirect object or something of the sort. For internal indirect objects to be acceptable, the act denoted by the symbolic construction must be one in which a change of state regarding the direct object noun phrase is effected:

80a. Sam promised to move his lover a mountain.
80b. Sam promised to crush his lover a mountain.
80c. ?Sam promised to climb his lover a mountain.
80d. *Sam promised to taste his lover her wine.
80e. *Sam promised to endure his daughter *American Bandstand*.

This constraint differentiates symbolic expressions from the performance verbs, unless one is willing to maintain the unlikely position that
playing a sonata effects a change on the sonata in some way that tasting
wine and enduring a television program do not affect the wine and the
program. In fact, it appears that it is exactly this condition of effecting
a change which accounts for the [?] by (80c). This sentence seems
perfectly all right if considered as a performance or demonstration of
skill, but not if considered a symbolic act. There is something about the
verb phrases of (80d,e) which makes it more difficult for one to conceive
of them as performances.

The usual term for the constructions under consideration, "benefactive," is a misnomer. As sentences like (81) show, these constructions
may refer to acts which certainly don't benefit the person they are
intended to impress, although they are, of course, performed "for his
benefit" in the sense that he is the intended audience.

> 81a. Kill a Commie for Christ.
> 81b. Kill me a dragon.
> 81c. Crush me a mountain.
> 81d. Cry me a river.

Many expressions which have been called benefactives are really
ambiguous between a symbolic sense and a creation sense. Thus (81b)
can be a request for a certain act of bravery, or a request for a dead
dragon (for instance, for dragon stew). Similarly (81d) can be a request
for a phenomenal crying jag, or merely a request for a river, as if crying
was the natural way to create one.

Constructions explicitly expressing acts which are considered actually
malefactive (that is, as having a harmful effect on the recipient or
audience, the indirect object) are not expressed in English with either
a *to*-dative or a *for*-dative. The closest English has to such a construction
is the somewhat colloquial "*on*-dative" as in (82), which may be a
positional variant of *do to*'s *to*-dative (cf. [83]):

> 82a. She played a trick on us.
> 82b. She played us a trick.

> 83a. She ran away on us.
> 83b. What she did to us was run away.
> 83c. What she did to us was: she ran away on us.

f   A note on other for-*phrases.* Before continuing the investigation of the syntax and semantics of *for*-dative verbs, it is necessary to distinguish several kinds of *for* $NP_{animate}$ phrases. The *for* $NP_{animate}$ phrases which can occur as internal datives are a small set of *for* $NP_{animate}$ phrases. Permitted are animate complements of

1. Creation and selection verbs (classes 1 and 2). Here the *for NP* phrase indicates the intended recipient of an object.

2. The symbolic construction (class 5). Here they indicate the intended "recipient" of a symbolic action.

3. Performance verbs (class 3). These *for NP* phrases indicate the intended percipient of an action.

4. Verbs of the *earn*-class (class 4). Here they indicate the recipient of a literal or figurative prize or reward.

Internal datives are not permitted as variants of *for* $NP_{animate}$ phrases which

5. Indicate a party substituted for by the subject of the dative-verb phrase:

   84a.   We are looking for someone who will teach Bob's students for him while he's on leave.
   84b.   *We are looking for someone who will teach Bob his students while he's on leave.

6. Indicate a party represented by the subject:

   85a.   Sen. Smith thanked the president for his constituents.
   85b.   *Sen. Smith thanked his constituents the president.

7. Indicate an individual employing the subject to perform the action represented by the verb phrase:

   86a.   I packed cakes for Mr Lubin.
   86b.   *I packed Mr Lubin cakes.

Assumptions about the subject's intention in performing the act are crucial to determining whether an internal dative is permitted. A sentence like (87)

   87.   J. baked Mr. Lubin cakes.

is appropriate if the cakes are intended as a gift to Mr Lubin, if the baking is intended as a performance for Mr Lubin, or if the baking is intended as a ritual act in honor of Mr Lubin; but not if J. was a substitute for Mr Lubin, or if J. was an employee of Mr Lubin. The *so do* test for ambiguity indicates that *for*-phrases are ambiguous as to which of the five or so meanings is intended, rather than vague. A sentence like (88)

88. J. baked cakes for Mr Lubin, and so did Sally.

is ungrammatical if J. got paid for it, and Sally did it to please him. If Sally merely didn't get paid, or did it for free, it might still be grammatical, indicating only that Sally was a crazy employee. In approaching paraphrases and semantic representations for *for*-dative sentences, we will not be concerned with *for* $NP_{animate}$ phrases for which the subject denotes a substitute, representative, or employee.

4   *General observations – the 'have' relationship*

It has been noticed by several investigators that most of the common dative-movement expressions involve the transitive relationship 'have' between the indirect object and the direct object. More precisely, the processes denoted by dative-movement expressions result in such a relationship. It is not by any means a single kind of 'having' which is involved here. In the most obvious cases, that is, the *take-*, *give-*, *send-*, and 'future having'-constructions of *to*-classes 1, 2, 3, and 5, it may be either the *have* of alienable possession, as in (89)

89. John has a 1969 Fiat.

which is applicable when the subject has any sort of alienable access to and/or responsibility for the object (he need not own it, or even use it), or it may be the *have* of alterable location, position, accompaniment, or whatever, as in (90):

90. I have your son (here, with me) (and you can have Red Chief back for $500).

It is in these senses of *have* that we can predict from (91a–d)

91a. Mary will bring Bill a lollipop.
91b. Mary will sell Bill a lollipop.
91c. Mary will mail Bill a lollipop.
91d. Mary will offer Bill a lollipop.

that Bill will (in [91d]: will be able to) have a lollipop. In either case, there is at least a potential physical relationship between the 'haver' and the 'had.'

It is primarily in the first sense of *have* that the subject of creation and selection verbs intends for the indirect object to have the direct object. When the 'creation' expression is, strictly speaking, an 'alteration' expression (e.g. *bake a chicken* as opposed to *bake a cake*), then it is an altered direct object which the subject intends for the indirect object to have. (I find it strangely redundant to speak of a *created* or *made object*, or a *baked cake*, and similarly contradictory to speak of an *unbaked cake*.) Thus in (92a–c)

92a. Jack carved Jill a statue.
92b. Jack bought Jill a Honda.
92c. Jack boiled Jill an egg.

it is respectively a statue, a Honda, and a boiled egg which Jack intended for Jill to have.

The sort of having involved in the *earn*-constructions of *for*-class 4 is either inalienable, non-inherent belonging, the same as that denoted by *have* in expressions like (93)

93. John has a good reputation.

or alienable possession, as in (89). In (94a) it is inalienable belonging, in (94b), alienable possession:

94a. John earned a good reputation for himself by sticking his neck out.
94b. John's essay won him a 1969 Fiat.

The kind of having involved in the communication expressions of *to*-class 4, and intended in the performance expressions of *for*-class 3, as in (95a–c)

95a. Peter will telephone Beverly the news.
95b. Peter will read the news to Beverly.
95c. Peter will play Beverly a Bach fugue.

is neither physical possession of any sort nor belonging, but possession which is perceptual, and again, inalienable. It is encoded in English by the word *have* in a variety of expressions, samples of which are found in (96):

96a. I have in mind a different plan.
96b. Do you have my address?
96c. Do you have it in sight yet?
96d. The air controller has a UFO on his console.
96e. I have it from Bill that there's a kilo on the way.
96f. I have a riddle for you.
96g. We had a recital of Tennyson's poetry by Miss Edelson.

It is this kind of having which is intended by the subject of *for*-class 5 (symbolic) constructions. I believe there is a sense of (97)

97. Jesse will have a lawman killed for him.

which demonstrates this kind of having, namely, the reading 'someone will kill a lawman for Jesse.' There is another sense, 'Jesse will have someone kill a lawman for him,' but this sense is irrelevant. In any case, with symbolic constructions, it is assumed by the agent that the indirect object will recognize the act performed for his appreciation *as* an act performed for his appreciation. In these constructions, it is assumed that the accomplishment of the act is to be presented to the indirect object as a sort of offering. In that the recognition necessary for the receipt of such an offering involves a sense of 'having' similar to that in (96), the symbolic constructions may be said to involve a 'have' relationship between the indirect object, and the direct object as affected by the subject's action, as with the creation and performance constructions.

In case 'having' should still seem a far-fetched way to describe the relation which the subject of the symbolic construction intends to prevail between the indirect object and the subject's action, it should be pointed out that in Japanese such constructions[1] are normally expressed with the ordinary words for 'give' and 'receive.' Thus

---

[1] Actually, the Japanese construction is not identical to the English. It is not restricted to describing actions which have an effect on the direct object, as the English construction is, but may be used for any sort of behavior, provided that it have been undertaken as a favor to the individual referred to by the 'dative' noun phrase. In the English construction it is not necessary that the action be undertaken as a favor to the indirect object. I am grateful to James McCawley for bringing the Japanese construction to my attention, and to Noriko Akatsuka for acting as an informant.

98a. St George ga   Mary no-tame-ni   ryuu   o
       'nom'   'of-sake-to'   dragon 'obj.'
   koroshite yatta
   killed   gave
   St George killed Mary a dragon.

98b. Mary   wa   St George ni ryuu   o
      'topic'   by dragon 'obj.'
   koroshite moratta.
   killed   received
   Mary had a dragon killed for her by St George.

Many expressions, though not all, which involve only one of the two indirect object forms, cannot be analyzed as resulting in any of the discussed 'have' relationships between the indirect object and the direct object. This is the case for the expressions in (99):

99a. I threw the ball to the 50-yard line.
   (*I threw the 50-yard line the ball.)

99b. I sold the house for $30,000.
   (*I sold $30,000 the house.)

99c. I wrote books for 6 months.
   (*I wrote 6 months books.)

99d. They fined John $10.
   (*They fined $10 to/for John.)

99e. We envied John his good looks.
   (*We envied John's good looks to/for him.)

99f. We forgave John his good looks.
   (*We forgave his good looks to/for him.)

99g. We elected John president.
   (*We elected president to/for John.)

99h. That will cost John 50 cents.
   (*That will cost 50 cents to/for John.)

It is clear that the points in space, sums of money, and durations of time which are the objects of *to* in (99a–c) cannot bear the relationship 'have' to objects or activities, as (99i–k) illustrate:

99i. *The 50-yard line has a ball.

99j. *$30,000 has a house.

99k. *Six months has books.

but it is not the case that the sentences of (99a–c) involve no 'have' relationship just because we say that only animates may 'have.' The inanimates in (100) all occur as the subject of *have* sentences as in (101):

    100a. We gave the door a kick.
    100b. We gave the house another coat of paint.
    100c. We gave that theory a thorough going-over.
    100d. They permit their tea-pots no more than two flaws.

    101a. We let the door have a kick.
    101b. The house now has one more coat of paint.
    101c. We let that theory have a thorough going-over.
    101d. Their tea-pots will never have more than two flaws.

In (99d–h), although the referent of the "indirect object" noun phrase *John* is animate, he does not in any sense of *have* come to 'have' (or even 'not have') the item of property denoted by the direct object as a result of the activity expressed by the subject and the verb.

In a sense, the 'have' relationship in dative-movement constructions is implicit in the term *dative*: the root is the Latin verb for 'give,' and successful giving results in getting ('coming to have') and having.

There are some cases where dative expressions, particularly *give*-expressions such as those cited in this chapter, section c.2.c above, have paraphrases or near-paraphrases with *get* or *let have*, but no corresponding sentences with *have*. For example:

    102a.   I gave John a punch in the nose.
    102b.   John got a punch in the nose from me.
    102c.   I let John have a punch in the nose.
    102d.   *John has a punch in the nose (from me).

    103a.   John gives me a pain in the neck.
    103b.   ?I get a pain in the neck from John.
    103c.   *John lets me have a pain in the neck.
    103d.   *I have a pain in the neck (from John).

It appears that *let have* occurs only with agents presumed to be capable of volitional causation, permission-granting, or enabling as subjects. This accounts for the difference between (102c) and (103c), since one cannot volitionally succeed in giving someone else a pain in the neck, although of course one can hope to have that effect. Paraphrases with *have* as the main verb appear to be restricted to cases where the effect is not an ephemeral state, but a permanent or at least physically perceivable one. This is why (104d) is good while (103d) is not; in (104d) the pain in the neck is a physical one.

104a. Trying to see around the couple in front of us gave me a pain in the neck.

104b. I got a pain in the neck from trying to see around the couple in front of us.

104c. *Trying to see around the couple in front of us let me have a pain in the neck.

104d. I have a pain in the neck from trying to see around the couple in front of us.

It appears also that *get* in (102b, 103b, 104b), rather than meaning 'come to have' means 'suffer' or 'experience.'

5 Constraints on dative movement

a Animateness of the dative noun phrase. In general, as demonstrated in (105–14), for the type of indirect object expression to be optional, the dative noun must be animate:

105a. John brought some flowers to the table.
105b. *John brought the table some flowers.

106a. *John gave a kick to the door.
106b. John gave the door a kick.

107a. John sent a letter to New York.
107b. *John sent New York a letter.

108a. ?John wired the news to New York.[1]
108b. *John wired New York the news.

109a. John assigned Private Smith to latrine duty.
109b. *John assigned latrine duty Private Smith.

110a. I fried an egg for the contest/breakfast/the record.
110b. *I fried the contest/breakfast/the record an egg.

---

[1] Apparently verbs of communication require that the indirect object be presupposed to be animate. Both (108a) and (108b) are acceptable if *New York* is taken as referring to some specific people in New York.

111a.   I found a cloth for the table.
111b.   *I found the table a cloth.

112a.   I sang a song for the audition.
112b.   *I sang the audition a song.

113a.   ?Advertising practices have won an international reputation for Coca-Cola.
113b.   Advertising practices have won Coca-Cola an international reputation.

114a.   John wants to kill a Commie for money.
114b.   *John wants to kill money a Commie.

although there are some exceptions, as in (115–16):

115a.   Give some consideration to sincerity.
115b.   Give sincerity some consideration.
115c.   They give a literal reading to the Constitution sometimes.
115d.   They give the Constitution a literal reading sometimes.

116a.   They allow three passengers to each car.
116b.   They allow each car three passengers.
116c.   John assigned the feature [+N] to *sincerity*.
116d.   John assigned *sincerity* the feature [+N].

All of the exceptions with optional indirect object type when the indirect object is inanimate, and the dubious (113a) as well, involve a 'have' relationship between the indirect object and the direct object. No such 'have' relationship holds for (105–8), (110), (112), or (114).

b   Animateness of the subject noun phrase. In general, in dative-movement constructions (that is, where the type of indirect object is optional), the subject must be animate:

117a.   The rain brought disaster to the farmers.
117b.   *The rain brought the farmers disaster.

118a.   *Eating liver gives lots of iron to you.
118b.   Eating liver gives you lots of iron.

119a.   ?The explosion hurled the jewels to Bond.
119b.   *The explosion hurled Bond the jewels.

120a.   *The bloodstains told a story of terror to us.
120b.   The bloodstains told us a story of terror.

121a. *Our diets permit fatty foods to us.

121b. Our diets permit us fatty foods.

122a. The sun baked these cookies for John.

122b. *The sun baked John these cookies.

123a. *Jan's money bought a teapot for her.

123b. ?Jan's money bought her a teapot.

124a. ?An overdose of LSD killed a dealer for the narcs last
       night.

124b. *An overdose of LSD killed the narcs a dealer last night.

although there are exceptions among the 'future having' verbs of
to-class 5:

125a. Your theory assigns the feature [+N] to *sincerity*.

125b. Your theory assigns *sincerity* the feature [+N].

One might think that the performance verbs by their nature permit
only animate subjects since (126a) is appropriate only if *the guitar*
refers to the guitarist; but there are musical instruments such as player
pianos and music boxes which play independently of a performer.
These, however, when they are subjects, do not permit datives at all,
as (126b,c) show. As (126d–g) demonstrate, these work syntactically
like the usual sort of musical instrument otherwise:

126a.   The guitar played "Blowing in the Wind" (for us).

126b. *The music box played Brahms' "Lullaby" for us.

126c. *The music box played us Brahms' "Lullaby."

126d.   Bobby played the music box for us.

126e.   Bobby played us the music box.

126f.   Bobby played Brahms' "Lullaby" for us on the music box.

126g.   Bobby played us Brahms' "Lullaby" on the music box.

Underlying animate subjects also seem to be required for the verbs of
for-class 4, the *earn*-class, as described above, but the surface inanimates
permit both of the indirect object types:

127a. Stunts like that will earn a bad reputation for you.

127b. Stunts like that will earn you a bad reputation.

c Existence presuppositions. A third general constraint on dative movement is that the speaker or referent of the subject of the commanding
world-creating verb (cf. Morgan 1969b) must assume that the referents

of the direct and indirect object noun phrases exist contemporaneously (i.e. in the same relevant world) with each other and with the subject, at the time referred to by the dative-movement verb. In simple sentences like (128) where there is no commanding world-creating verb, it is the speaker whose assumptions are relevant. Thus, if I believe that Jesus Christ exists in the sense of being able to appreciate actions performed for his benefit, or in his honor, I can say both (128a) and (128b). If I don't believe that he exists in that sense, I can still say (128a), but not (128b):

> 128a. Kill a Commie for Christ.
> 128b. Kill Christ a Commie.

It is not required that the referents of the subject, indirect object, and direct object NPs be assumed to co-exist with the speaker or subject of the world-creating verb, but only with each other, as demonstrated by (129a) and (129b), which are both grammatical for present-day speakers, regardless of their truth or falsity

> 129a. Brutus killed a Celt for Caesar in 49 B.C.
> 129b. Brutus killed Caesar a Celt in 49 B.C.

Here the time of co-existence is that of the main verb, first century B.C., not the time of the performative, twentieth century A.D. Likewise, in (130a) and (130b), the time of co-existence is the future, relative to the time of utterance:

> 130a. You are going to kill your next wife, whoever she may be, for Zorro.
> 130b. You are going to kill Zorro your next wife, whoever she may be.

At the time of utterance, there is no referent for the direct object NP.

In sentences with world-creating verbs which are overt, as in (131), or deleted or obscured as in (132), the co-existence is still at the time of the main verb, in the defined world:

> 131a. I want to dream that you kill a Gaul for Caesar.
> 131b. I want to dream that you kill Caesar a Gaul.

> 132a. You would have killed a Gaul for Caesar.
> 132b. You would have killed Caesar a Gaul.

In (131) this time is the present in the world of the dream. In (132) it is some time in the hypothetical world in which the referent of *you*, Gauls, and Caesar all exist.

That the subject must exist at the same time as the indirect object is demonstrated by (133):

133a.   The American ambassador baked a cake for James I.
133b.   *The American ambassador baked James I a cake.

Sentence (133a) might mean that the ambassador baked a cake to honor the memory of King James, but (133b) could only mean that he baked one which he intended to present to him. No one aware of the fact that James I died long before any American ambassadors could have been born could consider (133b) to be grammatical. Since it is the assumptions of the subject of the world-creating verb which are crucial, not those of the subject of the main verb, (133b) is ungrammatical even if the speaker knows that the ambassador in question thinks that James I lives next door to him. Since the co-existence of subject and indirect object is required as a presupposition of the subject of the commanding world-creating verb or the speaker, not as an assertion or a condition on absolute truth, speakers who find (133b) ungrammatical will find its negation, (134b), just as bad:

134a.   The American ambassador didn't bake a cake for James I.
134b.   *The American ambassador didn't bake James I a cake.

These speakers will find (134a) grammatical, even if they know it to be false.

This third general constraint on dative movement is fairly obvious for *to*-classes 1 and 3 (the *bring*- and *send*-classes), which describe the physical transfer of objects; non-existent objects cannot be transferred, and existent objects cannot be transferred to individuals who don't exist in the same world. Similar reasons make it obvious for most of the communication verbs of *to*-class 4 as well. One cannot speak to beings who do not (yet) exist, and while one may address epistles to them, one cannot write to them. Someone who does not believe in Santa Claus might say (135a) but he would hardly be likely to say (135b) (cf. also sec. C.2.*e* of this chapter, above):

135a.   Did you really write a thank-you note to Santa Claus?
135b.   Did you really write Santa Claus a thank-you note?

It is necessary to demonstrate that the co-existence constraint holds for the 'future having' verbs of *to*-class 5, since the verbs of this class all refer to times later than the activity they describe. But the constraint still refers to the time of the main verb, as demonstrated by (136) and (137):

136a. If I am elected, I promise a college education to any children born in this ward after I take office.

136b. If I am elected, I promise a college education to all the children in this ward.

136c. *If I am elected, I promise any children born in this ward after I take office a college education at the school of their choice.

136d. If I am elected, I promise all children in this ward a college education.

A will might read like (137a,b,d), but not like (137c).

137a. I leave my poker chips and all my debts to any children my wife may bear me.

137b. I leave my poker chips and all my debts to my children, however many they may be.

137c. *I leave any children my wife may bear me my poker chips and all my debts.

137d. I leave my children, however many they may be, my poker chips, and all my debts.

By their nature, many of the verbs of *to*-class 2, the *give*-class, require that the subject, indirect object, and direct object be assumed to co-exist. Such are *sell, loan, lend, give* (with concrete direct object), *advance, award, cede, concede, feed,* and *serve*:

138a. ?I expect to give my wealth to the grand-children of your great-grandchildren.

138b. *I expect to give the grand-children of your great-grand-children my wealth.

Others, such as *rent, lease,* and *entrust* permit indirect objects "from another world," but only as prepositional datives:

139a. I promise to lease my land to future generations at $1 an acre.

139b. *I promise to lease future generations my land at $1 an acre.

Still others, such as *pay*, have no co-existence requirement:

> 140a. I promise to pay \$1 a year to future generations of Sioux for the use of this land.
>
> 140b. I promise to pay future generations of Sioux \$1 a year for the use of this land.

In the case of the first, second, third, and fifth classes of non-literal *give*-expressions, the direct objects are not concrete noun phrases (e.g. pneumonia, a kiss, a rough time, a ride), and it does not make sense to speak of the referent of the direct object as "existing" much less as co-existing with something.

The creation, selection, performance, and symbolic expressions of *for*-classes 1–3 and 5 are all expressions denoting actions undertaken by an agent for the appreciation of another individual, denoted by the indirect object. There are many cases where the co-existence requirement fails to hold, but only with external datives:

> 141a. I bronzed your baby shoes for posterity.
>
> 141b. *I bronzed posterity your baby shoes.
>
> 142a. I bought a ring for my wife in case I should decide to marry.
>
> 142b. *I bought my wife a ring in case I should decide to marry.
>
> 143a. She's going to sing a song for her late lover.
>
> 143b. *She's going to sing her late lover a song.

This phenomenon was demonstrated for *for*-class 5 in (128–32). The case is not quite so clear for the *earn*-expressions of *for*-class 4. There does not seem to be any requirement of co-existence outside of the fact that the reconstructed animate subject is usually co-referential to the indirect object, as in (77–8). Where *earn*, etc. have non-co-referential animate subjects, the requirement does not hold:

> 144a. If you marry you will only be earning a place in the breadlines for your descendants.
>
> 144b. If you marry you will only be earning your descendants a place in the breadlines.
>
> 145a. Your going to jail will earn only abuse for whatever children you may beget.
>
> 145b. Your going to jail will earn whatever children you may beget nothing but abuse.

6   Paraphrases

In this section I will consider paraphrases for dative-movement constructions with the purpose of finding semantic representations for
them which will account for some of their properties – particularly the
'have' relationship, the co-existence requirements, and the requirements of animateness. In this chapter, section c.7, I will consider
syntactic evidence to support the claim that these verbs are structurally
complex. I do not pretend to present a complete or totally justified
semantic representation.

a   To-*class 1*. It is tempting at first to try to analyze the transfer verbs
(*to*-classes 1–3) as basically 'CAUSE to HAVE,' with in some cases presuppositions (class 2) or instrumental clauses (classes 1 and 3). Thus
sentences of the form of (146a) and (146b)

146a. Subject VERBed direct object (d.o.) to indirect object (i.o.).
146b. Subject VERBed i.o. d.o.

might have a source of the form of (146c):

146c. Subject CAUSED i.o. to HAVE d.o. BY VERB-ing d.o.

Including a clause in which the indirect object is the subject of a verb
HAVE, and the direct object is its object would account for the 'have'
relationship present in dative-movement constructions. Having such
a clause embedded as the complement of a verb CAUSE whose subject is
the subject of the surface sentence would account for the fact that this
relationship is the result of action by the subject.

However, this proposal is inadequate as it stands. For one thing, it
does not adequately paraphrase verbs of the *bring*-class; of the sentences
below, (147a) could refer to a situation where, because of some absurd
legal convention, ownership of the piano or responsibility for it

147a. John caused Mary to have the piano by dragging it.
147b. John dragged Mary the piano.

was transferred to Mary by the *fact* that John dragged it in a circle.
Sentence (147b), on the other hand, must refer to a situation in which
the piano goes from some place to Mary's presence, by being dragged
by John. Mary does not necessarily own it thereby, but merely has it

in the sense that she has charge of it. A closer paraphrase for *to*-class I
might be (148a) or (148b):

148a. Subject BRING/TAKE d.o. TO i.o. BY VERB-ing d.o.
148b. Subject CAUSE d.o. to COME/GO WITH subject TO i.o. BY
VERB-ing d.o.

the BRING/TAKE–COME/GO alternation depending on the speaker's presuppositions of his physical relation to the points involved in the
transfer (cf. Fillmore 1966). The sentences of (148) differ from (146c) in
two important ways: the underlying order is subject-direct object-*to*-
indirect object rather than subject-indirect object-direct object, and
the 'have' relationship is not asserted. Because of this latter difference,
(148) is adequate for the semantic representation of sentences such as
(149) which have no 'have' relationship, and no prepositionless counterpart:

149a. John dragged the piano to New York.
149b. *John dragged New York the piano.

and must be modified to include the 'have' relationship if we are to
maintain that the two dative-movement constructions have a single
source, perhaps something on the order of (150):

150. Subject CAUSE i.o. to HAVE d.o. BY CAUSE-ing d.o. to COME/GO
WITH subject TO i.o. (BY VERB-ing d.o.).

Of course, (150) represents a quite complex structure, and would
require several applications of predicate-raising and the often invoked
but never explicitly justified rule of instrumental verb formation (for
more on this rule and the use of the term "instrumental," cf. Appendix
III) to reduce it to an expression with a single surface predicate. Beyond
this, if (148) is the source for (149a), and (150) is the source for dative-
movement constructions homologous to (149a), is it possible that
sentences of the form of (151):

151. John dragged the piano to Mary.

are actually ambiguous as to whether they represent meanings like
(148) or meanings like (150)? It is. *Mary*, in (151), may refer to either a
person, or a place, the place where the person Mary is. Thus (151)
could be used in a situation where (147b) could be used, as well as in
situations where John drags the piano to Mary's presence, but does not

relinquish it to her. Sentence (147b) could not be used in the second kind. At any rate, on semantic grounds, both of the dative-movement constructions must involve a 'have' relationship between the indirect object and the direct object, which results from the subject's action on the direct object, while other constructions with external datives do not necessarily involve such a 'have' relationship.

One might object to (150) as a representation for *bring*-class verbs like *hand* and *pass* on the grounds that sentences like (152):

> 152a. John caused Mary to have the sugar by causing it to go with him to her by handing it.
> 152b. John caused Mary to have the sugar by causing it to go with him to her by passing it.

are ungrammatical or not equivalent to their dative counterparts:

> 153a. John handed Mary the sugar.
> 153b. John passed Mary the sugar.

Example (152a) is undoubtedly unacceptable as an English sentence, and *pass* in (152b), but not (153b) is more naturally interpreted as a kind of throwing action normally administered to a football. To maintain that a structure something like (152) is a source for (153) it is necessary to insist on PASS and HAND as abstract predicates, referring to the actions involved in handing (passing) something to someone as in (153), not as predicates with the exact syntactic and semantic properties of real verbs of the "same name." The fact that it may be necessary to postulate semantic predicates with different syntactic and semantic properties from the real lexical items we use to name them might appear to be a weakness in a theory in which the underlying syntactic representations of sentences are semantic representations, but it seems to be an unavoidable fact. I would speculate that it results more from the fact that natural language vocabularies are pitifully inadequate to describe with preciseness all of the events and objects in man's environment, than from any deficiency in linguistic theory.

b   *To-class 2*. Suppose, then, that (150) is an adequate representation for the constructions of *to*-class 1. It is woefully inadequate for *to*-class 2. For one thing, in cases like (154)

> 154a. John sold Mary the delicatessen.
> 154b. John conceded the point to Mary.

the referents of the direct object NPs do not move anywhere. One of them is, in fact, abstract and incapable of motion.[1] If the 'BY CAUSE-ing d.o. to COME/GO WITH subject TO i.o.' clause is removed, leaving a structure like (146c), the difficulties encountered there recur; (155) is applicable to a situation where John sells the store to someone entirely unconnected with Mary, while (154a) is not.

155. John caused Mary to have the delicatessen by selling it.

How then are these verbs to be represented?

It was mentioned earlier that these verbs mean basically 'give' or 'cause to have' with various conditions. The verbs of this class differ from each other mainly in what their direct objects can denote: money or other media of exchange (*pay, advance*), food (*deed*), awards (*award*), disputed points or objects (*concede*), responsibility (*entrust*); and in conditions on the causing to have: in exchange for something (*sell, rent, lease*), and on the having: for a limited period of time with possession reverting to the lender, who retains ownership throughout (*loan, lend, lease, rent*), before the scheduled time (*advance*), and so on. It is not clear whether there is any evidence that the conditions on the causing, the having, and the nature of the direct object are asserted rather than presupposed. One can construct sentences negating these verbs where these conditions are negated, although the 'causing to have' is not negated, as in (156):

156a. I couldn't sell him the car, so I gave it to him for frée.

156b. They couldn't rent the house to anyone, so they let us have it for the year for frée.

156c. I won't lend you the pencil; I'd rather give it to you for kéeps.

156d. They wouldn't advance us the money, so it was given to us
$$\begin{cases} \text{on páyday.} \\ \text{when we brought in the bílls.} \end{cases}$$

156e. We didn't award him $100 – the $100 we gave him was his sálary.

156f. We cannot pay you, but we wíll give you a valuable token of our appreciation.

---

[1] Notice that in these cases we can still say, idiomatically, *The delicatessen went to Mary*, and perhaps *The point went to Mary*, although we would not say in this situation *John caused the delicatessen to go to Mary*, or *John caused the point to go to Mary*. Constructions with *feed* have no counterparts with *go* or *cause to go*.

At first glance, one would take this to mean that the conditions are asserted, but it is not clear how to distinguish such cases from similarly constructed sentences or discourses in which the appropriateness of using a certain lexical item is at issue because of the assumptions which its use implies, as in (157):

> 157a. I don't thínk he's wrong – I knów
> { he is.
> { that he cannot be right. }
> 157b. John didn't bláme the murder on Bill. He thought the murder was jústified.

and from cases where what is at issue is whether the hearer has misunderstood because of some purely phonetic confusion, as in (158):

> 158a. I won't loan the paintings – I just want to ówn them.
> 158b. I didn't send him a Mahler – I lent him a dollar.

It is usually claimed that in such cases as (157) and (158a) there is extra stress on both of the contrasted verbs, but this is often effectively neutralized, either because the speaker has a small intensity range, or because various constraints force a verb that would not normally bear clause stress to do so. Thus if *for frée* and *for kéeps* in (156a) and (156d) were left off, or added as afterthoughts, clause stress would have to fall on *give* (as in their paraphrases in [159]) instead of on them, because prepositions and anaphoric expressions usually may not bear stress:

> 159a. I couldn't sell him the car, so I gáve ĭt tŏ hĭm. (Fŏr frée.)
> 159b. I won't lend you the pencil; I'd rather gíve ĭt tŏ yŏu. (Fŏr kéeps.)

Some additional evidence that the conditions on *to*-class 2 words must be made explicit somehow in their semantic representations is provided by the fact that when the conditions are made explicit, as in (160), the sentences which result are ungrammatically redundant, or nearly so:

> 160a. ?They sold us the car for a payment.
> 160b. ?They rented him the house in exchange for periodic payments.
> 160c. ?I'll lend you the pencil, but not forever.
> 160d. *They advanced us the money before the day we were supposed to get it.

160e. *They awarded him an award.
160f. *They paid him money. *They paid him a payment.
160g. *They fed him food. ?They fed him something to eat.

If the stated conditions are special cases of the general conditions, the sentences are grammatical:

161a. They sold the car for $1,000.
161b. They rented the house for $195 a month.
161c. I'll lend you the pencil for three weeks.
161d. They advanced us the money two days before the day we were supposed to get it.
161e. They awarded him a blue ribbon.
161f. They paid him $10. They paid him 10,000 trading stamps.
161g. They fed him some oatmeal.

as they are if the less restricted *give* is substituted in (160) for *sell*, *pay*, etc. In (160b), *lend* fits better than *give*, but this merely indicates that there are two conditions on *rent*, as mentioned above; that the 'having' is provisional (shared with *lend*), and that the transfer is effected in exchange for something. This does not provide evidence that the conditions are asserted rather than presupposed, or vice versa, because asserting the general condition results in redundancy when it is presupposed, as well as when it is asserted in semantic representation. Thus, in its literal use, the verb *hear* asserts 'perceive with the ears', and so it may not have the general condition 'with the ears' asserted as an instrumental phrase, as in (162a,b):

162a. *I heard it with my ears.
162b. *You can hear it with the ear.

But if this condition is satisfied in a way worthy of remark, then this particular way of 'perceiving with the ears' may be asserted, as in (162c,d):

162c. I heard it with my own ears – John wasn't hallucinating.
162d. You can hear it with the unaided ear – you don't need any kind of amplifier or hearing aid.

Similar phenomena are discussed in Appendix III. In contrast, anything presumed to be audible may be the object of *hear*, so that (163a–c) are grammatical sentences under normal conditions, and (163d,e) might be grammatical sentences for someone who claimed or pretended to have exceptionally good hearing, although (163f) never would be:

163a.   I heard a sound.
163b.   I heard a noise.
163c.   I heard John say that Bill was a coward.
163d.   I heard electricity coursing through the wires.
163e.   I heard the ants march down the sidewalk.
163f.   *I heard the Bible say "Thou shalt not kill."

But a noise described as *something audible* is not grammatical as the object of *hear*:

163g.   *I heard something audible.

unless perhaps it is elliptical for 'something audible under normal conditions,' in a situation where it is assumed that the conditions under which it was heard were not normal.

Presupposed propositions, asserted secondary propositions, and the conditions on at least some of the *give*-class verbs also work alike, and in contrast to implications (cf. p. 85, n. 1) and invited inferences[1] in that with the first three the presupposed or contained proposition may be asserted before the assertion which presupposes or contains it, but not after it. This is not true of implicative verbs or inference-inviting verbs, as is shown by the contrast between (164a–b, c–d, e–f) on the one hand and (164g–h, i–j) on the other:

164a.   It was true and I knew it.
164b.   *I knew it, and it was true.
164c.   Bill died and Mary killed him.
164d.   *Mary killed Bill and he died.
164e.   In our debates with Hubert, the immorality of the war was a disputed point, and he conceded it to us.
164f.   *In our debates with him, Hubert conceded the immorality of the war to us, and it was a disputed point.
164g.   *John kissed me and he managed to (kiss me).

---

[1] Cf. Geis and Zwicky 1971. A verb like *try* is said to invite the inference that its subject did not succeed in his endeavor, in that this is the usual inference drawn. For example, one would assume on hearing *John tried to kiss Mary* that John did not succeed in kissing Mary. However this inference is not a necessarily entailed or implied one, since it can be denied without contradiction and asserted without redundancy as in *John tried to kiss Mary, and he succeeded*, and *John tried to kiss Mary and he failed*.

164h. *John managed to kiss me, and he $\left\{\begin{array}{l}\text{did (kiss me)}\\ \text{kissed me.}\end{array}\right\}$

164i. *John failed to kiss me and he tried to (kiss me).

164j. John tried to kiss me, and he failed (to).

Conclusion: Neither (150) nor (146c) is adequate as a representation of the verbs of *to*-class 2. Rather, their meaning seems best represented as in (165):

165. Subject CAUSE i.o. to HAVE d.o. [in accordance with such and such condition i].

It is not clear whether the matter in brackets, the condition which must be fulfilled for the appropriate use of the lexical item, is presupposed or asserted.

For most of the classes of non-literal restricted *give*-expressions, I have been unable to propose semantic representations which are even partially justifiable on syntactic grounds, and in some cases I have been at a loss to find a set of paraphrases which are even semantically justified. The conclusions of my extremely frustrating research in this area are contained in Appendix v.

c To-class 3. Turning now to the *send*-class, it is clear that (146c) will be inadequate to characterize it, for reasons parallel to those given before: (166a) does not include cases included by (166b), where the causation may be magically direct or indefinitely indirect.

166a. John sent Mary the time bomb.

166b. John caused Mary to (come to) have the time bomb by sending it.

In addition, (166a) does not even indicate that Mary got the time bomb (although (147b) with *drag*, a *bring*-class verb, does indicate that she got the piano) so any paraphrase of these verbs which begins 'cause . . . to have' will be incorrect. Since most of these verbs, again in contrast to the verbs of the *bring*-class, indicate that the transmitter of the object did not accompany it to the referent of the dative NP, one might suppose that a representation on the order of (167) would delimit this class:

167. Subject CAUSE d.o. to GO FROM subject TO i.o. (BY VERB-ing d.o.).

The "FROM subject" specification is necessary to preclude the possibility of the subject's causing the direct object to go by taking it. It is incorrect to say (166a), for example, if it is known that John bore the bomb to Mary. But without further specification (167), like (148b), would represent non-dative-movement constructions such as (168a) – cf. (168b) – as well as the dative-movement verbs of *to*-class 3.

168a.   John threw the baseball to third base.
168b.   *John threw third base the baseball.

Thus it seems that the representation of these verbs must distinguish between a TO of location and a TO of possession, perhaps along the lines of Fillmore 1968, and specify only the latter. This TO would be the one that is realized in French, for instance, as *à* in cases like (169a) and not the one found in (169b).

169a.   Ce livre est à $\begin{Bmatrix} \text{Marie.} \\ \text{moi.} \end{Bmatrix}$

   this book is to $\begin{Bmatrix} \text{Marie} \\ \text{me} \end{Bmatrix}$

   This book is $\begin{Bmatrix} \text{Marie's.} \\ \text{mine.} \end{Bmatrix}$

169b.   Ce livre est à $\begin{Bmatrix} \text{Paris.} \\ \text{la bibliothèque.} \end{Bmatrix}$

   this book is to $\begin{Bmatrix} \text{Paris} \\ \text{the library} \end{Bmatrix}$

   This book is $\begin{Bmatrix} \text{in Paris.} \\ \text{at/in the library.} \end{Bmatrix}$

Distinguishing in this way between directional and dative uses of *send*-class verbs raises the possibility of similarly representing the difference between directional and dative senses of *bring*-class verbs (e.g. by [148b] with a TO of possession). And in fact, on closer examination, it appears that the claim is incorrect that the *bring*-class verbs are paraphrased by 'cause...to have' since one can say sentences like (170) without committing a contradiction.[1]

---

[1] Not all of the verbs I have been calling *bring*-class verbs work this way however. *Pass*, for instance, implies success if the dative NP is prepositionless, but not if it has a preposition, as evidenced by the difference in grammaticality between (1a) and (1b).

  1a.   *John passed me the peace pipe, but I $\begin{Bmatrix} \text{wouldn't} \\ \text{didn't} \end{Bmatrix}$ take it.

  1b.   John passed the peace pipe to me, but I $\begin{Bmatrix} \text{wouldn't} \\ \text{didn't} \end{Bmatrix}$ take it.

170a. I took Mary some flowers, but she wouldn't accept them.
170b. Max dragged me a sack of well-rotted manure, but I wouldn't take it.

I mentioned above that most of the verbs of the *send*-class may not be used in cases where the direct object goes with the subject to the indirect object. There is, however, a small class of verbs, including *push, lower, float, roll,* and perhaps some others,[1] which may be used when the subject does not accompany the direct object to the intended recipient, as well as when it does. If these verbs are ambiguous between these two senses, we must say that there are related homonyms which encode distinct semantic representations; one member belongs to the *bring*-class (1), and the other to the *send*-class (3). If these verbs are not ambiguous, but rather unspecified as to whether the subject accompanies the direct object, then it is necessary to say that they encode semantic representations which do not specify accompaniment or lack thereof, and that they belong to neither class 1 nor class 3. Unfortunately, the usual test for ambiguity does not resolve this problem. Ordinarily, if a verb is ambiguous between two senses, occurrences of the verb in different senses are not treated as identical for anaphoric reductions. Thus *pinch* may describe the action of squeezing a solid substance between two firmer objects, and it also has a sense which means about the same thing as *steal*. But one cannot pronominalize one sense with the other, and say non-facetiously, for instance, *John pinched a peach and so did Bill*, if John squeezed a peach between his thumb and first finger, and Bill stole one. Presented with such sentences as (171):

171a. John $\begin{Bmatrix} \text{pushed} \\ \text{rolled} \\ \text{floated} \end{Bmatrix}$ a ball to George and so did Paul.

171b. John $\begin{Bmatrix} \text{pushed} \\ \text{rolled} \\ \text{floated} \end{Bmatrix}$ George a ball and so did Paul.

If these judgments are correct (and I am not certain of them), then perhaps *pass* will have to be treated like *teach* (cf. chapter 4, sec. B). *Hand*, however, seems almost equally contradictory in either construction:

2a. *John handed me the peace pipe, but I didn't take it.
2b. ??John handed the peace pipe to me, but I didn't take it.

If they are both contradictory, then perhaps *hand* should be considered a *give*-class verb like *feed* and *lend*.

[1] Class membership appears to vary from speaker to speaker.

speakers find it difficult or impossible to say whether these sentences would be appropriate if John got the ball going and let it go, while Paul travelled with it, continuously or repeatedly directing or guiding its path. Implications of this inability to decide are discussed in chapter 6, section B.3.

d To-class 4. In order to account for the 'have' relationship and the fact that the subject is the immediate source, and the indirect object the recipient of whatever it is that the direct object denotes or describes, the denominal instrumental verbs of class 4a (the *radio*-class) would seem to require a semantic representation very similar to (167), differing only in that where (167) has "BY VERB-ing d.o.," it would have "BY MEANS of N." Actually, not all of these denominal instrumental verbs are necessarily communication verbs. One can wire money and flowers, and mail and relay packages of all descriptions. And one can merely send information, news, jokes, etc., although *send* is not a denominal verb. Furthermore, of the non-communication verbs of class 3 (the *send*-class), *ship* (and possibly others) is at least as denominal as the communication verbs, so it appears that denominal versus deverbal is not a real distinction between the physical transfer verbs of the *send*-class and the communication verbs of the *radio*-class.[1] It is necessary to say only that some verbs of class 3 are denominal instrumentals, and others are deverbal. None of the communication verbs is subject to the accompaniment vagueness (ambiguity?) of *push, roll, lower,* etc., since it is nonsense to speak of a person accompanying the information, etc. which he transmits by radio, telephone, etc. However, when a person does perform such transmissions, he does not necessarily cease to have the information, etc. which he transmits, so perhaps the semantic representation of class 4a verbs should not contain the "FROM subject" phrase of (167).

Of the communication verbs of class 4b (the *read*-class), all but *write* imply that the indirect object received the direct object as a result of the subject's action. In view of the fact that it was found necessary earlier to describe the meaning of *write* separately from the other verbs,

---

[1] The denominal sense of *ship* must be "SEND (AS) BY MEANS of a SHIP" rather than merely "SEND BY MEANS of a SHIP," since one can ship objects on trucks, trains, and airplanes, as well as on ships, boats, and barges. (Cf. Appendix III for further discussion of the representation of such verbs.) *Relay* is a similar case. I am not familiar enough with long-distance communication to say whether *radio, cable,* etc. have this property of being optionally figurative.

it may be wise to consider the semantic representation of *write* apart from *tell, cite, preach, read,* etc. The special cognitive sense of *have* that these verbs imply (cf. sec. c.4 of this chapter, above) will have to be provided for by any semantic representation that is to account for this implication. If, choosing an obviously *ad hoc* method, we say that these verbs are represented as in (172)

172. Subject CAUSE i.o. to HAVE_{cog} d.o. BY VERB-ing d.o.

it would wrongly imply that they were appropriate to (absurd) situations where the indirect object is unaware of the subject's action. If (172) was correct, it would be appropriate to say (173)

173. John cited Mary the facts about cancer in rats.

if John caused Mary to 'have' those facts by citing them in a book he wrote which she came to have. Sentences like (173) are only appropriate if the action was directed specifically to the indirect object, and in fact noticed by him, so it appears that a representation closer to (150) than to (146c) will be necessary, something on the order of:

174. Subject CAUSE i.o. to HAVE_{cog} d.o. BY CAUSE-ing d.o. to "GO" TO i.o. BY VERB-ing d.o.

It is necessary, however, to understand GO, as well as HAVE, in a metaphorical sense, since it does not refer here to a change in physical location, but merely to presence before an *additional* consciousness. This metaphorical GO is not an *ad hoc* creation for these communication verbs, but is necessary to explain the uses of such location and movement expressions as

175a. This theory came from a sixteenth-century text.
175b. I took these figures from the Merck manual.
175c. I got this joke from Morris.

It is apparently not necessary to include "FROM subject" in the semantic representation, as it was in (169), since when one tells a story, cites a statistic, etc., one does not cease to have what one relates, imparts, etc.

Alternatively, one might want to say here (and for class 4a as well) that the fact that the subject does not lose what he transmits to the direct object is expressed by a semantic representation on the order of (176):[1]

---

[1] A partially similar analysis was proposed by Gruber (1965: sec. 7.2) for a group of verbs including *tell, write, explain,* and *teach.*

176. Subject CAUSE i.o. to HAVE KNOWLEDGE of d.o. BY CAUSE-ing

$$\left\{\begin{matrix} \text{a RENDITION of} \\ \text{a FACSIMILE of} \\ \text{INFORMATION about} \end{matrix}\right\} \text{ d.o. to GO FROM subject TO i.o., BY}$$

VERB-ing d.o.

Such a representation would avoid the use of a special HAVE$_{cog}$, and would still specify the subject as the source of the ideas, etc. expressed by the direct object, without implying that as a result of imparting them to the indirect object, the subject ceased to 'have' them.

As for *write*, it was mentioned earlier (chapter 2, sec. C.2.*d*) that the *write* which is involved in dative-movement acts like a predicate which takes three arguments, a subject, a direct object, and an indirect object, the properties of which have some things in common with adverbs. It was also mentioned that this construction is used when the subject (1) assumes that the referent of the indirect object actually exists, and (2) intends for him to have the direct object. These semantic considerations suggest a paraphrase which includes a clause like (177a) or (177b)

177a. Subject INTEND i.o. to HAVE d.o.
177b. Subject INTEND d.o. to GO TO i.o.

but in order to account for the adverb-like properties of the indirect object phrase, it is necessary to put this intent specification not as a complement, subordinate clause, or conjunct to the predicate(s) which describes the activity of writing, but in a higher adverbial clause, as in (178):

178. [Subject] INTEND-ing d.o. to GO TO i.o., subject WRITE d.o.

e To-*class 5*. It is fairly obvious that the verbs of 'future having' (*promise, permit, bequeath*, etc.) cannot be paraphrased as simple instrumental causatives like (150, 165, 169, or 176); the 'have' relationship in *to*-class 5 is not asserted to exist as a result of the subject's action. Rather, the 'have' relationship is one which *may* (might) obtain at a time later than the action of the verb. Thus these verbs have paraphrases like the following:

179a. Subject COMMUNICATE to i.o. that subject WILL CAUSE i.o. to HAVE d.o. (*guarantee, promise*).

179b. Subject COMMUNICATE to i.o. that i.o. MAY HAVE d.o. (*permit, allow, offer, grant*).

179c. Subject ARRANGE that i.o. MAY HAVE d.o. (*assign, allot, bequeath, leave*).

179d. Subject IS OBLIGATED to CAUSE i.o. to HAVE d.o. (*owe*).

Although the semantic representations of sentences with these verbs must indicate or imply a 'have' relationship in the relative future, and half or more (e.g. *promise, permit, offer, allow, guarantee*) are normally complement-taking verbs, taking infinitival or sentential complements, I doubt that it is possible to find a single paraphrase type which will cover all of the verbs of this class in a non-trivial way.

f For-*classes 1-3, 5, and a further consideration of the intent clause.* The verbs of creation, selection, performance, and symbolic constructions (*for*-classes 1, 2, 3, and 5) are, like those of *to*-class 5, not causatives. The 'have' relationship is an intended one, as with *write*, not a resultant or predicted (promised, etc.) one. These verbs have an indirect object complement which has adverb-like properties rather than the adjectival properties of a post-nominal modifier. For instance, indirect object complements of these verbs may be preposed:

180a. I baked a cake for my brother.
180b. For my brother, I baked a cake.

181a. I chose the blue skirt for my daughter.
181b. For my daughter, I chose the blue skirt.

182a. I played the New World Symphony for my aunt.
182b. For my aunt, I played the New World Symphony.

183a. They killed a lamb for their leader.
183b. For their leader, they killed a lamb.

and relative clauses may be formed on the direct object nouns, without including the indirect objects, as (184) shows in comparison to (185):

184a. The cake (which) I baked (for) my brother was chocolate.
184b. The skirt (which) I chose (for) my daughter was red.
184c. The symphony (which) I played (for) my aunt was dull.
184d. The lamb (which) they killed (for) their leader had been shorn.

185a. ?The cake for my brother which Ĭ băked was chocolate.

185b. ?The skirt for my daughter which Ĭ chŏse was red.

185c. ?The symphony for my aunt which Ĭ plăyed was dull.

185d. *The lamb for their leader which thĕy kĭlled had been shorn.

This suggests that the position of an intent clause in the semantic representation will be similar to its position in the paraphrase of *write* sentences. A paraphrase for these classes on the order of (186a) or (186b) is a reasonable guess:

186a. [Subject] INTEND-ing i.o. to HAVE d.o., subject VERB d.o.

186b. [Subject] INTEND-ing d.o. to GO TO i.o., subject VERB d.o.

It is not obvious whether "i.o. HAVE d.o." or "d.o. GO TO i.o." is more correct, since *x went to y* in the non-volitional and non-physical sense of *go* which is intended here entails that y had x as a result of the change. It may be that the paraphrase with HAVE is more correct, at least for selection verbs, because these may be used when the subject makes a selection from among things which are already "to" the indirect object – things which the indirect object already owns. This is often the case with *find* and *choose*.

Write is the only *to*-dative verb for which the suggested semantic representation shares structural features with the semantic representations suggested for these *for*-dative verbs. Interestingly enough, it also shares a rather obscure syntactic property with these verbs. When the direct object of *to*-dative verbs is deleted as understood, as in

187a. I did it because they paid me.

187b. They were kind, and fed him.

187c. As soon as they heard the news, they wired us.

the indirect object never has a preposition:

188a. *They paid to me.

188b. *They fed to him.

188c. *They wired to us.

When the direct object of *for*-datives is deleted, the indirect object must have a preposition:[1]

189a. Mary cooks for us.

---

[1] Bruce Fraser has pointed out to me (personal communication) that particle verbs almost never permit deletions of the direct object, regardless of the type of indirect

189b. Mrs Smith chose for us.
189c. Sally danced for us.
189d. The girls were willing to kill for him.

190a. *Mary cooks us.
190b. *Mrs Smith chose us. (Ungrammatical if intended to mean the same as [189b].)
190c. *Sally danced us.
190d. *The girls were willing to kill him. (Ungrammatical if intended to mean the same as [189d].)

In American English at least, *write*, a *to*-dative verb, may have either a preposition, like the *for*-datives, or no preposition, like the *to*-datives, when the direct object is deleted:

191a. As soon as he heard the news, he wrote to us.
191b. As soon as he heard the news, he wrote us.

It is proper here to raise the question: do the indirect objects of other classes of dative-movement verbs have adverb-like properties, and if so, how are they to be accounted for? They do have the adverb-like property of being preposable, although preposing the indirect objects sometimes results in an awkward-sounding sentence:

192a. To John, I brought a typewriter.
192b. To John, I awarded three merit badges.
192c. To Mary, John sent a dozen roses.
192d. To the general, John wired news of the invasion.
192e. To the old man, the aide read a book of jokes.
192f. To Danny, I promised an ice-cream cone.

Furthermore, the semantic representations of most sentences with dative-movement constructions require a statement of the subject's

---

object, as illustrated by the following sentences:

1a. They dished out the stew to us.
1b. They dished us out the stew.
1c. *They dished out to us.
1d. *They dished us out.

2a. They picked out a site for us.
2b. They picked us out a site.
2c. *They picked out for us.
2d. *They picked us out.

intention in performing the action described. It is inappropriate to say (193), for example:

193a. I told a dirty joke to my mother.
193b. I brought my teacher an apple.

if the recipients got the transmitted items from you without your intending it, for example, if your mother overheard you telling the joke to a friend, or if your teacher took the apple (away) from you, or even if you had intended to eat the apple yourself, but changed your mind, and intending your teacher to have it, gave it to him. I conclude that on semantic grounds, an adverbial[1] clause stating the subject's intent that the indirect object have the direct object, such as is prefixed to the assertions in (178) and (186), is necessary in the semantic representation of sentences with all of the dative-movement verbs except those of the *earn*-class.[2]

It is, of course, true that adverbs like *unintentionally* may be inserted into dative-movement sentences without yielding a contradiction, for example:

194a. She unintentionally sent her sister the letter she wrote to her aunt.
194b. She unintentionally sent that letter to her sister.

These sentences are interpreted as involving the subject's intentionally sending something, although she may have been mistaken about its identity or contents. Adverbs like *unintentionally* (and *intentionally* as well, for it can be inserted without resulting in a redundant sentence) are always interpreted as describing a higher level impulse/decision (I cannot find a non-loaded expression for the concept I have in mind) to act. Examples of this are provided by (195, 196):

195. She $\begin{Bmatrix} \text{unintentionally} \\ \text{mistakenly} \\ \text{unknowingly} \end{Bmatrix}$ got into a situation in which she intentionally sent the wrong letter to her sister.

---

[1] The intent clause must be adverbial rather than predicative because intent is not the main assertion in dative-movement sentences. Arguments were given in chapter 3, sec. c.2.*e*, and at the beginning of this section that the intent clause is not like an adjective which modifies only the direct object of the sentence.

[2] It is not intuitively obvious what the form of the intent clause would be for verbs of promising. The difficulty is, of course, in representing reports of insincere promises, e.g. *Mary promised Billy a car, but she never had any intention of getting him one.*

196. She $\begin{Bmatrix} \text{intentionally} \\ \text{deliberately} \\ \text{knowingly} \end{Bmatrix}$ got into a situation in which she inten-

tionally sent the wrong letter to her sister.

sentences which would be appropriate to describe intentional and deliberate trips to the mailbox under the influence of LSD ingested respectively unintentionally/mistakenly/unknowingly or intentionally/deliberately/knowingly.

Austin (1956) and Searle (1969) claim that adverbs like *intentionally* and *unintentionally* are appropriate only when it is aberrant (Austin) or noteworthy (Searle) for the action in question to be intentional or unintentional, respectively. I am not, of course, proposing that *intentionally* be derived from the same sort of representation as represents intention in dative-movement constructions, but if their claims are interpreted as a claim that the intentionality we attribute to the subject of all dative-movement constructions except those of the *earn*-class is a matter of cultural standards rather than a linguistic matter, then we have no explanation for the conditions under which sentences like (193) are inappropriate.

Turning now to the representation of the adverbial intent clause, G. Lakoff (1965:Appendix F) described several kinds of adverbial phrases as being main verbs in "deep" structure, because they were the main assertion of the declarative sentences which they occurred in, and were negated and questioned when the sentence was negated or questioned, the surface main clause being presupposed to be true in all three cases. Assuming here, as I believe Lakoff did, that the highest predicate below the performative in "deep" or semantic structure is the "main" predicate and primary assertion of the sentence, I will argue that on semantic grounds the intent adverbials in question cannot be higher adverbials of the sort Lakoff described if his description of them is correct. To say (197a)

197a. John brought Mary a flower.

is not the same as saying (197b)

197b. John intended Mary to have a flower in bringing her one.

Still, some sort of intent clause appears to be necessary to distinguish the underlying representation of promises from that of predictions that the subject will cause the indirect object to have the direct object.

for in the former it is asserted that he brought her a flower, while in the latter that is merely presupposed. Unlike the locative and manner adverbials Lakoff described, the intent adverbials in question are not the main assertions of their sentences, and they are not negated or questioned when the dative-movement construction is negated or questioned. A sentence like (198a) does not assert that Jerry didn't intend Emily to have a cake, and (198b) doesn't ask whether he intended her to have one.

> 198a. Jerry didn't bake Emily a cake.
> 198b. Did Jerry bake Emily a cake?

Trying to stick a single negative in (197b) to represent the negation of (197a) produces ludicrous results.

Since the intent clause is not a main assertion like the higher adverbials, it is fair to ask whether it is presupposed like the sentential constituent of preposed temporal adverbial clauses. For instance, the speaker of (199)

> 199. After John got married he became lazy.

assumes that John got married, and asserts that he became lazy after doing so. It appears that the intent clause is not merely presupposed, however, for if it were, a speaker would be wrong to use (198a,b) unless he presupposed that Jerry intended for Emily to have a cake, and this is not the case. It is proper to use (198a), for instance, when it is known that Jerry had no intention of baking a cake at all. I conclude that an intent clause is present as an assertion in the semantic representation of these verbs, but as a secondary assertion, e.g. in a preposable adverbial clause, rather than in a main clause. Exactly how such an adverbial clause is attached in semantic representation to the verbs or clauses it modifies remains a mystery to me.

It is worth noting in this regard that the subject's intent that the indirect object have the direct object can be negated in a secondary assertion, without negating the action of the main verb, as in (200):

> 200a. Jerry sent the package, but not to his father.
> 200b. Jerry sent the package, but not to New York.
> 200c. Jerry baked a cake, but not for Emily.

Of course, as is shown by (200b), and by the fact that (200c) is six ways ambiguous, and not just the three of creation, performance, and symbolic action (cf. sec. c.3.*f* of this chapter, above), this kind of negation is not limited to dative-movement constructions. But it does include the dative-movement constructions; there are readings of (200c) which are equivalent to (198a).

An assertion of intent on the subject's part suggests an explanation of several syntactic properties of dative-movement verbs. It will account for the fact that the subject in dative-movement constructions must be animate, since only animate beings are (usually) assumed to be capable of intending. Second, it will explain why the referents of the dative and accusative noun phrases must be presupposed by the subject and the speaker or subject of the commanding world-creating verb to exist contemporaneously with each other, since the use of *intend*, as in *x intends y to have z* implies that x believes that y and z exist. This presupposition is part of the meaning of *intend*, and distinguishes it from other verbs of wanting such as *want, wish,* and *hope*. Third, it will explain why sentences with an animate subject for a verb which does not require an animate subject are ambiguous with respect to intent. Unintending "animate" subjects are really understood as nominalizations with the meaning 'the way x is,' or 'the way x acted,' and interact with the mind–body distinction. Thus (201a), with a verb phrase which does not require an animate subject (cf. [202]) is ambiguous as to whether the subject intended the result of his action:

201a. Mary gave John an inferiority complex.
201b. Mary gave John an inferiority complex because she hated him.
201c. Mary gave John an inferiority complex, and was quite upset when she learned of it.

202. Having a smart older sister gave John an inferiority complex.

Fourth, the 'intending to have' clause makes it unnecessary to postulate two distinct underlying TOs to distinguish between directional and dative senses of *bring-* and *send*-class verbs. Such a clause would be nonsense with the directional uses (e.g. *Intending Germany to have a package, John caused a package to go to Germany*) in exactly the same way as the prepositionless datives of (149b) and (168b) are:

149b. *John dragged New York the piano.
168b. *John threw third base the baseball.

Finally, if a higher adverbial clause is the proper way to account for the preposability of indirect object phrases with prepositions, then it will account for this property of dative-movement verbs.

But prefixing an intent clause to the semantic representations of all sentences with dative-movement constructions raises another question: what accounts for the preposition *for* in some classes and *to* in others? One might be able to make a case for *to*-datives originating in "INTEND d.o. to GO TO i.o." clauses, and *for*-datives originating in "INTEND i.o. to HAVE d.o." clauses, but the arguments I know of are rather tenuous (cf. discussion of [186] above), and it will not be possible to resolve the question here.

In suggesting (186) as a semantic representation for dative-movement constructions with verbs from *for*-classes 1–3, 5, I have not offered descriptions of the various verb classes, but only schemata for dative constructions with their members. It is relatively easy to characterize and label these classes intuitively, but much more difficult to define them rigorously. One might expect, for instance, that the creation verbs are defined as "MAKE by VERB-ing" so that constructions with them encode semantic representations of the form:

> 203. INTEND-ing i.o. to HAVE d.o., subject MAKE d.o. by VERB-ing.

This works well enough for *bake, knit, sew,* and some others, but it is nonsense to say that the sentences of (204) with *build, fry, roast,* correspond to those of (205):

> 204a. John built Mary a house.
> 204b. John fried an egg for Mary.
> 204c. John roasted Mary a chicken.

> 205a. Intending Mary to have a house, John made a house by building.
> 205b. Intending Mary to have an egg, John made an egg by frying.
> 205c. Intending Mary to have a chicken, John made a chicken by roasting.

A representation for sentences (204b,c) on the order of (206)

> 206. INTEND-ing i.o. to HAVE a VERBed d.o., subject MAKE VERBed d.o. BY VERB-ing d.o.

might be more accurate, but it is also circular, and nonsense as far as (204a) is concerned. It does seem that the differentiating criteria (e.g. "BY VERB-ing") are asserted rather than presupposed since they may be negated and questioned when the constructions are negated and questioned. Thus, if John asks Mary, "Did you fry me an egg?" she must answer "no" if she cooked an egg for him by boiling it, denying the method of cooking, but not necessarily the fact that she cooked it. It may be the case that such verbs are names for physically and cognitively complex, but linguistically unitary 'making' activities,[1] so that rather than it being the case that clauses containing them encode representations like (203), they encode representations like (207):

207. INTEND-ing i.o. to HAVE d.o. subject VERB$_i$ d.o.

provided that VERB$_i$ refers to an activity assumed by the speaker to be "creative" (cf. the discussion in sec. c.3.*a* of this chapter, above).

As mentioned above, the selection verbs encode the notion 'get' in some very loose sense – one can find, choose, buy, etc. something without taking possession of it physically. Thus *find* (with an indirect object) means 'get by searching' and *buy* means something like 'get by paying money' or 'get by agreeing to pay money.' But it is hard to say what *choose*, *pick* (*out*), etc. mean, without being circular. It does appear to be clear that the criteria differentiating among the selection verbs are presupposed rather than asserted, since they hold in questions and negations (i.e. they are not questioned or negated). Thus it is improper to answer "no" to the question, "Did you find me my shoelaces?" or "Did you pick us out the vanilla ice-cream?" if you didn't even look for the shoelaces, or if there was no choice of ice-cream flavors.

Performance verbs are likewise difficult to paraphrase uniformly. *Dance*, *play* (a composition), and perhaps *sing* mean 'perform' or 'give a rendition of' but *play* (an instrument) means 'perform on' or 'give a rendition on,' and *play* (on a phonograph, tape recorder, etc.) is different still. The differentiating criteria seem to be asserted rather than presupposed, since a question like "Did Mary play you 'Let it Be'?" asks specifically if she played it on some instrument (musical or

[1] Thus while *fry* refers to a kind of cooking in fat, above the heat, for a relatively short period of time (for other examples, cf. Lehrer 1969), it would not have the semantic representation COOK IN FAT, ABOVE THE HEAT, FOR A SHORT TIME, but would represent a single simple predicate. The exact boundaries of the meaning of such words are not clear, and may vary from speaker to speaker depending on personal experience. For instance, if you scramble eggs in butter, is that 'frying'? A dietician would probably say that it is, but try and convince someone who wants a fried egg 'easy-over' of it! Is the stir-frying characteristic of Chinese cuisine 'frying'? Compare the discussion of *banana* in Morgan 1969a.

electronic), and must be answered "no" if she caused a rendition of "Let it Be" to be heard by singing it.

The verbs which occur in the symbolic construction remain a rather ill-defined class, so it will be impossible for me to add anything here to what was said above (see sec. c.3.*e* of this chapter, above). Still, it should be clear that the verbs of *for*-classes 1–3, 5 differ from other dative-movement verbs in important ways (e.g. they are not causatives), but share certain important semantic and syntactic properties with them (e.g. intent clauses), and nonetheless differ from each other in important ways (for example, in what is presupposed and what is asserted).

g For-*class 4*. The verbs of the *earn*-class (*for*-class 4) are a comparatively coherent bunch in terms of semantics, encoding something like (208):

> 208. Subject CAUSE i.o. to (COME to) HAVE d.o. BY MERIT/EFFORT.[1]

These verbs are causatives; they assert that the indirect object 'has' the direct object as a result of some property of an inanimate subject, or some action of an animate subject. They do not require an intent clause on semantic grounds; inanimate subjects are incapable of intent, and for many sentences with animate subjects, a prefixed intent clause could be contrary to the sense of the sentence, as in (209a) – cf. (209b):

> 209a. John earned a bad name for himself by swearing a lot.
> 209b. Intending (for himself) to have a bad name, John caused himself to come to have one by swearing a lot.

It was mentioned in this chapter, section c.3, that inanimate surface subjects of *for*-class 4 verbs are always understood as action nominalizations which have animate subjects. This is reasonable, given a semantic representation like (208), because inanimate objects cannot be causative agents or catalysts, although events and situations can. The fact that the subject of the nominalization must be animate is not, however, explained, unless by the requirement as in (208) that the causation be by merit (inanimate surface subject) or effort (animate subject), since merit,

---

[1] *Merit* is not the best word here, since it wrongly excludes negative and neutral qualities. *Deserve* is appropriately neutral, but does not have a suitable nominalization. Likewise, *effort* is inaccurate because it excludes unintentional and irrelevantly motivated actions. The verb *do* is appropriately neutral, but it excludes qualities, and lacks a suitable nominalization, as *deed* refers only to intentional acts.

deserving, effort, and doing are predicable ultimately only of animates. The restriction to causation by quality or action is apparently asserted, since the existence of a determining quality or action may be questioned or negated when the construction is questioned or negated. Thus, if asked, "Did John earn himself a bad reputation?" it is proper to say "no" if John was unintentionally the source of misunderstandings leading to his getting a bad reputation (effort questioned and denied).[1] Likewise, if asked, "Did the publication of John's article win him fame and glory?" one may appropriately say "no," if one knows that John became famous because his mother took out ads in *The New York Times* because he finally got his article published (merit questioned and denied).

7   Syntactic justification

In this section, I will present syntactic evidence, primarily from the scope of adverbs and quantifiers, to support the claim that various dative-movement verbs are structurally complex in a way that supports certain aspects of the semantic representations proposed in section c.6 of this chapter, above. This evidence is summarized in Appendix II.

a   Time adverbs. When some kinds of adverbial phrases, such as time adverbials, modify some kinds of dative-movement verbs, such as *to*-class I verbs like *take*, they modify simultaneously several aspects of the action the verb describes. Thus (210):

210.   John took his advisor the first chapter on Monday.

asserts that the first chapter got to John's advisor on Monday, that it went on Monday, and that John initiated on Monday the event of its going. It would be inappropriate to use (210) if John started out on Monday but didn't get to his advisor with the chapter until Tuesday, or if he started out on Sunday and got it to him on Monday. The time adverb may be preposed without affecting the interpretation. Verbs of the *give*-class (2) are like this also, but the *send*-class verbs (3) do not behave this way. The time adverb modifies only the causation and the initiation of the going. Thus, we may say (211):

211.   Mary sent her father the letter on Monday (so he won't have it yet).

[1] One must answer "yes," however, if John's actions, intentional or not, were properly understood as reflecting badly on his character.

even if we know that the indirect object couldn't have the letter yet, and even if we know that the letter has gone no further than the local post office, just so long as we know that the transfer was begun on Monday. The direct object must have gone from the subject's control on Monday; if the extent of Mary's 'sending' was to leave the letter for the mailman to pick up on Tuesday, it would be wrong to assert (211). For syntactic representations to represent the difference in scope of adverbs in *bring-* and *give-* class verbs and *send*-class verbs, it is necessary for them to be at least complex enough to distinguish predicates of causing, going, and having. The rest of this section will describe the scopes of various kinds of adverbs with the several classes of dative-movement verbs, demonstrating that the verbs are structurally complex, having at least some of the predicates proposed in section c.6, and that there are clear and usually systematic differences among the classes.

Time adverbs modifying the verbs of *to*-class 4b (the *read*-class), and *for*-class 4 (the *earn*-class), refer simultaneously to both the causation and the beginning of the effect, the 'having.' In a sense, the actions described by these verbs must be conceived of as instantaneous; it would be wrong, for instance, to assert (212)

212a. John told Mort a joke on Monday.
212b. That joke earned Mort $6,000 on Monday.

if the causation began on Monday, but was not complete until Tuesday, or if it began on Sunday but was not complete until Monday. This might be the case if the joke was a very long one. In such cases, it is necessary to choose a time adverb which includes both the time of the beginning of the causation, and the time at which the effect is complete, as in (213):

213a. John told Mort a joke last week.
213b. That joke earned Mort $6,000 last week.

To-class 4a (the *radio*-class) is quite different from *to*-class 4b. Time adverbs with these verbs have different scopes depending on the indirect object type. Thus, in (214a), John may have sent the wire,

214a. John wired the news to his mother on Monday.
214b. John wired his mother the news on Monday.

but his mother may not have yet received it. In (214b), however, it is necessary that the news have been both sent and received at times included in the time adverb. This is demonstrated again by the difference between (215a) and (215b):

215a. John wired the news to his mother yesterday, but she can't have received it yet.

215b. *John wired his mother the news yesterday, but she can't have received it yet.

(Actually this property is limited to a semantically defined subclass of *to*-class 4a (cf. Appendix I), namely those verbs which do not describe direct and instantaneous transmission of information or other relevant commodity.

The scope of time adverbs with the promise and permission verbs of *to*-class 5 is ambiguous. Thus (216):

216. Tricky Dick $\left\{ \begin{array}{l} \text{promised} \\ \text{offered} \\ \text{permitted} \end{array} \right\}$ Judy a new car on Thursday.

may mean either that Tricky Dick said on Thursday to Judy that she would or could have a new car, or that he said to her that on Thursday she could have a new car. If the adverb is preposed, or if the dative is external, as in (217), the sentence is no longer ambiguous, and has only the first reading:

217a. On Thursday, Tricky Dick promised Judy a new car.

217b. Tricky Dick promised a new car to Judy on Thursday.

It is generally the case that adverbs can be preposed only to the head of the clause they modify,[1] as illustrated by the fact that (218a) and (218b)

---

[1] A provocative discussion of this may be found in Keyser 1968. A small but interesting class of exceptions to this was brought to my attention by Jerry Morgan. It is illustrated by the following examples.

1.   When John comes home, I think I'll have to fire him.

2a.   If Mary doesn't go home, Harry says he'll hit her.

2b.   ??If Mary was in California, Harry says he'll hit her.

3a.   Before you leave, I hope you'll visit the garden.

3b.   *Before you leave, I hope it'll rain.

4.   When you grow up, I hope your children treat you the way you treat me.

5a.   Before you leave, I'm afraid I'll have to take those gloves.

5b.   *Before you leave, I'm surprised I'll have to take those gloves.

5c.   *Before you leave, the boss is afraid I'll have to take those gloves.

6a.   After you leave, you realize I'll have you followed.

6b.   *After you left, you realize I would have you followed.

6c.   *After you leave, Archie realizes I'll have you followed.

below are synonymous, while (219c), where the adverb has been preposed to the head of a higher clause, is not synonymous with (219a)
and (219b), and again by the fact that (220d,e) are ungrammatical, but
not for semantic reasons, as the acceptability of (220a–c) testifies:

218a.   John said on Thursday that Martha could have a new
         phone.
218b.   On Thursday, John said that Martha could have a new
         phone.

219a.   John said that Martha could have a new phone on Friday.
219b.   John said that on Friday, Martha could have a new phone.
219c.   On Friday, John said that Martha could have a new phone.

220a.   John said on Thursday that Martha could have a new
         phone on Friday.
220b.   On Thursday, John said that Martha could have a new
         phone on Friday.
220c.   On Thursday, John said that on Friday, Martha could
         have a new phone.
220d.   *On Thursday, on Friday, John said that Martha could
         have a new phone.
220e.   *On Friday, on Thursday, John said that Martha could have
         a new phone.

The fact that (217a) does not have the ambiguity of (216) is predicted by
a syntactic representation of sentences with these verbs which, like (179a)
and (179b), is such that a time adverb could have as its scope a clause
whose main verb was a verb of saying, or alternatively, a clause whose
main verb was a verb of having.

7a.   When John comes home, Mary says she won't hit him.
7b.   *When John comes home, Mary doesn't say she'll hit him.

8a.   After you leave, you realize I won't have you followed.
8b.   *After you leave, you don't realize I'll have you followed.

9.   After you leave, I think you realize I'll have you followed.

10a.   Before you leave, I'm pleased to give you this token of our appreciation.
10b.   *Before you leave, I'm eager to give you this token of our appreciation.

I will not attempt to characterize here the conditions under which adverb-preposing
may 'skip' a clause, but a connection with performative verbs is suggested by the
restrictions on tense (illustrated by (2b) and (6b)), on negativity (illustrated by (7)
and (8)), by restrictions on subjects (illustrated by (5c) and (6c), but cf. (2a) and (6a)),
and by the fact that emotive verbs which permit embedded performatives occur here,
(10a), while other emotive verbs do not, (10b). Notice that (9) shows that more
than one clause of the appropriate type may be jumped over.

Because the verbs of this class are verbs which refer to 'having' in the future, they may take adverbs referring to the future, as in (221):

221a.   Tricky Dick promised Judy a new car tomorrow.
221b.   *Tomorrow Tricky Dick promised Judy a new car.

The ungrammaticality of (221b) is predicted by the fact that adverbs generally move up only to the head of their own clause; here, with a past tense verb, *tomorrow* can modify only HAVE, not SAY. The time adverb cannot simultaneously modify both the saying (etc.) and the having. *Today* (in [222a]) means 'later today,' and (222b) is ungrammatical – inappropriate in any situation:

222a.   I promise you a spoonful today.
222b.   *I promise you a spoonful right now.

With the arrangement verbs of this class (*assign, allot, bequeath, leave*), punctative time adverbs refer only to the time of the arrangement, as in (223):

223.   They assigned Bob a new office on Thursday.

Sentence (223) cannot mean that they arranged on Monday that on Thursday Bob could have a new office. The scope of durative time adverbs, on the other hand, is restricted to the verb of having. Thus (224a)

224a.   They will assign Bob a new office beginning Monday.
224b.   They will assign Bob a new office for the next six months.

means that sometime before Monday they will arrange that beginning on Monday, Bob will have a new office. It may not mean that on Monday they will begin to assign him a new office. Similarly, (224b) does not mean that they will spend the next six months assigning an office, but that Bob's new office will be his for the next six months. *Bequeath* and *leave* seem to contain a reference to the time when the indirect object's 'having' begins (i.e. they mean roughly 'subject arranges that indirect object may have d.o. when subject dies') so that the only durative adverbs which would not contradict this time adverb are redundant, as in (225):

225.   *Scrooge left his niece all of his stock beginning when he dies.

With *owe*, neither punctative nor durative time adverbs may modify

anything but the time at or during which the obligation is in effect.
Thus (226a)

226a.   Hy owed her a dollar on Friday.
226b.   *Hy owes her a dollar for three weeks.
226c.   *Hy owes her a dollar beginning Monday.

cannot be used on Thursday to describe a situation in which Hy became
obligated on Wednesday to pay her a dollar on Friday, and (226b,c),
with durative adverbs, are ungrammatical in the sense 'Hy is presently
obligated to cause her to have a dollar for three weeks (beginning
Monday).'

With the creation, selection, performance, and symbolic expressions
of *for*-classes 1–3 and 5, time adverbs as in (227) refer only to the time
of the making, selecting, performing or doing, respectively, and not to
the time of intending or the intended time of having:

227a.   George fried Martha a fritter on Monday.
227b.   George chose Martha a new gown on Monday.
227c.   George played Martha a sonata on Monday.
227d.   George killed Martha a Tory on Monday.

When the adverb is preposed, its scope remains the same.

b   Place adverbs. As with the time adverbs, with an adverb of place,
such as *in Urbana*, dative-movement constructions with verbs of the
bring-, *give-*, *send-*, *read-*, and *earn*-classes have only a reading in which
the causation, movement (if any), and consequent having all occur as
described by that adverb.[1] Thus, one cannot use (228a–d):

228a.   Jack brought Jill a joint in Urbana.
228b.   Jack sold Jill a joint in Urbana.
228c.   Jack shoved Betty a hoe on the patio.
228d.   Jack told Jill a story in Urbana.
228e.   Jack's pranks earned him notoriety in Urbana.

if Jack was not in Urbana (or on the patio) when he initiated the transfer,

---

[1] Verbs of the *bring-* and *radio*-classes, and perhaps a few others, such as *send*, have a
reading with a prepositional dative such that the time adverb refers only to the
indirect object's having the direct object. For instance, *Jack brought a joint to Jill in
Urbana* could be used if Jack came from L.A. with a joint which he gave to Jill, who
was in Urbana. The place expression here is not preposable, and is not found when
the indirect object is separated from it, as when it is prepositionless and internal,
so it is probably a reduced relative clause on the indirect object.

or when the transfer was completed. In (228e), it must have been in Urbana that Jack became notorious, and he must have been notorious in Urbana. It is necessary to disregard relative clause readings, such as 'Jack brought Jill a joint which was in Urbana,' throughout this section (C.7), since they are irrelevant to the issues at hand. They have different properties (e.g. the relative phrase does not prepose, while the adverbial phrases often do), and I have tried therefore to use sentences for which relative clause readings would be farfetched or ungrammatical.

With place adverbs, verbs of the *radio*-class (4a) do not behave like those of the classes just discussed, and this provides some syntactic evidence that the internal structure of *to*-classes 4a and 4b is not very similar, as indeed the semantic details I have suggested indicate. (Recall that 4a and 4b also differed with respect to the scope of time adverbs.) Constructions with verbs of the *radio*-class have the reading shared by the other classes, but they also have a reading in which only the causation must be covered by the time adverb. Thus (229):

229. Jack wired Mary the news in California.

may refer either to a situation in which Jack in Los Angeles sent Mary in San Francisco a wire by California Western Union, or to one where Jack in Los Angeles sent the wire to Mary in Hawaii. Although the adverb preposes with both of these readings, they are distinct. A sentence with one reading conjoined to a sentence with the other cannot be reduced by *so do*-reduction. The same reading must be intended in both clauses of (230):

230. Jack wired his sister the news in California, and so did Bill.

Notice that, given the restriction on adverb-preposing that it not skip over a clause boundary, the preposability on these two readings seems to provide evidence against an analysis of these verbs in which "CAUSE d.o. to GO TO i.o." is embedded beneath "CAUSE i.o. to HAVE d.o." Presumably, preposability on both readings would be consistent with an analysis where CAUSE and GO were the highest predicates.

The development of communication satellites makes possible a situation in which a message can be sent by one person to a person at another point in a large area by going out of that area and coming back in. It is not clear to me whether a sentence like (231) could be used in such a situation:

231. Jack relayed the story to his editor in Brazil.

All of the 'future having' verbs of *to*-class 5 have a reading with place adverbs such that it is only the place of the communicating or arranging, etc. which is referred to. With *owe*, the adverb apparently specifies the place where the subject is bound by the obligation, as in (232):

232. She owes Ma Bell $4.00 in Chicago.

These adverbs are all preposable. The promise and permission verbs have an additional reading, under which it is the having which is specified as to place. Thus (233a):

233a. Jack promised Jill a kiss in Chicago.
233b. FDR offered them a chicken in every pot.

has the reading 'Jack told Jill that in Chicago she would get a kiss,' and (233b) can only mean that FDR said that they could have, in every pot, a chicken. With these readings, the adverbs are not preposable, except in very emphatic sentences. As with time adverbs, when the indirect object is an external prepositional phrase, only the first, higher-verb, reading is present, so (234), which has only the second reading, is ungrammatical even with an emphatic reading:

234. *In every pot, FDR offered a chicken to them.

As with the time adverbs, the creation, selection, performance, and symbolic constructions of *for*-classes 1–3 and 5 have with place adverbs only a reading in which the place of the making, selecting, performing or doing is specified. These adverbs may be preposed freely.

c   Source adverbs. Adverbs denoting origin, such as *from Urbana*, impose rather different readings from place adverbs, and rather different classifications on dative-movement constructions. With source adverbs, the verbs of the *bring*-class are different from all other dative-movement verbs in that the adverb refers to the going as in (235), and not to the causing or having:

235. Jack brought the Ming vase to Jill from Urbana.

The *give*-class verbs of *to*-class 2, and the promise, permission, and arrangement verbs of *to*-class 5, on the other hand, have only a reading in which only the place of the causation, communication, etc. is referred to, as in (236):

236a. Jack sold Mary a house (in Urbana) from Chicago.
236b. Jack promised Mary a house (in Urbana) from Chicago.

236c. Jack granted Mary a house (in Urbana) from Chicago.

236d. Jack assigned the soldiers their positions from his office.

These adverbs are preposable, as is the one in (235).

The sending and communication verbs of *to*-classes 3, 4a, and 4b are similar to those of *to*-class 2 except that the adverb describes the spatial origin of both the causation and the movement. Thus, for the sentences of (237):

237a. Jack mailed a package to Mary from Urbana.

237b. Jack wired the news to Mary from Urbana.

237c. Jack read the news to Mary from Urbana.

to be appropriate, Jack must have been in Urbana, and the package (237a) or news transmitter (237b,c) must also have been in Urbana. It would be improper to use these sentences if Jack was in Urbana and caused the package (news) to be sent to Mary from Ann Arbor. It would also be wrong to use them if Jack was in Ann Arbor when he caused the package (news) to be sent from Urbana.

As might be expected, the creation, selection, performance, and symbolic expressions of *for*-classes 1–3 and 5 all behave alike, and have only a reading in which the adverb modifies only the origin of the making, selecting, performing, etc., as in (238):

238a. Jack baked Marge a pie from his study.

238b. Jack chose Marge a coat from his office.

238c. Jack played Marge a song from his bed.

238d. Heinrich killed the Fuehrer a subversive from his switchboard.

The readings of these sentences are similar to the readings of sentences with these verbs and simple place-at-which adverbs, except that here the link between the subject and the direct object is less direct; the direct object may be in a totally different place from the subject, at least in (238a,b,d), with the action being performed more or less by remote control.

Owe seems to have no non-relative clause readings with a source adverb, and indirect object expressions with *earn* (or *gain*) are compatible with source adverbs only when they have animate agentive subjects, and do not have unstressed prepositional phrase indirect objects:

239a. Jack earned $\left\{ \begin{array}{l} \text{himself} \\ \text{his favorite charity} \end{array} \right\}$ \$100 from his basement darkroom.

239b. *Jack's photography earned him $100 from his basement darkroom.

239c. ??Jack earned $100 for $\left\{\begin{array}{l}\text{his favorite charity}\\ \text{himself}\end{array}\right\}$ from his basement darkroom.

The scope of the source adverb in (239a) is the causation only.

d Until. There are at least four distinct readings of *until*-clauses and phrases which occur with dative-movement verbs, and several classes permit more than one reading. In generic sentences with dative-movement verbs of the *bring-*, *give-*, *read-*, and *earn*-classes, *until* clauses may have a reading of repeated causing, having and (sometimes) movement, which ceased at the time specified in the *until*-clause. Sentences (240a–d) all have this reading:

240a. Dave brought us *The Daily News* until Thursday.
240b. The doctor gave us lollipops until we were six.
240c. She cited statistics to us until you rescued us.
240d. John's haircut won him respect and admiration until everyone started copying it.

This reading is preserved when the adverbial phrase or clause is preposed. In generic and non-generic sentences with dative-movement verbs of the *give-*, *send-* and *earn*-classes, and of the selection and 'future having' constructions, the *until*-clause may be read as describing the time when the having will cease, saying nothing about the time or duration of the causing or transfer. This is the usual reading for the sentences of (241):

241a. John lent his hoe to Jill until Monday.
241b. John sent his hoe to Jill until Monday.
241c. They promised Jill a free room until she gets a job.
241d. They permitted Jill a free room until she gets a job.
241e. They assigned Jill control of their estate until their son is twenty-one.
241f. They owe her room and board until Monday.
241g. They found a bed for her until Monday.
241h. The Democratic Convention won political control for the Republicans until 1972.

These adverbs are not preposable.

A third reading, in which the adverb modifies the causing and the going but not the having, is found in sentences describing habitual or repeated action with verbs of the *send-* and *radio-*classes, as in (242):

242a. Bob forwarded Mary her mail until yesterday, so she probably won't have all of it yet.

242b. Bob wired the news to Mary until yesterday, so she probably doesn't know of the events of this morning.

Sentences (242a,b) are inappropriate if Bob engaged in only one causative act whose effect was that the mail or news be sent every so often; Bob must have engaged in a causative act for each occurrence of the mail's (news') going. The *until*-phrase is preposable on this reading.

A fourth reading, in which only the time of cessation of the activity of making, choosing, performing, saying, etc., is referred to is found in sentences describing repeated or continuing activity with the verbs of *for*-classes 1–3 and *to*-class 5. This is the usual reading of (243a–g), although many of these sentences also have the second reading mentioned.

243a. They made him cakes until they ran out of flour.

243b. They chose clothes for her until they ran out of money.

243c. They sang songs for her until they were hoarse.

243d. Tom promised his girlfriends money until they caught on.

243e. He permitted his cronies positions of power until the BGA caught on.

243f. He assigned positions of power to his cronies until the BGA caught on.

243g. He owed them $1,000 until the government voided all debts.

The meaning of these sentences on the fourth reading is not altered if the adverbial clause is preposed. *Until*-clauses have a similar reading with the symbolic constructions of *for*-class 5, but they seem to be compatible with them only when the dative phrase is prepositional:

244a. They shaved subversives for the Grand Wizard until the townspeople arrived.

244b. ?They shaved the Grand Wizard subversives until the townspeople arrived.

e   Almost. In sentences with most dative-movement verbs, the adverb *almost* refers to the initiation of transfer or activity almost being effected, as in (245):

245a. John almost brought Martha a bouquet, but he forgot to buy one.

245b. John almost sold his ward to some white-slavers, but he chickened out.

245c. John almost sent the President a bomb, but he chickened out.

245d. John almost wired Martha the news, but we stopped him in time.

245e. John almost told Martha that joke, but we stopped him in time.

245f. John almost promised (bequeathed) his son a ring, but he stopped in time.

245g. John almost baked Martha a cake, but he remembered that he wasn't supposed to.

245h. John almost chose Martha a dress, but he remembered that he wasn't supposed to.

245i. John almost sang Martha a song, but he remembered his vows not to.

245j. Paul almost killed Jesse a lawman, but his gun wasn't loaded.

With verbs of the *give*-class, however, it is ambiguous, and may refer instead to an attempted transfer almost succeeding, as in (246):

246a. John almost sold his ward to some white-slavers, but the notary was out of town.

246b. Joan almost paid the deliveryman $10.50, but he gave her back $5.00.

246c. They almost advanced us $1.50, but we insisted on $11.50.

Verbs of *for*-class 4, the '*earn*'-class, have exclusively this reading, as in (247):

247a. John's book almost won him a Newberry Prize.

247b. They almost won their team the pennant.

On this reading, *almost* VERB has the reading 'almost succeed in VERB-ing' or 'cause that (i.o.) almost have.'[1] Verbs of other classes do not have

---

[1] McCawley has pointed out to me that an exclusively internal scope for *almost* is not limited to this small class of dative-movement verbs, but occurs elsewhere as well, e.g. in *I almost reached Pittsburgh*. It seems to be typical of many verbs which Vendler (1967) calls achievement verbs (e.g. *recognize, identify, lose, find, reach*).

this second reading. It is wrong, for instance, to use (248a and b), if John got the ball, story, etc. going, but it failed to get all the way to Nora.

248a. John almost took Nora the ball.
248b. John almost sent Nora the ball.
248c. John almost wired Nora the story.
248d. John almost told Nora the story.

Likewise, it would be wrong to use (249a–c) if John said (arranged, etc.) that Nora would/could almost have $1,000, or that she would/could have almost $1,000:

249a. John almost promised Nora $1,000.
249b. John almost allowed Nora $1,000.
249c. John almost left Nora $1,000.

On the other hand, the latter reading is marginally found with *owe* and the verbs of the *earn*-class. Thus, the sentences of (250) are occasionally equivalent to those of (251):

250a. John almost owed the government $1,000.
250b. John almost earned his company $1,000 in royalties.
250c. John almost won his team enough to go to Florida.

251a. John was obligated to remit to the government almost $1,000.
251b. John brought it about that his company had almost $1,000 in royalties.
251c. John brought it about that his team had almost enough to go to Florida.

f Again *and* another. All of the dative-movement verbs occur in constructions with *again* or *another* to indicate that the activity involving subject, indirect object, and direct object (or a counterpart of the direct object) was repeated, as in (252):

252a. John took Mary the book again.
252b. John took Mary another book.
252c. John bought Mary a book again.
252d. John bought another book for Mary.

With *another*, these verbs are ambiguous, having an additional reading where the action is not necessarily a repeated one, but rather brings about an effect which duplicates a previously existing situation in which the indirect object had the direct object or a counterpart of it. This reading may be found in the sentences of (253):

253a. John broke the watch his grandfather gave him, so his jeweler lent him another one.

253b. After Mary lost her ticket, Travelers' Aid bought her another one.

253c. John lost the cake I bought him, so I baked another one for him.

Again also occurs with this reading, but apparently only with some verbs of *to*-class 5 and *for*-class 4, as in (254):

254a. As soon as his new boss saw how distraught Jon was, she promised (permitted, assigned) him a single office again.

254b. As soon as his new boss saw how distraught Jon was, she agreed that she owed him a single one again.

254c. Good behavior will earn first offenders the right to vote again.

This reading is impossible if *again* occurs before the dative-movement verb, as in (255):

255a. She again promised him a single office.

255b. Again she promised him a single office.

In such positions, *again* has only the reading of a repetition of the action involving the subject, indirect object, and direct object.

g   *Summary and conclusions.* In sections c.7.*a–f* of this chapter, evidence was presented that in many constructions with dative-movement verbs the scope of adverbs and quantifiers was frequently only a part of what was asserted in the expression. This was the case every time an adverb or quantifier referred only to the causation (saying, arranging, etc.) or the going, or the having, or to the causation and the going, but not the resultant having. In several cases, there was an ambiguity of scope. Each such case of sublexical adverb or quantifier scope is evidence that the lexical items in question are derived from structured semantic representations containing predicates of causing, having, etc., to which the adverb or quantifier is bound, because if it is not assumed that the ambiguity arises in the lexicalization of structures identical except for the position (scope in semantic representation) of the adverb, it must be the case that for each ambiguity there are two separate homonymous lexical items which differ in the interpreted scope of particular kinds of adverbs. If structured semantic representations, or remote structures, are not assumed, these differences must be considered idiosyncratic properties of lexical items, and there is no way of predicting them or accounting for them. In fact, the claim that they are idiosyncratic is a claim that they are in principle unpredictable and unexplainable.

But in several cases the adverb could be preposed if it modified a predicate of causation, saying, making, performing, etc. – in all cases, the highest predicate in the postulated assertion – but not if it modified only a predicate of having or going. This is predicted by the fact that adverbs generally can be preposed only to the head of their own clauses. This provides strong motivation for the claim that the verbs involved have structures in which a predicate of having or going (or both) is embedded as the complement of a predicate of causing. Further motivation for the proposed semantic representation of promise and permission verbs was provided by the fact that the proposed paraphrases predicted correctly that the scope of time adverbs could not simultaneously include all aspects of the meaning, since one element was *specified* as referring to a time in the future relative to the time of another. In some cases, there was no obvious logical or pragmatic reason why the scope of an adverb should be less than the entire assertion, as in the case of *until*-clauses with *send*-class verbs, or why it could not be less, as in the case of time adverbs with *bring*-class verbs, but a much more detailed study than I have been able to offer here of the semantics and syntax of the proposed paraphrases would be necessary before a definitive claim could be made that the scope of adverbs is in some cases unpredictable, and therefore unpredictable in general.

Since for each class of dative-movement verbs, evidence was presented that at least one adverb or quantifier has sublexical scope, it may be concluded that all of the dative-movement verbs have complex, non-atomic remote structures, containing at least the predicates whose clauses are modified by the relevant adverb or quantifier. The adverb and quantifier data do not justify any of the paraphrases suggested in section c.6 of this chapter, in their entirety, but they do at least demonstrate that all of the dative-movement verbs are syntactically as well as semantically complex, and they do provide evidence for the inclusion of predicates of causing, going, having, saying, arranging, etc. as suggested in section c.6.

In addition, the fact that no two *to*-classes of dative-movement verbs have the same readings or ambiguities with adverbs and quantifiers, as is quite clear from Appendix II, offers syntactic support for discriminating the six to nine classes from one another, as was done on semantic grounds in section c.6. Likewise, the fact that with adverbs and quantifiers the creation, selection, performance, and symbolic *for*-constructions behave alike in all respects but one, and are consistently different from the *earn*-class constructions, supports having similar remote structures for them quite distinct from that of *for*-class 4.

The predicates of intent and having are, in addition, independently motivated in that they provide a source for the constraints (cf. secs. c.4–5 of this chapter, above) on the animateness of the subject, for the speaker's assumptions about the co-existence of the subject and the direct and indirect objects, and for the 'have' relationship which exists as a result of the activity described (*to*-classes 1–4, *for*-class 4), as predicted (*to*-class 5), or as intended (*for*-classes 1–3, 5). The fact that *for*-class 4 verbs are the only ones which on semantic grounds do not require an intent clause, and in addition are the only ones for which the requirement that the subject be animate and the assumptions about existence do not hold is corroborating evidence that the relation between intent and the other constraints, discussed in section c.6.*f*, is not accidental.

D   Summary and conclusions

Section A of this chapter outlined syntactic phenomena which first (historically) prevented formulation of a single, general rule of dative movement. Section B outlined additional lexical obstacles to a single rule, either governed or ungoverned. In sections c.1–3, an attempt was made to characterize the verbs which participate in the dative-movement alternation. Sections c.4–5 described additional constraints on dative-movement constructions, and in sections c.6–7 an attempt was made to provide and justify semantic representations which would account for the semantic properties of dative-movement constructions and for some of the contraints on them.

The first thing that is clear from an examination of the semantic representations suggested by the paraphrases in section c.6 is that if these semantic representations are correct, the dative-movement phenomena cannot be characterized as a single transformational rule applying to a class of verbs specifiable by a single (generalized) derived semantic structure. Most of the verb classes require an intent clause, but the *earn*-class (*for*-class 4) does not. Most of the *to*-dative verbs are causatives, but *to*-class 5 verbs are not. Some of them in fact appear not to involve the notion of causation at all. The only thing that the verbs of the creation, selection, performance, and symbolic constructions (*for*-classes 1–3 and 5) have in common is the intent clause. They have nothing in common with *for*-class 4 (the *earn*-class), which is in fact most similar to *to*-class 2 (the *give*-class). The only thing which all of the semantic representations would have in common is the embedded structure:

but it is clear that a notation specifying only this and variables, such as [X HAVE]$_\text{V}$ or even X[Y HAVE]$_\text{V}$ Z, would specify a class of verbs much larger than the class of dative-movement verbs, and would include *deprive* ('cause to not have'), *accept* ('agree to have'), *demand* ('ask to have' as in *demand something from someone*), and the like.

Furthermore, even if the exact details of the semantic representations I have suggested are not correct, and it is possible to find one or a small number of generalized semantic notations which will uniquely specify the class of dative-movement verbs, the constraints on dative-movement are such that some define the $V\ NP_i\ NP_j$ constructions which alternate with $V\ NP_j\ Prep\ NP_i$ constructions (e.g. the animate subject constraint on verbs of the *give-*, *read-*, and permission classes [*to*-classes 2, 4b, and 5b]), while others define the $V\ NP_i\ Prep\ NP_j$ constructions which alternate with $V\ NP_j\ NP_i$ constructions (e.g. the animate subject constraint on the *bring-*, *send-*, and creation classes [*to*-classes 1 and 3, and *for*-class 1], the existence assumption in the promise, arrangement, creation, selection, performance, and symbolic constructions (*to*-classes 5a and 5c, *for*-classes 1–3 and 5), the assumptions of creative intent and normalness in *for*-class 1, and the constraint on properties of the object in the performance constructions of *for*-class 3).[1] This

---

[1] It would be possible, of course, to describe a $V\ NP\ NP \rightarrow V\ NP\ Prep\ NP$ transformation which occurs optionally "if such-and-such is the case" as a

$$V\ NP\ Prep\ NP \rightarrow V\ NP\ NP$$

transformation, but it would require a doubly negative condition: "unless such-and-such is not the case." For example, one could say that the structures underlying sentences like

1. Joe baked Laurie oatmeal cookies.   (*cont.*)

implies that there would be at least two dative-movement rules, one of which optionally converted structures that would otherwise be realized as $V\ NP_i\ NP_j$ into $V\ NP_j\ to\ NP_i$, and one or more others which converted structures which would otherwise be realized as $V\ NP_i\ Prep\ NP_j$ into $V\ NP_j\ NP_i$. My postulating two dative-movement rules which are converses bears a resemblance to Fillmore's grammar of indirect object constructions, in having two indirect object movement rules which work in opposite directions, but there are interesting and important differences. The reason Fillmore had two rules is that he had different deep structures for *to*-datives and *for*-datives so that he could have his passive rule apply to one kind of Verb Phrase but not the other. His optional *to*-deletion rule, and subsequent obligatory *to* NP-extraposition rule are in their effect equivalent to a single optional NP-intraposition rule, so his rules are not really converses of each other. In effect, both of them optionally convert a structure with a prepositional phrase indirect object to a structure with an internal prepositionless indirect object. I have attempted to show that, for reasons quite independent of the possible passives of dative-movement constructions, it appears that some constraints limit $V\ NP_i\ NP_j \rightarrow V\ NP_j\ Prep\ NP_i$ transformations, while others limit $V\ NP_i\ Prep\ NP_j \rightarrow V\ NP_j\ NP_i$, although I have not offered *specific* dative-movement rules, because it seemed pointless to do so when it is not clear to me how the remote structures which appear to me to be necessary are reduced to a stage where dative-movement rules could apply. It is not at all clear why some dative-movement constructions (e.g. *to*-classes 2 and 5b) should be $V\ NP_i\ NP_j$ before they are optionally converted to $V\ NP_j\ to\ NP_i$, while others (e.g. *to*-classes 1, 3, 5a, and 5c) should be $V\ NP_i\ to\ NP_j$ before they are optionally converted to $V\ NP_j\ NP_i$. Nonetheless, it appears that such is the case, and that there is a separate dative-movement rule for each of the fourteen or so classes of dative-movement verbs.[1]

---

may be realized as sentences like

    2. Joe baked oatmeal cookies for Laurie.

unless the subject is not animate. But conditions like this are so complex cognitively that it is hard to believe that they could have any counterpart in the internalized grammars of human beings.

[1] It is plausible that the *bring*- and *send*-classes, and perhaps the *radio*-class, could be treated together. Likewise, the promise and arrangement classes and the creation and performance constructions, and possibly the selection and symbolic constructions as well, for the purpose of the dative movement itself. I do not see at present how any other reductions could be made, without resorting to lists.

There is another possibility besides rules moving dative noun phrases, and that is: rules deleting dative noun phrases. Such rules would presumably relate structures which would otherwise have the form of (256a) to structures like (256b) or (256c). Whether this may be

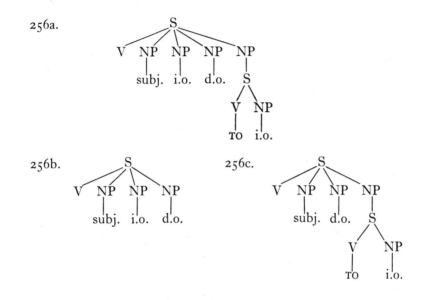

256a.

256b.   256c.

done with independently motivated transformational rules, such as Equi-NP-deletion, and what assumptions it will require regarding the organization of rules in a grammar is at present still a matter for con-jecture. The point remains, however, that even if derivations can be justified which produce (256b,c) from the kinds of representations suggested in section c.6 of this chapter, without the use of *ad hoc* rules, the restrictions on 'dative-movement' described in this chapter will have to be translated into that many equivalent restrictions on the deletion rule or rules, producing in effect, that many more rules. The effect of adding a number of rules to the grammar which all do essen-tially the same thing is the same, regardless of whether or not they are,

---

I have no evidence that any of these classes would require more than one rule. It appears that if there was evidence that one constraint limited an extraposing con-version, in a single class, while a different constraint limited an intraposing con-version for the same class, one would have to choose between two complex rules, each with both a simple condition and a doubly negative condition, or else *arbitrarily* order two single-condition rules, in order to prevent them from applying to an infinite number of times to each other's output.

strictly speaking, dative-movement rules. For convenience, I will continue to speak here of dative-movement rules.

It seems thus that there is not *a* dative-movement rule, but a "conspiracy" of dative-movement rules of two kinds, which makes it appear that there is a single rule. Notice that in any case, other rules are necessary to produce structures which are more or less of the same form as the two types of output of these rules. That is, English requires rules to derive other, non-dative-movement expressions of the form *V NP NP* and *V NP Prep NP*. The nomination/declaration expressions of (257), the judgment expressions of (258), and the economic transaction expressions of (259) are all examples of *V NP NP* expressions which bear no relation to any *V NP Prep NP* expressions:

257a. They elected Dick president.
257b. They called him a jerk.
257c. The playwright made the hero an Eskimo.
257d. The playwright made an Eskimo the hero.
257e. They named their son Fafnir.

258a. They consider him their leader.
258b. They believed him an enemy of the people.

259a. That cost him ten shillings.
259b. They fined him ten shillings.
259c. They charged him ten shillings.

Likewise, the locative expressions of (149) and (168), the favor, substitution, and employment expressions in (84–6), and the assortment of *V NP for NP*[inanimate] expressions in (260) are not related to any *V NP NP* expressions.

260a. Larry fried an egg for breakfast.
260b. Mike wrote a poem for English 102.
260c. Barb took the car for some bean curd.
260d. Wendy took Cyndy for a hamburger.
260e. Jan took the lamp-post for a hatrack.

There are probably also other, unrelated, movement rules relating such *V NP NP* and *V NP Prep NP* sentences as those in (261–2):

261a. She forgave him his self-assurance.
261b. She forgave him for his self-assurance.

262a. She envied him his self-assurance.
262b. She envied him for his self-assurance.

263a. They made the kitchen a cozy place.
263b. They made the kitchen into a cozy place.
263c. They made a cozy place of the kitchen.

The notion of grammatical conspiracy was introduced into print within generative grammar in Ross 1969. Ross used it to refer to situations where several independently required phonological rules and/or level constraints all have the same effect. The effect towards which the rules, etc. conspire is referred to as a target structure. In the case of a dative-movement conspiracy, both of the output structures, *V NP NP* and *V NP Prep NP*, are target structures. The illusion of a single dative-movement rule is a consequence of the existence of this conspiracy for these target structures, but it is not itself a target structure. Evidence is presented, however, in chapter 4, section B, for an apparently unrelated set of rules which make it falsely appear that there is a dative-movement rule operating with *teach* and certain kinds of objects.

Although some conspiracies appear to have "ulterior motives," such as the avoidance of articulatorily difficult sequences of sounds, the effect of others, such as that described in the introduction to Green 1970, is to avoid syntactic or phonological constructions which do not appear to be particularly difficult to produce or understand. Still others, which also seem to have no motivation, appear to exist merely to effect an arbitrary limitation on the number of surface level structures. This type is exemplified by syntactic conspiracies, such as the dative-movement conspiracy and the one presented in the main section of Green 1970, which from diverse remote structures produce forms which are indistinguishable at the surface level. The existence of such target structure conspiracies is no doubt related to the apparent fact that human languages are typically much more limited in their inventories of syntagms and perceptually distinct phonological segments, and consequently more ambiguous, than they logically need to be. For instance, no human language uses all of the sounds and combinations of sounds which the vocal organs are capable of producing and the ear is capable of distinguishing. Languages are full of homophonous and nearly homophonous forms and ambiguous forms, some of which are even quite opposite in meaning. Thus the expression *a shelled crab* may mean either 'a crab which has been endowed with a shell' or 'a crab whose shell has been removed.' Likewise with *a boned leg of lamb*. Similarly, certain expressions with the adjective *last*, such as *her last husband*, require either an assumption that there will probably be more, or an assumption that there will not be any more. Although artificial languages can be invented with relative ease which are less ambiguous, and sacrifice economy of forms for greater precision, the fact remains that natural languages are still full of such potentially confusing syncretisms. This suggests that the preference for a smaller number of forms is something which is required by the limitations of the human language processing mechanism, whatever form it might have.

4   Target structures

Introduction

At the end of chapter 3 it was claimed that the evidence presented argues against treating as a unitary phenomenon the dative-movement alternation between constructions with a prepositionless indirect object preceding the direct object, and constructions where the indirect object is preceded by *to* or *for*, and follows the direct object. Rather it was claimed that this evidence pointed to the existence of several independent but similar alternations. It was pointed out that in any case there have to be several independent rules creating different kinds of *V NP NP* constructions, *V NP to NP* constructions, and *V NP for NP* constructions, and it was suggested that conspiracies of this sort, where several independently required rules or constraints operate to produce constructions or forms which are indistinguishable at the surface level alone, were a reflection of the fact that human languages are typically much more limited than they logically need to be. No explanation was offered for this fact, but it was suggested that the preference for a smaller number of forms might be a requirement of the human language-processing capacity.

It is the purpose of this chapter to argue that conspiracies of rules and constraints are a widespread and long-recognized phenomenon in grammar (sec. A), and to describe another target-structure conspiracy. In particular, section B describes a lexical and semantic conspiracy which produces two surface structures which appear to be related by a dative-movement rule, but which in fact must come from separate semantic sources, since their meanings differ in systematic ways. A description of an additional syntactic target-structure conspiracy which produces a single surface structure from at least five distinct remote structures may be found in Green 1970, and Green To appear.

A   Kinds of conspiracies

Phonological conspiracies have been focused on in recent papers by Ross, Kisseberth, and Kim.[1] These papers describe in detail situations

---

[1] Ross 1969; Kisseberth 1969, 1970a,b; and Kim 1970.

where certain structural properties of a language's phonological system cannot be attributed to any single part of the system, be it surface output constraint, morphophonemic rule, or underlying morpheme structure condition. Investigating phenomena as diverse as stress patterns, syllable structure, cluster types, and other intra-unit segment-segment constraints, these linguists found that it was not just that they couldn't formulate a single constraint or rule which would predict the correct forms, it was that for independent reasons they had to have several rules or constraints, all of which would, in whole or in part, predict the correct forms. Kisseberth, for instance, argues (1970a:298) that "in addition to a morpheme structure condition which blocks triliteral clusters within the morpheme, Yawelmani also possesses two rules of consonant reduction and a rule of Vowel Epenthesis, all of which function to break up triliteral clusters."

Morphological and syntactic conspiracies have a long tradition in grammatical studies; whoever discovered the syntactic and semantic differences between the apparently identical subjective and objective genitive forms discovered a conspiracy. The philological term *syncretism* has been used for a long time to describe the union or fusion into one of two or more originally different inflectional forms. Many of the structuralists were concerned with systematic differences among languages, and some, particularly among the Prague linguists, investigated conspiracies involved in these differences. Vilém Mathesius, for instance, in his article on linguistic characterology, discussed the claim (1928:61) that "compared with Modern German or with any of the Modern Slavonic languages, e.g. Modern Czech, Modern English shows a characteristic tendency for the thematical conception of the subject" (that is, the claim that the tendency in English to express the psychological subject as grammatical subject exceeds such tendencies in other languages), concluding that the highly developed passive, "psych-movement" (cf. Postal 1968), and subject-raising constructions which contribute to (or in our terms "conspire toward") this tendency, were made possible by a weakened conception of action in the Modern English verb (1928:66).

B   The *Teach* Conspiracy

1   Introduction: *the non-parallelism of* give *and* teach

It was argued above that there must be several distinct, and in some cases converse, optional dative-movement rules, which "conspire" to produce outputs which appear as if they could be related by means of a single optional rule. In addition, I will now claim, different semantic structures and rules "conspire" to produce surface structures which are identical to the output of these rules, but which cannot have been produced by any of them. The reason for this is that the meanings mapped on to them differ in systematic ways, and axiomatically, transformations do not describe the derivation of semantically distinct sentences as proceeding from one to the other, or even both from the same source. The particular case with which I will demonstrate this claim is the verb *teach*, but, as I will show, *show* provides a parallel case.

At first glance it appears that sentences which have been assumed by all writers on the topic, myself included, to involve dative movement, such as (1a,b) are paralleled by sentences with *teach*, as in (2a,b):

1a. Mary gave John an apple.
1b. Mary gave an apple to John.

2a. Mary taught John linguistics.
2b. Mary taught linguistics to John.

Both (1) and (2) have animate subjects; both have indirect objects which may occur directly after the verb or preceded by the direct object and a preposition *to*. One can even claim that the sentences are similar in that both sets describe situations involving the passing of something from the subject to the indirect object – on the one hand, a piece of fruit, on the other, some understanding of linguistics. But this comparison fails to hold in any strong sense. For while sentences (1a) and (1b) are, as far as I can tell, synonymous with each other, (2a) does not mean the same thing as (2b). Sentence (2a) implies or entails that John learned linguistics, while (2b) merely states that he was a student of linguistics, and is neutral as to whether his teacher Mary had any success in her efforts. This is even clearer in such sentences as:

3a. I'm going to teach them linguistics come hell or high water.
3b. I'm going to teach linguistics to them come hell or high water.

Sentence (3a) is a vow to succeed at imparting an understanding of the study or the nature of language, while (3b) is a vow to obtain an opportunity to lecture on linguistics, typically a job or the assignment of a particular course. Or consider the fact that while such sentences as (4a) and (4b) are contradictions:

4a. I gave John a nickel, but I didn't give anything to him.
4b. I gave a nickel to John, but I didn't give him anything.

sentence (5a) is quite meaningful:

> 5a. In 1955 they taught arithmetic to children, but they didn't teach them anything.

as the bookkeeper of any bank will testify. Sentence (5b), like (4), is contradictory:

> 5b. In 1955 they taught children arithmetic, but they didn't teach anything to them.

It seems clear, then, that while *give someone something* and *give something to someone* are synonymous, *teach someone something* (hereafter *teach₁*) and *teach something to someone* (*teach₂*) are not.[1]

Similar facts obtain for *show*. Sentence (6a) implies that Fido perceived the bone, while (6b) leaves this open.

> 6a. John showed Fido a bone.
> 6b. John showed a bone to Fido.

Likewise (7a) reports the effect on Sam of some behavior of Greta's relating to him, while (7b) reports only that Greta pointed out to him some linguistic or philological description for the purpose of having him take it in. In (7a), Greta's behavior was not necessarily undertaken for the purpose of having Sam understand the meaning of true love.

> 7a. Greta showed Sam the meaning of true love.
> 7b. Greta showed the meaning of true love to Sam.[2]

Furthermore, the distributions of *teach₂* and *show₂* are restricted in the kinds of subjects and direct objects they can have, in ways in which *teach₁* and *show₁* are not restricted.[3] *Teach₁* and *show₁* may have abstract subjects, but *teach₂* and *show₂* may not, as (8–11) show:

> 8a. Several mistakes taught John the secrets of Chinese cooking.
> 8b. Being criticized taught John criticism.

---

[1] There is apparently a class of expressions in which *teach* occurs with either kind of indirect object, with no difference in meaning. Broadly speaking, this class includes *teach* with such direct objects as *a dirty word, a French song, the Lord's Prayer*, and *Finnish proverbs*, but the exact class of permitted direct objects seems to vary considerably from speaker to speaker, and my own judgments are unclear, so I am unable to characterize the sense of *teach* involved, and say how it fits into the scheme of *to*-datives described in chapter 3, secs. c.2 and c.6.

[2] These examples were suggested by Irwin Howard.

[3] Many of the semantic and distributional facts noted here about *teach* were observed independently by Gruber (1965, sec. 7.2). His interpretation and analysis differ significantly from the conclusions I present in this section.

9a. A little experience will show Mary the absurdity of that claim.

9b. Interviewing personnel managers will show Mary the meaning of sexism.

10a. *Several mistakes taught the secrets of Chinese cooking to John.

10b. *Being criticized taught criticism to John.

11a. *A little experience will show the absurdity of that claim to Mary.

11b. *Interviewing personnel managers will show the meaning of sexism to Mary.

$Teach_1$ and $show_1$ may have a wide range of abstract objects, but the abstract noun phrases which may occur as objects of $teach_2$ and $show_2$ are severely limited, as demonstrated by (12–15):

12a. Greta taught John responsibility.

12b. Greta taught John the orientation of carbon atoms in sugar.

12c. Greta taught John that Columbus discovered America.

12d. Greta taught John when to remain quiet.

12e. Greta taught John how to swim.

12f. Greta taught John to swim.

12g. Greta taught John to shake hands firmly.

13a. Gladys showed Sam true happiness.

13b. Gladys showed Sam the consequences of carelessness.

13c. Gladys showed Sam that oil and water don't mix.

13d. Gladys showed Sam when to shift gears.

13e. Gladys showed Sam how to shift gears.

14a. *Greta taught responsibility to John.

14b. *Greta taught the orientation of carbon atoms in sugar to John.

14c. *Greta taught that Columbus discovered America to John.[1]

---

[1] It might be supposed that the non-occurrence of final *to*-phrases with abstract objects as in (14c) and (15c) (and others) follows from output conditions or constraints proposed in Ross 1967, namely, his (3.27):

(3.27) Grammatical sentences containing an internal NP which exhaustively dominates S are unacceptable.

and his output condition on post-verbal constituents (3.41), which prefers indirect object phrases to precede complex noun phrases. Ross's (3.41) predicts that (1a)

14d. *Greta taught when to remain quiet to John.

14e. *Greta taught how to swim to John.

14f. *Greta taught to swim to John.

14g. *Greta taught to shake hands firmly to John.

15a. *Gladys showed true happiness to Sam.

15b. *Gladys showed the consequences of carelessness to Sam.

15c. *Gladys showed that oil and water don't mix to Sam.

15d. *Gladys showed when to shift gears to Sam.

15e. *Gladys showed how to shift gears to Sam.

Apparently, then, the semantic difference between *teach₁* and *show₁*, on the one hand, and *teach₂* and *show₂*, on the other, is not due to a coincidence in lexical idiosyncracies of these verbs, but is correlated with systematic facts about their syntactic distributions. The simplest explanation for this correlation, it seems to me, would be found in a justified analysis in which *teach₁* and *show₁* result from underlying structures different from those underlying *teach₂* and *show₂*, and in which the syntactic differences follow naturally from the semantically justified structures. In this chapter, section B.2, I will sketch a possible analysis of this sort and show that it is at least plausible and motivated, but space does not permit the inclusion of a rigorous semantic and syntactic justification.

2   An analysis

Teach was mentioned in chapter 3, section c.2.*e*, as an apparent *to*-class 4 verb, like *write*, and in fact, there are similarities between *teach₂* and three-argument *write* and between *teach₁* and two-argument *write*. Associated with *teach₂* (and *show₂*) and three-argument *write*, but not with *teach₁* (*show₁*) or two-argument *write*, is the implication or contextual condition that the subject intends for the indirect object to

---

will be preferred to (1b), but I find them equally unacceptable:

1a. *Mary taught to John that cows can have kittens.

1b. *Mary taught that cows can have kittens to John.

While Ross's (3.27) will predict that (1b) is unacceptable, since it contains an internal NP exhaustively dominating an S, it does not explain why (2) is just as bad:

2. *What Mary taught to John is that cows can have kittens.

since that NP is no longer internal, and the output condition is not violated. Compare to *(2) the grammatical (3):

3. What Mary taught John is that cows can have kittens.

come to have control of the direct object, or otherwise internalize whatever beliefs, attitudes, understandings, or skills are denoted by the direct object. You can teach someone something without intending to, but when you say that you are teaching something *to* someone, you indicate an intent (weak though it might be) to impart to your pupil whatever it is you are teaching. With *teach$_2$* and *show$_2$*, as with three-argument *write*, the indirect object behaves like an adverb in that it may be preposed, as shown in (16):

16a. To John, Mary taught linguistics.
16b. To Fido, Sam showed a bone.

The indirect objects of *teach$_1$* and *show$_1$* may not be preposed, just as the indirect object of two-argument *write* could not be:

17a. ?*John, Mary taught linguistics.
17b. *John, Mary taught that Columbus discovered America.
17c. *John, Mary taught how to swim.
17d. *John, Mary taught to shake hands firmly.

18a. *Sam, Gladys showed true happiness.
18b. *Sam, Gladys showed the consequences of carelessness.
18c. *Sam, Gladys showed that oil and water don't mix.
18d. *Sam, Gladys showed when to shift gears.

That the ungrammaticality of (17–18) is not the result of some surface structure condition which prohibits prepositionless indirect objects from standing before the subject can be seen from the fact that (19–20), where the indirect object has a preposition, are just as unacceptable as (17–18):

19a. *To John, Mary taught that Columbus discovered America.
19b. *To John, Mary taught how to swim.
19c. *To John, Mary taught to shake hands firmly.

20a. *To Sam, Gladys showed true happiness.
20b. *To Sam, Gladys showed the consequences of carelessness.
20c. *To Sam, Gladys showed that oil and water don't mix.
20d. *To Sam, Gladys showed when to shift gears.

These parallelisms between *teach$_2$*, *show$_2$*, and three-argument *write* suggest that one could use the arguments which supported the proposed underlying structure for three-argument *write* to support a similar underlying structure for *teach*$_2$ and *show*$_2$, that is, one containing a subordinate intent clause, and a main clause with a simple transitive verb, as in (21) and (22):

21. Subject INTENDING indirect object to "LEARN" direct object, subject TEACH direct object.

22. Subject INTENDING indirect object to "PERCEIVE" direct object, subject MAKE-MANIFEST direct object.

TEACH in (21) would be defined as meaning 'give instructions (in).' There is some evidence that the inference of intent derivable from sentences like (2b) is possible because the semantic representation of (2b) includes a secondary (that is, subordinate) assertion of intent, as in (21). This evidence is that attaching the adverb *unintentionally* to (2b), as in (23)

23. Mary unintentionally taught linguistics to John.

results in a sentence which at worst is ungrammatical and which at best implies that Mary intended to teach him something, but not linguistics. Attaching *unintentionally* to (2a) does not necessarily have this effect; a sentence like (24):

24. Mary unintentionally taught John linguistics.

is interpretable as implying that she meant to teach him something else, or that she never had any intention of teaching him anything. Sentence (23) cannot have the latter interpretation.

Teach$_1$ and *show*$_1$ differ from *teach*$_2$ and *show*$_2$ not only in not requiring the assumption of intention, but also in indicating that the indirect object changes in some way as a result of the subject's behavior (if the subject denotes an animate being), or of its interpretation of the subject (if the subject is abstract). The simplest way to represent such a semantic relation between the animate subject and the indirect object is with causative and inchoative predicates, as in (25) and (26):

25. Subject CAUSE i.o. to "LEARN" d.o. BY TEACHING d.o.

26. Subject CAUSE i.o. to "PERCEIVE" d.o. BY MAKING MANIFEST d.o.

Presumably the rules required for instrumental verb formation (cf. Appendix III) would serve to form a simple transitive verb of these predicates. LEARN and PERCEIVE are not to be taken as necessarily representing primitive semantic notions. Both *learn* and *perceive* denote the inchoation of a mental state, and conceivably the putative semantic predicates with those labels should be replaced by an inchoative predicate like COME and some sort of cognitive or perceptual HAVE (cf. chapter 3, secs. c.4 and c.6.*d*).

Unfortunately, as with some of the rejected causative proposals of chapter 3, paraphrases based on (25) and (26) would be appropriate to a wider class of cases than *teach*$_1$ and *show*$_1$ are appropriate to, since these verbs are inappropriate if the causation is magically direct or indefinitely indirect. For instance, (2a) would be inappropriate if John came to know linguistics as a magical result of Mary's teaching linguistics to his second cousin in a distant city, or even if her teaching linguistics to someone other than John initiated a chain of events leading ultimately to John's learning linguistics. But (27) would be appropriate to describe these situations:

27. Mary caused John to learn linguistics by teaching it.

A similar demonstration can be made for *show*$_1$. The problem seems to lie in the English word *cause*, which is applicable to a much wider variety of situations than the causative element in *teach*$_1$ and *show*$_1$. The kind of causation involved in *teach*$_1$ and *show*$_1$ is apparently quite close to the kind of cause which Collingwood (1940:285–312) described as a lever which triggers some natural event. You cannot teach someone something at will, by some purely voluntary effort on your part. Teaching$_1$ and showing$_1$, whether by an agent – perhaps catalyst would be a better word – or by some experience, involves the setting into motion of an involuntary process. The limited sort of causation that is involved in *teach*$_1$ and *show*$_1$ is perhaps expressed in English better by the non-persuasion sense of the verb *get* than by *cause*.

Philosophers have for a long time recognized different types of causation, so it should not surprise us that the 'CAUSE' ('CAUSE$_{get}$,' say) which we will have to assume as part of *teach*$_1$ and *show*$_1$ differs from the 'CAUSE' ('CAUSE$_c$') which we understand in such causatives as *melt*. For instance, (28a) and (28b), unlike (2a) and (27) can be used under the same conditions:

28a. John melted the copper.
28b. John caused the copper to melt.

and the causation can be indefinitely indirect, or mystically and immediately direct; one could say (28a) and (28b) whether John melted the copper by holding it in a furnace, by setting off a nuclear reaction in a city five miles away, or by magic. Among the syntactic reflexes of this difference between the causative in *melt* and the causative in *teach*$_1$ is the fact that with an animate subject, expressions encoding 'CAUSE$_{get}$' can be paraphrased by expressions with an inchoative verb and *from*, while expressions including 'CAUSE$_c$' have no such paraphrases. Sentence (29) is appropriate to just those situations where (2a) is appropriate, but (30), far from being equivalent to (28a), is ungrammatical:

29.   John learned linguistics from Mary.

30.   *The copper melted from John.

What is interesting is that semantically different "CAUSE"s function differently syntactically, but similarly in terms of derivational morphology: both of them are involved in the derivation of unmarked causative verbs. For example, if an analysis of *teach*$_1$ as including whatever underlies the inchoative *learn*, in the complement of a causative predicate, can be supported, we get as a bonus a way to explain naturally the fact that in children's speech, some non-standard dialects, and older stages of English,[1] a natural way to say (31a) is (31b) and never, for example, (31c), with non-inchoative *know*:

31a.   John learned that from Mary.
31b.   Mary learned John that.
31c.   *Mary knowed John that.

Not totally irrelevant here is the cross-linguistic fact that in standard French the same verb, *apprendre*, is used for 'learn' and for 'teach$_1$.' 'Teach$_2$' is expressed by an entirely different verb, *enseigner*.

The purpose of the foregoing discussion has been to show (1) that there is semantic justification for wanting to derive *teach*$_2$ and *show*$_2$ from something like (21) and (22), and to derive *show*$_1$ and *teach*$_1$ with an animate agent as subject from structures semantically and structurally similar to *get to learn* (inchoative *perceive*) *by teaching*$_2$ (*showing*$_2$), or *cause to come* [naturally] *to accept* (*be aware*) *by teaching*$_2$ (*showing*$_2$), and (2) that the rules required for such derivations do not differ from rules required for derivations motivated elsewhere (e.g. in chapter 2, sec. B.2.*c*, chapter 3, sec. C.6, and Appendix III). However, there is no

---

[1] Some random citations from the *Oxford English Dictionary*: Þus lernyd he me (*c.* 1440). The frequent practice of this exercise must have learned them . . . to become excellent horsemen (1801). I shall lerne hem a new daunce (*c.* 1420).

semantic justification for deriving $teach_1$ with an abstract subject from such a structure. Because $teach_2$ requires an animate subject, it would be absurd to say that, for example, (8a) was equivalent to any of the sentences in (32):

8a. Several mistakes taught John the secrets of Chinese cooking.

32a. Several mistakes got John to learn the secrets of Chinese cooking by teaching them.

32b. Several mistakes caused John to learn the secrets of Chinese cooking by teaching them.

32c. Several mistakes caused John to come to have the secrets of Chinese cooking by teaching them.

We could, however, say that when $teach_1$ has an abstract subject, rather than being derived from a structure with an instrumental clause with the content 'by teaching Direct Object,' it is derived from a similar structure with an instrumental clause with the content 'as by teaching Direct Object.' This proposal is not made merely to save the proposed analysis of $teach_1$, but is a particular subcase of something that will be required for a large number of cases where instrumental verbs, causative and otherwise, are understood as including either a particular instrumental clause or phrase, or such a clause or phrase introduced by a predicate of comparison. For instance, expressions such as (33a–d) can be interpreted literally, in which case they are equivalent to those in (34), or they may be interpreted figuratively:

33a. She pinned him to the floor.
33b. He's been hammering on it all morning.
33c. Mop up the spilled milk.
33d. She painted the scratch.

34a. She flattened him against the floor with pins.
34b. He's been striking it with a hammer all morning.
34c. Clean up the spilled milk with a mop.
34d. She covered the scratch with paint.

In the figurative senses of (33a–d), as in (35), these verbs may occur with phrases that indicate the actual instrument or means used, as in (36):

35a. She flattened him against the floor as with pins.
35b. He's been striking it as with a hammer all morning.

35c. Clean up the spilled milk as with a mop.

35d. She covered the scratch as with paint.

36a. She pinned him to the floor with her bare hands.

36b. He's been hammering on it all morning with a shoe.

36c. Mop up the spilled milk with a paper towel.

36d. She painted the scratch with iodine.

If these verbs are interpreted literally, an instrumental phrase may be almost unacceptably redundant, as in (37)

37. She painted the scratch with paint.

or contradictory, as (36d) would be if *painted* was interpreted as 'cover with paint.'

Actually, the sentences of (33) are vague as to whether they involve a figurative sense or a literal one, rather than ambiguous, as is demonstrated by the fact that (38) is appropriate if the speaker knows that John used a mop, while Bill used a paper towel:

38. John mopped up his spilled milk, and so did Bill.

This means, I conclude, that the 'as'-predicate required for *teach*$_1$ with an abstract subject is deleted in the course of the derivation, before lexical insertion, or that there is one lexical entry for the two senses of *teach*$_1$, which is vague or contains the 'as'-predicate as an optional element.

As the sentences of (36) show, the 'figurative' senses of instrumental verbs are not restricted to abstract subjects. The claim that *teach* in sentences like (8) bears the same relation to *teach* in (12a) as, say, *paint* in (36d) bears to *paint* in (33d) predicts that *teach*$_1$ with an animate noun phrase as subject will be vague as to which of the senses is intended. It is clear that sentences like (12a):

12a. Greta taught John responsibility.

and (12d,g) as well, are appropriate if John learned from Greta's example rather than from explicit instruction from her, and in fact, sentences like (39) show that they are vague.

39. Greta taught her son responsibility, and so did Gladys.

It would be appropriate to use sentence (39), even if one knew that Greta taught by example, and Gladys by lectures.

3 *Summary*

I have tried to show that the apparent parallelism of (2a) and (2b) with (1a) and (1b) is illusory – the effect of one or more conspiracies. Sentences (1a) and (1b) are apparently derived by a dative-movement rule from the same underlying structure, but (2a) and (2b) must be derived from sources which are different from each other, for reasons both semantic and syntactic. The specific abstract analyses which were proposed for sentences with $teach_1$ and $teach_2$ were motivated by syntactic as well as semantic properties of the forms being considered. I have tried to show that the homophony of the *teach*s in (2a), (2b), and (8) is not accidental, but that the rules relating $teach_2$ and the two senses of $teach_1$ to one another, regardless of whether they are pre-lexical transformational rules, or static implicational rules which provide structure in the lexicon, are independently required rules.

5 Internal politics; the interaction of constraints

In chapter 3, several observations were made about the generality of the dative-movement alternations, some general, applying to assumptions about situations as a whole, and to large, open classes of verbs, others more particular, applying to smaller classes of originally metaphorical or idiomatic expressions, and perhaps to individual lexical items as well. The illusion of a single dative-movement rule was attributed to conspiracies in favor of the two dative constructions. This chapter will describe a sort of power politics process in which some constraints give way to other, more general ones, and favored forms are suppressed under the influence of constraints not peculiar to dative movement.[1] Section A will treat output conditions, section B, idiomatic forms, and section C, constraints concerning reflexive forms.

A Output conditions

1 Definite anaphora
In the earliest days of generative grammar, it was observed that there was an interaction between dative movement and pronominalization, regardless of whether it was a transformational rule or a set of conditions on acceptable surface structures, which produced paradigms such as (1) and (2) in full surface clauses:[2]

  1a. They gave the boy the book.
  1b. They gave the book to the boy.

---

[1] The contents of secs. A and B were published in the *Papers from the Seventh Regional Meeting of the Chicago Linguistic Society*, as part of my article 'Some Implications of an Interaction among Constraints.'

[2] For some reason, imperative forms such as *Give him it!* and *Find me it!* are not quite as awkward as (1g) and (2g), and (1g) and (2g) are not as awkward as (1e) and (2e). This may be related to the fact that positions closer to the end of the sentence are preferred in English for "heavier" (more complex, and sometimes longer) expressions (cf. Ross 1967: chapter III). There is most contrast among NPs in (1e) and (2e), least in the imperative forms cited, perhaps because the verbs are short as well, and there are no overt subjects.

1c.   They gave him the book.

1d.   They gave the book to him.

1e.   *They gave the boy it.

1f.   They gave it to the boy.

1g.   *They gave him it.

1h.   They gave it to him.

2a.   They bought the girl the book.

2b.   They bought the book for the girl.

2c.   They bought her the book.

2d.   They bought the book for her.

2e.   *They bought the girl it.

2f.   They bought it for the girl.

2g.   *They bought her it.

2h.   They bought it for her.

Something prevents sentences with anaphoric (and therefore normally unstressed) pronouns as direct objects from being acceptable if the pronouns follow the indirect object. Since a similar constraint is in effect where other rules, e.g. particle movement and inversion,[1] as in (3):

3a.   I put out the cat.

3b.   I put the cat out.

3c.   *I put out it.

3d.   I put it out.

3e.   The cat went out.

3f.   Out went the cat.

3g.   It went out.

3h.   *Out went it.

rearrange the verb phrase constituents[2] so that a noun phrase is the rightmost element, Ross (1967: chap. III) concluded that the paradigm gaps in (1), (2), and (3) were not due to some complex ordering relation

---

[1] I am indebted to Fred Lupke for the observation that this phenomenon occurs with inversion.

[2] Apparently this constraint must be phrased in terms of verb phrase constituents or be a derivational constraint referring to cyclic application to lower sentences, rather than being phrased in terms of surface clauses, since sentences of the form *NP-V-NP-Pronoun-Adverb*, *NP-V-Particle-Pronoun-Adverb*, and *Particle-V-Pronoun* are as bad as if the adverb was not there:

   1. *They gave the boy it yesterday.

   2. *I put out it at midnight.

   3. *Out went it then.

among rules and blocking conditions on them, but to a simple, language-specific condition on output, which said that certain forms, e.g. *V NP Pronoun* and *V Particle Pronoun*, were awkward, and to be avoided. This did not, of course, explain why they were awkward; nor will I.

It was noted in chapter 3 that a host of expressions with *give* had only forms where a prepositionless indirect object preceded the direct object. The simultaneous existence of two surface structure constraints, one against *Verb-Indirect Object-Anaphoric Direct Object* sequences, and one against *give-Direct-Object-Indirect Object* constructions, raises an interesting question: what happens when one of these restricted *give*-expressions has a direct object which must be an anaphoric pronoun? The answer is clear. We get sentences like the (a) sentences of (4–6), and never ones like the (b) sentences, despite the fact that sentences with similar noun phrase order are unacceptable if the direct object is a full, non-anaphoric noun phrase, as in the (c) sentences:

4a. Martha gave John trench-mouth, and he gave it to Ted.
4b. *Martha gave John trench-mouth, and he gave Ted it.
4c. *John gave trench-mouth to Ted.
4d. John gave Ted trench-mouth.

5a. Walt gave Dick the finger, and he gave it to Ted, too.
5b. *Walt gave Dick the finger, and he gave Ted it, too.
5c. *Walt gave the finger to Ted.
5d. Walt gave Ted the finger.

6a. Walt gave Dick the answer, and he gave it to Ted, too.
6b. *Walt gave Dick the answer, and he gave Ted it, too.
6c. *Walt gave the answer to Ted.
6d. Walt gave Ted the answer.

The general constraint on the position of pronouns prevails. It requires in the instance at hand that if the direct object is an anaphoric pronoun it precede a prepositional indirect object even though this order is generally to be avoided with these expressions. Non-pronominal anaphoric noun phrases have the same distribution as anaphoric pronouns. Thus, similar to (4a) and (4b) we find:

7a. Martha gave John trench-mouth, and he gave the stuff to Ted.
7b. *Martha gave John trench-mouth, and he gave Ted the stuff.

Notice that just as the anaphor position constraint does not apply to indefinite pronouns,[1] permitting therefore such forms as (8b) and (8c) in contrast to (1e) and (1g):

8a. They gave a book to the girl.
8b. They gave the boy one too.
8c. They gave themselves one too.

these *give*-expressions do not tolerate the unpreferred order if the direct object is an indefinite pronoun, as (9–13) illustrate:

9a. Liz gave Richard a black eye, and he gave her one.
9b. *Liz gave Richard a black eye, and he gave one to her.
9c. Liz gave Richard a black eye, and he gave her a shiner too.
9d. *Liz gave Richard a black eye, and he gave a shiner to her too.

10a. Barney gave Helen a kick, and then she gave him one.
10b. *Barney gave Helen a kick, and then she gave one to him.

11a. The students gave the first speaker some flak, and they gave the second speaker some too.
11b. *The students gave the first speaker some flak, and they gave some to the second speaker too.

12a. Max unwittingly gave me an idea, so I was glad to learn I had given him one.
12b. *Max unwittingly gave me an idea, so I was glad to learn I had given one to him.

13a. On Tuesdays, Max gives me a ride, and on Fridays I give him one.

13b. *On Tuesdays, Max gives me a ride, and on Fridays I give one to him.

Some indefinite direct objects are not as bad as others when the indirect objects have prepositions, and these permit indefinite direct object pronouns with prepositional indirect objects just as easily. Thus (14a) and (14b) are both better than (15a) and (15b):

14a. Christine gave an infection to Alex.
14b. And he gave one to Ruby.

---

[1] Two adjacent indefinite pronouns, however, as in (1) and (2) is as awkward as two definite pronouns:

1. *They gave a book to a tramp, so we gave one one.
2. *They gave some books to a tramp, so we gave one some.
3. They gave some books to a tramp, so we gave some to one.

15a. *Martha gave a piece of her mind to John.
15b. *Martha gave John a piece of her mind, and then she gave one
to Richard.

It is clear at any rate, that the possibility of a given anaphoric form depends both on the constraints on the position of anaphora in general, and on expression-specific restrictions on noun phrase order.

If pronominalization (still one of the least understood of grammatical phenomena) is taken to be a set of conditions on anaphoric relations at various stages in a derivation, as work done since 1967 has suggested,[1] rather than a single rule turning some fully specified full noun phrases into pronouns, then it makes sense to account for the *give*-expression phenomena by saying that dative movement is not permitted for this sub-class of *to*-class 2 expressions only in a theory which permits constraints on derivations to be stated in terms of pairs of derivations. That is, if pronominalization is not a rule, one cannot block dative movement here by making it contingent on the application of a pronominalization rule. One would require a constraint on derivations which said essentially:

16. A derivation is ill-formed if the *to*-class 2 dative-movement rule applies to a member of these subclasses [appropriately described – cf. chapter 2, sec. c.2.c for the outlines of a characterization], unless failure to undergo this rule would result in a violation of the output condition on anaphor position.

Such a derivational constraint is somewhat suspect in that it must refer to a general constraint as well as to a specific rule, and explicitly depends on avoiding a violation of that constraint. Furthermore, it does not even claim to explain the restrictions on *give*-expressions or relate them to other restrictions or target structures in English. It does, however, state the facts, which is no mean accomplishment, and there is something very plausible about it in that the violation of the restriction on *give*-expressions is permitted only when the result is indistinguishable from a well-formed surface structure with a different meaning. After all, there is no surface-structure way to distinguish between *John gave it to her* where *it* refers to a case of beer, and *John gave it to her*, where *it*

---

[1] Cf., for instance, G. Lakoff 1968, 1969b; Bach, 1969, Forthcoming; McCawley 1970a; Postal 1970; Karttunen 1969.

refers to a case of pneumonia. One might suppose that the constraint would be better stated as a transderivational constraint like (17):

17. A derivation is ill-formed if the *to*-class 2 dative-movement rule applies to a member of these subclasses [appropriately described], unless the result is indistinguishable from that of a well-formed derivation with a different semantic representation.

However, there are many cases where a surface string is well-formed for one meaning, and ill-formed for another *a priori* possible meaning,[1] so there is no reason to believe that (17) is any more "natural" than (16).

Actually, violations of constraints on dative forms, however they are to be formulated, are not limited to *give*-expressions, but occur also with the "negative verbs of future having" mentioned in chapter 3, section c.2.*f*.[2] Thus, while we ordinarily cannot say the (b) versions of sentences such as (18–19), with external indirect objects:

18a. Ted denied Kim the opportunity to march.
18b. *Ted denied the opportunity to march to Kim.

19a. The brass refused Tony the promotion.
19b. *The brass refused the promotion to Tony.

---

[1] For instance, (1) is grammatical as a generic statement or an instruction, but not as a promise; (2), with no contrastive stress or facetious intent is grammatical if the second occurrence of *John* has a referent different from the first, but ungrammatical if they refer to the same person:

   1. You promise me your undying love.
   2. John brought John's book.

[2] *Spare* must be excluded from a consideration of dative-movement verbs, since even with pronominal direct objects, it does not have a paraphrase with *to* where the direct object precedes the indirect object. Rather, as the examples below show, it has paraphrases with prepositionless indirect object, and *from* preceding the "direct object," both with full noun phrase direct objects, and with pronominal direct objects.

   1. This will spare you embarrassment.
   2. *This will spare embarrassment to you.
   3. This will spare you from embarrassment.
   4. *I don't think the other will spare you it.
   5. *I don't think the other will spare it to you.
   6. I don't think the other will spare you from it.

Semantically, *spare* differs from *deny* and *refuse* in that the direct object, the thing which the subject arranges that the indirect object will not have, is assumed to be considered undesirable by the indirect object with *spare*, while with *deny* and *refuse* it is something assumed to be considered desirable by the indirect object. In cases where *deny* and *refuse* are communication verbs (cf. discussion of examples [18–21] below), the direct object is usually something which has been in fact requested by or in behalf of the indirect object.

when the direct object is a referential pronoun, forms with external indirect object are preferred to ones with internal indirect object, as in (20–1):

20a.   *Ted gave Joey permission to march, but he denied Kim it.
20b.   Ted gave Joey permission to march, but he denied it to Kim.

21a.   *The brass gave Martin permission to sit, but they denied Tony it.
21b.   The brass gave Martin permission to sit, but they denied it to Tony.

It is not obvious whether *deny* and *refuse* should be considered as belonging to one of the subclasses of *to*-class 5 already described, or whether they form one or more classes of their own. From an "engineering point of view," one might re-define *to*-class 5a or 5b or 5c as containing an optional negative between the modal predicate and the predicate of having, but is not clear what modal or modals would be semantically justified for the semantic representations of these verbs; nor is it clear whether *deny* and *refuse* are communication verbs or arrangement verbs, or just what. One might think that *deny*, for instance, was a communication verb in (20b), but an arrangement verb in (18a). In any case, since it is not clear what semantic class *deny* and *refuse* belong in, it is impossible to say whether or not the derivational constraints regarding them are a subcase of (16). They could not be a subcase of (17), it should be pointed out, even if *deny* and *refuse* are "exceptions" to the same kind of rule as the *give*-expressions, since in forms like (22):

22a.   He denied it to her.
22b.   He refused it to her.

deny and *refuse* could not be considered as having different meanings from *deny* and *refuse* in (20) and (21).

2   *Complex noun phrases*
A second instance in which the constraints on dative expressions interact with another output condition is found where the indirect object is a complex noun phrase which sounds awkward preceding a short and non-complex direct object as in (23):

23a.   The Snopes brats gave every single kid who lived within two blocks of them the mumps.

23b. He threatened to give anyone who attempted to reveal where they had been a beating.

23c. We gave all of the American soldiers we saw the peace sign.

23d. That gave all of us who had read the assignments faithfully an idea.

23e. We gave each of the crying, ragged, long-neglected children a ride.

23f. The brass denied some of the airmen who wanted to join the American Servicemen's Union the opportunity to do it.

23g. The brass refused some of the airmen who joined the ASU promotions.

Complex NP Shift would result in ungrammatical sentences with prepositionless indirect objects directly following the direct objects, as in (24):

24a. *The Snopes brats gave the mumps every single kid who lived within two blocks of them.

24b. *He threatened to give a beating anyone who attempted to reveal where they had been.

24c. *We gave the peace sign all of the American soldiers we saw.

24d. *That gave an idea all of us who had read the assignments faithfully.

24e. *We gave a ride each of the crying, ragged, long-neglected children.

24f. *The brass denied the opportunity to join the ASU some of the airmen who wanted to do it.

24g. *The brass refused promotions some of the airmen who joined the ASU.

but for some speakers at least, dative movement is exceptionally allowed to apply, and yield sentences like (25):

25a. The Snopes brats gave the mumps to every single kid who lived within two blocks of them.

25b. He threatened to give a beating to anyone who attempted to reveal where they had been.

25c. We gave the peace sign to all of the American soldiers we saw.

25d. That gave an idea to all of us who had read the assignments faithfully.

25e. We gave a ride to each of the crying, ragged, long-neglected children.

25f. The brass denied the opportunity to join the ASU to some of the airmen who wanted to do it.

25g. The brass refused promotions to some of the airmen who joined the ASU.

Other speakers find the sentences of (25) quite as awkward as those of (23). For those speakers for whom the sentences of (25) are significantly better than those of (23), the surface-structure restrictions on *give*-expressions are overruled in another case. For them a transderivational constraint with the content of (26) is required.

26. A derivation is ill-formed if the *to*-class 2 dative-movement rule applies to a member of such-and-such subclass(es) [appropriately described], unless failure to undergo this rule would result in a violation of the output condition on the position of complex noun phrases.

As before, it is impossible to say whether (26) could be expanded to include *deny* and *refuse*, or whether they require a separate derivational constraint. It would, perhaps, be possible to combine (26) and (16) into a transderivational constraint of the form of (27):

27. A derivation is ill-formed if the *to*-class 2 dative-movement rule applies to a member of such-and-such subclass(es) [appropriately described], unless failure to undergo this rule would result in a violation of a (semantically or lexically) more general output condition.

but it remains to be seen just which output conditions, if any, may be violated by the restrictions on *give*-expressions. Notice, at any rate, that (17) could not be generalized to include the violations which preserve the output condition on the position of complex noun phrases, since in this case the output of the dative-movement rule applying to these *give*-expressions would be in fact distinguishable (i.e. by the complexity of the indirect object noun phrase) from the output of derivations where dative movement would be ordinarily permitted.

3   NP-movements

On the other hand, (17) is not entirely out of line, and may in fact be necessary in addition to transderivational constraints like (16) and (26), or (27), since something like it is necessary to account for the fact that sentences like (28) and (29), where the *give*-expression has been broken up by the removal of the direct object, are much better than their counterparts in (30).

28a. The infection which Martha gave to John nearly killed him.
28b. The shove which Liz gave to Richard shocked us all.
28c. The flak which Joan gave to Ed utterly decimated him.
28d. The idea which Bill gave to Sue caused her to rewrite her thesis.
28e. The ride Mack gave to Ellen ended in disaster.

29a. What kind of infection did Martha give to John?
29b. How hard a shove did Liz give to Richard anyway?
29c. What sort of flak did Joan give to Ed?
29d. Which idea did Bill give to Sue?
29e. How long a ride did Mack give to Ellen?

30a. *Martha gave an infection to John.
30b. *Liz gave a shove to Richard.
30c. *Joan gave some flak to Ed.
30d. *Bill gave an idea to Sue.
30e. *Mack gave a ride to Ellen.

In (28), relative-clause formation has left the clause containing *give* bereft of any indication that it is restricted in regard to dative movement. WH-adjective question formation has done the same in (29). Failure of dative movement to apply in these cases would not violate any output conditions, as it would in simple clauses with pronouns and complex noun phrases, and in both (28) and (29) the clause containing *give*, though not the sentence as a whole, is indistinguishable at the surface level from clauses where dative movement might have applied freely.[1]

---

[1] It is true that WH-noun questions with restricted *give*-expressions are strange if the indirect object is prepositional as in (1):

    1. What are you going to give to him?

That is, if A has been talking about giving B a black eye, and C comes up, having heard only snatches of the conversation, and asks A, "What are you going to give to him?" A may have a difficult time answering if he does not like to ride roughshod over his presuppositions and the rules of his grammar. He cannot properly answer with (2), since the form of (1) precludes the sense of *give* which would occur in a full response, that is, (3). Nor can he say (4), since it has the *sound* of a contradiction. Perhaps he could say (5), but probably he would prefer to avoid answering the

It was pointed out earlier that (17) did not cover violations of restrictions on *deny* and *refuse*. Thus (17) makes no prediction that *deny*- and *refuse*-expressions will permit prepositional indirect objects if the direct object is transposed out of the constituent containing the verb and the indirect object. And, in fact, as (31) and (32) show, this does not happen; expressions with prepositional indirect objects are very awkward or ungrammatical even when the direct object does not occur following the verb.

31a. ?*The opportunity which the brass denied to the airmen became a bone of contention.

31b. The opportunity which the brass denied the airmen became a bone of contention.

31c. ?*The promotions which the brass refused to the airmen were the subject of a congressional inquiry.

31d. The promotions which the brass refused the airmen were the subject of a congressional inquiry.

32a. ?*What opportunity did the brass deny to those airmen?

32b. What opportunity did the brass deny those airmen?

32c. ?*Which promotions did the brass refuse to those airmen?

32d. Which promotions did the brass refuse those airmen?

---

question directly at all, and instead merely inform C of what he (A) actually said, as by (6).

2. A black eye.

3. *I am going to give a black eye to him.

4. I'm not going to give anything to him; I'm going to give him a black eye.

5. I'm not going to give anything to him; I'm going to blacken his eye.

6. I said I'm going to give B a black eye.

The fact that WH-noun questions of the form of (1) may not be interpreted as questions about restricted *give* seems to be a general fact about non-literal expressions and presuppositions, rather than a fact about *give*-expressions. In sentences like (7a) and (7b), for instance,

7a. Whát is Max going to kick?

7b. Whát do you want me to lend you?

it is always assumed that it is the literal sense of *kick* and *lend*, respectively, which is being used, and they may not be answered by "the bucket" or "an ear."

It should be pointed out that the restricted *give*-expressions are not idioms in exactly the same sense that *kick the bucket* and *lend someone an ear* are because they may be questioned, if the indirect object is internal, as in (8):

8. Whát are you going to give him? A black eye.

There is no question of output conditions being directly violated in the mere form of (1) or (8), since both are fully grammatical.

This situation is quite consistent with (17), although it does not actually provide evidence for its correctness.

B   Idioms

The restrictions on some non-literal *give*-expressions, and their inter-action with other constraints raises the question: what about idioms with other dative-movement verbs, and real idioms with *give*? Do they all obey the same constraints? I regret that I am unable to answer this in an unequivocal way. I have found little but chaos in the idiom data I have collected, although admittedly I have not attempted a systematic semantic analysis of the idioms involved. Verbs from *to*-classes 1, 3, and 4 are involved in such idioms as *bring word, drop a line,* and *read the riot act.* Other *to*-class 2 words occur in such idioms as *pay attention, lend an ear, lend a hand,* and idiomatic expressions with *give,* which do not fit into the categories described in chapter 3. These include *give the ax, give a wide berth, give a bad name, give birth,* and *give rise.* Of these last, only *give a bad name* involves a real semantic 'have' relation-ship, and *give birth* and *give rise* do not even have idiomatic paraphrases with *let have.*

Some of these idioms, such as *give rise, give birth,* and *pay attention* may never have a prepositionless internal indirect object, regardless of its form, as (33–5) illustrate.

33a.   Mao's silence has given rise to an absurd rumor.
33b.   *Mao's silence has given an absurd rumor rise.
33c.   Mao's silence gave rise to it.
33d.   *Mao's silence gave it rise.

34a.   Sarah gave birth to a son.
34b.   *Sarah gave a son birth.
34c.   Sarah gave birth to him in May.
34d.   *Sarah gave him birth in May.

35a.   Pay attention to Mr Fawkes.
35b.   *Pay Mr Fawkes attention.
35c.   Pay attention to me.
35d.   *Pay me attention.

It might be supposed that (33b,d) are ungrammatical because dative movement requires an animate indirect object, but this would not explain the fact that (34b,d) and (35b,d), which have animate indirect objects, are also ungrammatical. It might be supposed that (33b,d) and (34b) are ungrammatical because the indirect objects are non-referential, but referentiality was not found to be a requirement of dative movement in chapter 3, and it would not explain why (34d) and (35b,d), with unambiguously referential noun phrases, are ungrammatical.

Then, some idioms, such as *bring word*, permit a pronominal indirect object in either position, but permit fuller noun phrases only as external prepositional indirect objects, as illustrated in (36):

36a. Bring us word of any new developments.

36b. Bring word to us of any new developments.

36c. *You are to bring General Custard word of any new developments.

36d. You are to bring word to General Custard of any new developments.

36e. *You are to bring our government word of any new developments.

36f. You are to bring word to our government of any new developments.

Other idioms, such as *lend a hand*, permit only internal prepositionless indirect objects if the indirect object is a pronoun, but accept other kinds of noun phrases in either position, as in (37).

37a. Lend me a hand; I'd help you if you needed it.

37b. *Lend a hand to me; I'd help you.

37c. Lend John a hand; he'd help you.

37d. Lend a hand to John; he'd help you.

37e. Lend the new students a hand; they'd help you.

37f. Lend a hand to the new students; they'd help you.

Still others have different tolerances. An attempt is made in Appendix IV to present an organized view of the chaotic facts in my own speech.

To return to the question of whether any generalizations can be made about restricted *give*-expressions and real idioms, the semantic coherence of the five classes of restricted *give*-expressions, in the face of the speaker-to-speaker variation of permitted indirect object types (cf. sec. A.2) suggests that while the restriction is general and regular for these classes, at least some of the conditions on it, the amnesties stated as (16), (17), (26), and (27), may be idiosyncratic, and learned either as exceptions, or more or less randomly. (Difficulty in learning would support the former view, widespread idiolectal variation the latter view.) The apparently unsystematic gradience of the "dative" idioms with respect to indirect object types, on the other hand, and the speaker-to-speaker variation, along with the fact that these expressions are patently idiomatic – in most cases neither the verb nor the noun has its literal meaning – suggest that the restrictions are truly idiosyncratic, and that the expressions are truly idiomatic lexical items, learned one by one, and more or less exceptional in everything except morphology. Consider, for instance, the difference in my speech between *send word* and *bring word*, as shown in Appendix IV, or that between *pay attention* and *give attention*.

The claim that idioms are to be considered exceptional lexical items, rather than members of classes of expressions like the *give*-expressions, which are merely restricted syntactically by a general constraint, implies that the constraints governing syntactically restricted classes are in nature, scope, or function different from the allegedly idiosyncratic constraints on exceptions, and that the constraints on idioms are more similar to the constraints on exceptions than to the constraints on restricted expressions. Is this in fact the case?

It was demonstrated above that the constraint on *give*-expressions was vetoed by the more general constraints on pronoun position and position of heavy noun phrases, and neutralized by NP-movement rules which transported out of their immediate clause what would be the crucial evidence for violation of the constraint. But the restrictions on the relative order and form of the objects of the apparently exceptional verbs I have examined are not overruled by the more general constraints I mentioned, nor neutralized by NP-movements. Thus *tug*, *lift*, *report*, *delegate*, and *obtain*, five apparently exceptional verbs which seem to take only prepositional indirect objects, as mentioned in chapter 3, may not have internal prepositionless indirect objects even at the cost of awkwardness arising from violation of constraints on the ordering of heavy noun phrases, as (38–9) show. And NP-movements do not make it acceptable to omit the preposition, as (40–1) show. Of course, this would be predicted by the claim that it is the verbs, rather than expressions consisting of verbs and direct objects, which are exceptionally restricted.

38a. ?John tugged the cookie jar whose contents he desired to consume to me.

38b. ?Jacob lifted the tray of paint which I intended to use to paint the ceiling to me.

38c. ?Richard reported the death of a man they were depending on to them.

38d. ?They delegated responsibility for seeing that there was money in the treasury to me.

38e. ?Dick can obtain anything a party boss could possibly desire for you.

39a. ?*John tugged me the cookie jar whose contents he desired to consume.

39b. ?*Jacob lifted me the tray of paint which I intended to use to paint the ceiling.

39c. *Richard reported them the death of a man they were depending on.

39d. *They delegated me responsibility for seeing that there was money in the treasury.

39e. *Dick can obtain you anything a party boss could possibly desire.

40a. *The cookie jar John tugged me was empty.

40b. *The paint tray Jacob lifted me was empty.

40c. *The death which Richard reported them turned out to be a hoax.

40d. *The responsibility they delegated me was quite sobering.

40e. *The assistance Dick can obtain you is unlimited.

41a. ?*What did John tug you?

41b. *What did Jacob lift you?

41c. *What did Richard report them?

41d. *What did they delegate you?

41e. *What can Dick obtain you?

To take another case, the indirect object of *allow*, as mentioned in chapter 3, must always be internal and prepositionless. As demonstrated by (42a), this constraint may not be violated to accommodate the more general constraint on anaphor position. Sentence (42a) is as bad as (43). Sentences (42b–c) show that the restriction is not loosened to accommodate the constraint on position of heavy noun phrases, and (42d–g) show that NP-movements, as expected by now, do not neutralize it.

42a. *The chairman allowed Jim the floor, and then he allowed it to Mary.

42b. ??The chairman allowed the person who had been wanting to speak longest the floor.

42c. ??The chairman allowed the floor to the person who had been wanting to speak the longest.

42d. *The amount of time which the chairman allowed to Jim was insufficient.

42e. The amount of time which the chairman allowed Jim was insufficient.

42f. *How much time did the chairman allow to Jim?

42g. How much time did the chairman allow Jim?

43. *The chairman allowed the floor to Mary.

Since the idioms are verb + object constructions, like the restricted *give*-expressions, *a priori* one would expect them to behave like the *give*-expressions, ignoring their restrictions when verb and object are separated, and relaxing them when they threaten to violate more general constraints. The facts are not as clear as they might be, since the idioms in question are "islands"[1] (cf. Postal 1969) with respect to pronominalization, and consequently this phenomenon cannot be used in comparison. But the position of complex noun phrases and NP-movements can be examined, and as (44c–f, 45c–f) demonstrate, the idioms in question are indeed like the *give*-expressions in that if the direct object has been separated from the verb, an indirect object of the usually unpreferred prepositionless type is much more nearly acceptable than if the direct object had not been removed from its place within the clause. However, as (44a,b) and (45a,b) show, the constraint on the position of heavy noun phrases is not strong enough to

---

[1] That is, as (1a–c) demonstrate, it is not possible to pronominalize only the direct object of one of these idioms. Rather, one must pronominalize the whole idiom as in (2a–c):

1a. *Marcus brought word of the successes to the general, and Publius brought
$\begin{Bmatrix} \text{it} \\ \text{some} \\ \text{one} \end{Bmatrix}$ to him too.

1b. *The hippie lent the workers a hand, and he lent one to the old ladies too.

1c. *The president gave his secretary the ax, and he gave it to the cook too.

2a. Marcus brought word of the successes to the general, and so did Publius.

2b. The hippie lent the workers a hand, and he did the same for the old ladies.

2c. The president gave his secretary the ax, and he did the same to/with the cook.

override the specific requirements of these idioms, so they are in this respect more like the exceptional verbs discussed above.

44a.   Pay closer attention than you have ever before to Mr Fawkes.

44b.   *Pay Mr Fawkes closer attention than you have ever before.

44c.   The amount of attention they paid to the lecturer was not very flattering to him.

44d.   ?The amount of attention they paid the lecturer was not very flattering to him.

44e.   How much attention did they pay to you?

44f.   ?How much attention did they pay you?

45a.   ?Have you sent word of the defeat which the government has been hoping for to the generals?

45b.   ??Have you sent the generals word of the defeat which the government has been hoping for?

45c.   Word of the defeat, which we sent to the generals at 9:00, surprised them.

45d.   ?Word of the defeat, which we sent the generals at 9:00, surprised them.

45e.   What sort of "word" was sent to the generals?

45f.   *What sort of "word" was sent the generals?

Of course, I have only discussed two idioms here, the clearest two I could find. To secure my point I would have to show that it is in general the case that the specific requirements on idioms are stronger than some more general constraints, but weak enough to be at least loosened, if not suspended, by removing the direct object noun phrase. But because with most idioms my judgments of acceptability for determining the normal requirements fluctuate, as do they in cases concerning the data crucial here, it has seemed futile to attempt such an undertaking.

C   Reflexive forms

1   Direct object–indirect object co-reference
A third area in which we may expect interaction between constraints on dative movement and other grammatical constraints concerns reflexive pronouns. Postal (1968:chap. xv) observed that there is a regular but unexplained constraint in English against co-referential

noun phrase clausemates in the verb phrase or predicate of a sentence, as in (46):

46a. I struck the belt with itself.
46b. The slave-dealers sold Mary to herself.
46c. The slave-dealers bought Mary from herself.

These sentences are impeccable semantically; something syntactic about them is ill-formed. The extent to which this constraint holds for *to*-dative constructions in my speech may be seen from examples (47–51).

47a. ?*Bill dragged Barbarella to herself.
47b. *Bill dragged Barbarella herself.

48a. ?The slave-dealers sold Mary to herself.
48b. *The slave-dealers sold Mary herself.

49a. ?*Bill pushed Barbarella to herself.
49b. *Bill pushed Barbarella herself.

50a. ?Sue quoted John to himself.
50b. ?*Sue quoted John himself.

51a. *Wonderwoman promised Batman to himself.
51b. ?*Wonderwoman promised Batman himself.

The meanings of the verbs in (47), (49), and (51) (*to*-classes 1, 3, and 5) preclude interpretations where the indirect object and the direct object refer to the identical object or being, but these sentences are ungrammatical even when the indirect and direct objects are non-identical but co-referential counterparts, as in dreams and science-fiction where one may meet up with a different version of oneself.

Morgan 1969a, for instance, discusses a time-travel situation which can be described most naturally by a sentence which is syntactically ill-formed if applied to a normal state of affairs. Normally, one describes the action of grasping one's own flesh between the first digits of the thumb and first finger by saying, "I pinched myself." One cannot describe this action by saying "I was pinched by myself." Imagine then, a trip through time to visit one's former self. One might pinch the former self, to see if it has substance, and one could describe this also by "I pinched myself." Again, one could certainly not say "I was pinched by myself." But suppose that the former self pinches the self from the "real" world. The "real" one could not now use "I pinched myself" to describe this. He would have to say, "I was pinched by myself."

No matter what distribution of "selves" one imposes on (47–51), they remain ungrammatical. Postal's observation that the constraint concerns clausemate noun phrases in the verb phrase of a sentence, is supported by the fact that (52a–c), passives of (48), (50), and (51), where the co-referential noun phrases are no longer both in the predicate, are much more acceptable than (48), (50), and (51).

52a. Mary was sold to herself by the slave-dealers.

52b. John was quoted to himself by Sue.

52c. Batman was promised to himself by Wonderwoman.

The fact that the passives of (47) and (49), given as (53a,b), are as ungrammatical as the actives, remains unexplained

53a. *Barbarella was dragged to herself (by Bill).

53b. *Barbarella was pushed to herself (by Bill).

but the differential behavior of *sell* and *quote*, on the one hand, and *drag* and *push*, on the other, supports the suggestion in chapter 3, section D, that the *give-* and *read*-classes (*to*-classes 2 and 4b) undergo dative-movement rules which are topologically similar to each other but different from those which apply to the *bring-* and *send*-classes (*to*-classes 1 and 3).

Interpreting sentences with verbs of *for*-classes 1–4 and co-referential direct and indirect objects is more difficult because it requires suspending the normal assumptions about what sorts of objects can be created, performed, earned, etc., or about what sorts of things are capable of perception, as illustrated by (54) to (57):

54a. ?*John carved a statue for itself.

54b. *John carved a statue itself.

54c. ?*Gepetto$_i$ carved Pinocchio$_j$ for himself$_j$.

54d. *Gepetto$_i$ carved Pinocchio$_j$ himself$_j$.

55a. *The Smiths bought the slave for himself.

55b. ?*The Smiths bought the slave himself.

56a. ?*John played the sonata for itself.

56b. *John played the sonata itself.

57a. ?*The designer of the prize earned it for itself.

57b. *The designer of the prize earned it itself.[1]

---

[1] I find (54a,c), (55b), (56a), and (57a) almost impossible to understand as intended, even suspending the requisite presuppositions. The others, marked with an asterisk, I find totally ungrammatical in the intended sense.

In addition, the contemporaneous existence constraint on *for*-class 1–3 dative movement requires that the indirect object exist prior to the existence of the direct object, asserted to be produced in (54) and (56), but the assertions of the verbs in (54b) and (54d) contradict this. Nonetheless, (55) and (57) are still well-formed semantically, but atrocious sentences. As for *for*-class 5, we may observe that (58a,b) with reflexive pronouns are ungrammatical, but (58c), with co-reference between indirect object and direct object, but no reflexive, is grammatical.[1]

58a. *Sandra killed the chairman of the Martyr's League for himself.

58b. *Sandra killed the chairman of the Martyr's League himself.

58c. Sandra killed the chairman$_i$ of the Martyr's League for him$_i$.

This suggests that the *for* NP phrase in the structure of *for*-class 5 expressions is not in the same clause as the direct object at the time of reflexivization (that is, at the time at which the clausemate condition is relevant for a co-reference relationship holding between two noun phrases). Non-reflexive pronouns as the indirect or direct objects (whichever follows the other) are no better than reflexive ones for (47) to (57).

It may be remarked that the sentences of (50) are not quite as bad as the other sentences I have called ungrammatical. I do not know how to explain this, but it may be related to an additional curious and unexplained fact about sentences like (50a). Contrary to the severe general prohibition against anaphoric pronouns preceding and commanding their antecedents (cf. Langacker 1969; Ross 1967), as in (59)

59. *She sent him$_i$ to John$_i$'s desk.

the version of (50a) with the anaphoric relations reversed as in (60a) is approximately as acceptable as (50a).

60a. ?Sue quoted himself to John, but he remained obstinate.

60b. *Sue quoted himself John, but he remained obstinate.

Sentence (60b), however, is not nearly as acceptable as (50b), and this difference is also unexplained.

---

[1] Independent constraints on the order of pronouns and their antecedents, and on the position of anaphoric pronouns preclude the existence of a form with an internal prepositionless indirect object such as (1) or (2) below:

1. Sandra killed him$_i$ the chairman$_i$ of the ML.

2. Sandra killed the chairman of the ML him.

2   *Subject–indirect object co-reference*

It appears that there are restrictions on the occurrence of co-referential noun phrases as subjects and indirect objects, as well as restrictions on co-referential direct and indirect objects. Among the *to*-dative verbs, only the communication and 'future having' verbs of classes 4 and 5 occur readily with reflexive pronouns which mark what we may call "absolute co-reference" – identity of two or more noun phrases in world (cf. chapter 3, sec. c.5.*c*, and Morgan 1969b), reference and aspect (agent or location or object, or will or actions or some combination). That is, sentences like (61) to (64) are quite normal, although the (b) versions may be preferred to the (a) versions.

61a.   Susan wired a dozen roses to herself.
61b.   Susan wired herself a dozen roses.

62a.   ?Bill read a story to himself.
62b.   Bill read himself a story.

63a.   ?Bill promised a vacation to himself.
63b.   Bill promised himself a vacation.

64a.   Bill owes a vacation to himself.
64b.   Bill owes himself a vacation.

With verbs of *to*-class 5, the indirect object refers to a being which must exist in the same world as the subject (recall the discussion of example [136c] in chapter 3), even though it is assumed that a version of it will also exist in a future world. If cross-world co-reference is assumed, to permit counterparts to encounter each other, (62a,b) are both ungrammatical for me, but my intuitions are vague regarding the others.

One might assume that sentences with at least some of the *bring*- and *send*-class verbs of *to*-classes 1 and 3 would be acceptable with reflexives marking same-world co-reference, if not same-aspect co-reference. Assuming this, one would expect to be able to use (65) and (66)

65a.   Ralph dragged a rock to himself.
65b.   Ralph dragged himself a rock.

66a.   Edgar tossed a rock to himself.
66b.   Edgar tossed himself a rock.

to describe respectively situations where Ralph reached out for a rock, and grasping it, pulled it along the ground until it was at his side, and where Edgar tossed a rock up in the air and caught it again, either remaining in place, or running a few steps forward. I find (65b), (66a), and (66b) all totally inappropriate, but (65a) does not seem so bad.[1] Furthermore, a form like (65a) but with a non-reflexive anaphoric pronoun, e.g. (67):

67. Ralph$_i$ dragged a rock to him$_i$.

is just as appropriate or inappropriate as (65a).[2] This is not entirely surprising in view of the fact that many speakers including me find sentences like (68a,b) about equally as appropriate (as each other, and as [65a] and [67]) for describing the situation described above:

68a. Ralph put a rock near himself.
68b. Ralph$_i$ put a rock near him$_i$.

What is totally surprising to me is that if I assume cross-world co-reference between the subjects and indirect objects in (65) and (66), then (65b), (66a), and (66b) become acceptable, and (65a) becomes totally unacceptable. This is reminiscent of the reversal of grammaticality judgments on passive sentences with reflexive agents (section c.1 above), but I know of no other semantic or syntactic property which the *bring*-class verbs have in common with *pinch*, which they don't also share with the *send*-verbs, or with the *give*-verbs, which also are unvaryingly ungrammatical in constructions with co-referential subject and indirect object; sentences like (69–70) are uniformly ungrammatical[3] regardless of whether co-reference is assumed to be in the same world or across worlds:

[1] Another speaker finds (66a) appropriate if Edgar runs to catch the rock, but not if he remains in place. I have not been able to investigate what sort of variations occur in such data from a reasonable sample of speakers.
[2] The corresponding version of (65b), e.g. *Ralph$_i$ dragged him$_i$ a rock* does not have the same range of meaning as (65a) or (67), but means approximately 'Ralph did himself the favor of dragging a rock (to some unspecified location).'
[3] Why these sentences should be ungrammatical, particularly with an assumption of cross-world co-reference, is a mystery to me, and an interesting question in its own right. Only a few *give*-expressions permit reflexive indirect objects, e.g.:

　　1. I gave myself a pinch.
　　2. John gave himself a turn at the telescope.

and these are only good with same-world co-reference. Others which are nonsensical if same-world co-reference is assumed remain so assuming cross-world co-reference, e.g.:

　　3. I gave myself the peace sign.
　　4. I gave myself an idea.

69a. *Mandrake gave the magic wand to himself.
69b. *Mandrake gave himself the magic wand.

70a. *John sold stock in a krypton mine to himself.
70b. *John sold himself stock in a krypton mine.

The *for*-dative verbs do not seem to be nearly as restricted as the *to*-datives. Thus both the (a) and (b) versions of sentences (71–4), with verbs of *for*-classes 1–4 are perfectly appropriate, even when absolute co-reference is assumed.

71a. Bill baked a cake for himself.
71b. Bill baked himself a cake.

72a. Bill bought some tea for himself.
72b. Bill bought himself some tea.

73a. Bill played a lullaby for himself.
73b. Bill played himself a lullaby.

74a. Bill earned $1,000 for himself by avoiding the middleman.
74b. Bill earned himself $1,000 by avoiding the middleman.

As for *for*-class 5, I find sentences with an external indirect object, like (75a), somewhat less acceptable than sentences with an internal indirect object, like (75b):

75a. ?*Grace killed a male chauvinist for herself.
75b.   Grace killed herself a male chauvinist.

All of the *for*-dative verbs, in contrast to the *to*-datives, may occur with non-reflexive co-referential indirect object pronouns, but only in certain colloquial, rural, or substandard types of speech, and, for no apparent reason, only if the indirect object is internal, as illustrated in (76–80).[1]

76a. *I baked a cake for me.
76b.   I baked me a cake.

77a. *Shall we buy some tea for us?
77b.   Shall we buy us some tea?

---

[1] For some reason, second person pronouns, as in *Where are you going to find you an island? I bet you're gonna kill you a honkie*, sound very strange in this construction. I don't think this reason is entirely semantic, since the *we* and *us* in (77b) are inclusive, referring to the speaker (first person) and the hearer (second person).

78a.   *Bill$_i$ played a lullaby for him$_i$.
78b.   Bill$_i$ played him$_i$ a lullaby.

79a.   *Bill$_i$ earned \$1,000 for him$_i$.
79b.   Bill$_i$ earned him$_i$ \$1,000.

80a.   *We ought to kill a male chauvinist for us.
80b.   We ought to kill us a male chauvinist.

Some *to*-dative verbs, it will be recalled, permit non-reflexive co-referential indirect object pronouns, as in (67), but they occur only when the indirect object is external, and are not limited to colloquial varieties of speech. This distribution of pronominal forms surely reflects the similarity of the *for*-dative verb classes to each other, and a difference in syntactic structure at some level between them and the *to*-datives, in addition to their differences in semantic representation.

3   Subject–direct object co-reference

As sentences (81–9) show, verbs of *to*-classes 2, 3, 4b, and 5, and *for*-classes 1–3, and 5 (i.e. all except the verbs of the *bring-*, *radio-*, and *earn-*classes) occur easily in dative constructions where the direct object is a reflexive pronoun and the subject and direct object are co-referential in the same world, if not always in the same aspect. For example, in (83) the subject noun phrase refers to John as a volitional agent, whereas the object noun phrase refers to John as a physical object which happens to be the "container" for John's "will."

81a.   *John carried himself to the dean.
81b.   *John$_i$ carried the dean himself$_i$.

82a.   Simon sold himself to the slave-dealers.
82b.   *Simon sold the slave-dealers himself.

83a.   John shipped himself to his sister.
83b.   *John shipped his sister himself.

84a.   Richard quoted himself to Thelma.
84b.   ?*Richard quoted Thelma himself.

85a.   Steve promised himself to Summer.
85b.   *Steve promised Summer himself.

86a.   This cake will bake itself for Mandrake.
86b.   *This cake will bake Mandrake itself.

87a.   Sue chose herself for Harry.
87b.   ?*Sue chose Harry herself.

88a.   The Sonata Sympathique will play itself for its composer.
88b.   ?*The Sonata Sympathique will play its composer itself.

89a.   The fanatics killed themselves for their leader.
89b.   *The fanatics killed their leader themselves.

If we imagine a verb *microwave* which would mean 'send an exact replica of by microwaves,' and so be a member of *to*-class 4a, we can see that verbs of this class also permit direct objects co-referential to the subject, if the indirect object is external, as (90) shows:

90a.   John microwaved himself to Mary.
90b.   *John microwaved Mary himself.

The fact that (81a) is ungrammatical if same-world co-reference is assumed may be attributed to the fact that the meaning of verbs of its class (the *bring*-class) requires that the subject and direct object noun phrases refer to separate entities, one capable of going with the other. Assuming cross-world co-reference doesn't help, as might be predicted from the fact that co-referential subject and indirect object likewise could not occur with *bring*-class verbs, apparently as a result of their meaning, as described in chapter 3, section c.6.*a*.

One other class of dative constructions seems to be totally impossible with co-referential subject and direct object, and that is the *earn*-class, *for*-class 4, as demonstrated in (91):

91a.   *The prize is good enough to earn itself for its designer.
91b.   *The prize is good enough to earn its designer itself.

Conceivably the ungrammaticality of (91) follows in some way from the ungrammaticality of (57), since both sets of sentences seem to be well-formed semantically, and presumably would, if used at all, be used in very similar situations.

The fact that the (b) sentences of (81–90) are all unacceptable is probably a reflection of the output condition on pronoun position which, as discussed earlier, "blacklists" structures with pronominal direct objects following internal indirect objects. Notice that it cannot be claimed that the reason the (b) sentences are unacceptable is simply that a prepositionless reflexive form is in string-final position, because sentences with the same order which result from other derivations and may have different surface structure are perfectly acceptable. For example, the (b) sentences of (81–5, 87, 89, 90) are acceptable as stylistic variants of the emphatic sentences (92a–h) respectively:

92a. John himself carried the dean.

92b. Simon himself sold the slave-dealers.

92c. John himself shipped his sister.

92d. Richard himself quoted Thelma.

92e. Steve himself promised Summer.

92f. Sue herself chose Harry.

92g. The fanatics themselves killed their leader.

92h. John himself microwaved Mary.

6   *Summary and conclusions*

A   Summaries

1   Goals and hypotheses

The original goal of this work was to make a case for the position that it is not accidental that generalizations about the syntactic properties of verbs must often be made in semantic terms. I hoped to demonstrate the utility of assuming that there are natural explanations for phenomena described in terms of deep structure constraints (Perlmutter 1968), structural description features, redundancy rules, and rule government, and I also hoped to demonstrate that these explanations are stated most easily in terms of the meaning of lexical items, that is, in terms of the occurrence of particular semantic predicates in the underlying representation of sentences, and in terms of the structural relations of the elements in underlying and derived representations. It appeared to me that the notions of redundancy rule, structural description feature, and deep structure constraint were necessitated by the concepts of rule government implied by or described in Chomsky 1965 and Lakoff 1965, so my plan was to re-examine the notions 'exception to a rule' and 'rule government,' and provide new analyses in terms of the structural relations of semantic elements, for several syntactic phenomena believed to be exception-ridden, requiring governed rules for their description.

2   Research

The notion of exception which developed has been discussed in chapter 1, section A.2 and chapter 2, section D.4. The evolution of the approach to governed rules as rules which are regular for a semantic class was described in chapter 2, sections A–B. Chapter 2, sections C–D.3 and D.5 described the approach itself, and chapter 2, section D.6 described some of its implications. The attempt to demonstrate its validity and utility for *several* supposedly governed rules had to be abandoned as much too large an undertaking. Instead, a single phenomenon, dative movement,

194

was chosen from among the proposed rules which were generally conceded to be governed in the sense of Chomsky and Lakoff. A survey of the general and particular semantic properties of the expressions involved in dative-movement alternations was presented in chapter 3. The semantic investigations did not cover all conceivable aspects of meaning. I would not say that I merely scratched the surface – *gouge* is probably a more accurate word – but I did make an effort to restrict my investigation to what appeared to be relevant details of the semantics. The following conclusions were reached:

1. It is necessary to define on the order of fifteen or twenty distinct semantic classes of expressions in order to characterize the set of all and only those expressions subject to a dative-movement alternation.

2. In terms of syntactic properties which are obviously related to dative movement (e.g. presuppositions required for an alternation to be possible, direction of dative movement, possibility of passives with the indirect object as subject) as well as ones which *a priori* would be considered unrelated (e.g. deletion of indirect object, deletion of direct object), these classes are remarkably distinct from one another, and remarkably homogeneous internally, although, of course, there are properties which are shared by several classes, and properties which are not distributed uniformly within a class.

3. As a result of this, it is necessary to postulate several rules of "Dative Movement," distinct not only in the class of verbs they apply to, but in the direction of the movement of the indirect object noun phrase, and in the conditions on them (assumptions of the speaker and subjects of world-creating verbs) as well.

These conclusions led to what appears to be a *reductio ad absurdum* of the hypothesis that governed rules are those which apply to classes of expressions which must be described in semantic terms – after all, seven to fifteen distinct rules which all describe the "simple" alternation between *V NP Prep NP* and *V NP NP* constructions is not impressive as a generalization. I claimed, and attempted to substantiate in chapter 4, that rather than being a *reductio ad absurdum* the illusion of one or two simple dative-movement rules was but another example of the independently justified notion of linguistic conspiracy in favor of particular target structures. In chapter 4, section B, I provided another example of the effects of this particular conspiracy – the illusion of a dative-movement rule operating where in fact no such rule operates at all.

The existence of apparent surface-structure restrictions on several kinds of verbal expressions which one would expect to be subject to a dative-movement alternation raised the question of constraints interacting with each other: what happens when conformity to one constraint entails violation of another constraint? This question was studied in some detail in chapter 5, sections A and B, where it was concluded that the constraints on some restricted verbs of 'future having,' and on some non-literal expressions with *give* relaxed to accommodate other more general constraints, while the constraints on true idioms did not, although, as with the *give*-expressions, if the objects were separated from their verbs by NP-movement rules the constraints no longer held. At the other extreme, verbs to which dative movement did not apply, even though they fell within a semantic class to which a dative-movement rule applied, that is, exceptions to dative-movement rules, appeared to be quite steadfast when they confronted general constraints. The restrictions on exceptions, although their scopes might vary from verb to verb, were absolute. It was also concluded that some sort of transderivational constraints were necessary to describe these interactions of constraints. The exact number and form of such constraints was discussed, but not conclusively determined. No single derivational constraint could be found which described the interactions, nor any set of non-overlapping constraints.

Chapter 5, section C, considered the interaction of dative movement and constraints on the position of reflexive pronouns. The differential behavior of the various classes of dative-movement verbs with respect to these constraints provided unexpected evidence for structural details (e.g. of *to*-class 5 representations), and similarities (e.g. of *to*-classes 2 and 4b), and differences (e.g. between *to*-classes 1 and 2, on the one hand, and 3, on the other) postulated in chapter 3, as well as for semantic details (e.g. of *to*-classes 1–3), and for several of the constraints discussed there. In addition, it was concluded that at some intermediate stage the *for*-datives were as a group much more similar to each other than to any of the *to*-datives. Other differential behavior appeared to be quite mysterious.

B   Evaluation

1   Support of the semantic basis of syntactic properties

The study of dative movement presented in chapter 3 provides strong support for the hypothesis that governed rules are rules which apply across the board to constructions commanded by particular semantic classes of lexical items. The set of verbs and verbal expressions subject to dative-movement alternations was found to be characterizable with a high degree of accuracy as the membership of a relatively small number of classes rigorously definable only in semantic terms. I am not aware of any verbs involved in dative-movement alternations which do not fit in one of the classes described in chapter 3. Admittedly I was not able to define rigorously all of the classes; some (e.g. the symbolic constructions of *for*-class 5) were particularly hard to pin down, but impressionistic limits were put forth where more formal ones were beyond reach. A very small number of verbs were found which fit in the semantic classes described but appeared not to participate in dative-movement alternations. The nature of these putative exceptions is discussed in section B.3 below.

Particularly compelling evidence for the semantic nature of governed rules is provided by several facts discussed in chapter 3. First, the membership of more than one class of dative-movement verbs depends not on what sort of activity the verb describes, as is usually the case (cf. the *bring-* and *send-*classes), but on how the activity is perceived by the speaker. For example, a verb's membership in *for*-class 1 depends on whether it is perceived as describing an action intended by its agent (the animate subject of the main verb) as a creative or artistic act. If such a criterion is not semantic, I cannot imagine what would be.[1]

Furthermore, it seems to be the case with these verbs that dative movement is impossible if the activity described by the main verb is considered not to be expected relative to the known behavior of the

---

[1] Undoubtedly there exist philosophers, and possibly linguists as well, who claim that semantics maps meaning on to the real world, and who would say that such a criterion is in fact not semantic at all, but rather psychological, and outside the province of linguistics, because it concerns an individual's perception of reality rather than the reality itself. But this is an erroneous way of thinking, and it amazes me that it should have persisted for so long. One of the goals of linguistics is to describe the principles of languages used by speakers of natural languages, that is, by flesh-and-blood human beings. People are not limited in their use of language to what is real and true and presently existing. They talk about what they believe and assume to be true, and about what they would like to be true, and about what might be true if certain things were true which they know not to be true, and so on. No theory of semantics can be of any use to linguistics unless it is based on the assumptions and beliefs of the actual users of language relative to what they are talking about, rather than being based on the rather uninteresting subcase of what actually happens to be true. Detailed arguments to this effect can be found in Morgan Forthcoming.

agent. This is clearly a case of the possibility of application for a syntactic rule being determined by a semantic criterion – assumptions of the speaker or other subject of a world-creating verb about the event the speaker is referring to. Assumptions about an agent's intent are similarly necessary in determining the well-formedness of sentences like (1):

  1. Sam promised to climb his lover a mountain.

where the putative dative-movement verb, in this case *climb*, does not describe an activity which is felt to produce a change in its object. Sentence (1) is well-formed if Sam's climbing the mountain is considered an artistic performance, but not if it is considered a favor or a symbolic act.

Another case of the relevance for syntactic rules of language users' assumptions is discussed in chapter 3, section C.3.*f*. Not all noun phrases which occur preceded by *for* in the complement of a verb belonging to a dative-movement class participate in dative-movement alternations, even if they are animate. In order to occur before the direct object, without a preposition, they must be considered as denoting intended recipients or percipients of intended gifts, performances, or symbolic acts. If they are considered to denote employers, or individuals substituted for or represented by another, they must occur with the preposition *for*.

Fifth, four classes of expressions with *give*, which are weakly restricted with respect to the possibility of dative movement, must be described in semantic terms, because they differ in this property from literal expressions with *give*, and from real idioms with *give* as well, as described in chapter 5, sections A and B. They cannot be considered a class of *non-alternating* expressions derived by optional lexical or syntactic rules from expressions not containing *give*, since under certain conditions, namely when the objects are separated from the verbs, they participate freely in dative-movement alternations. It is clear that the semantic representations of sentences with these expressions are closely related to the semantic representations of literal expressions with *give*. Both assert causation and imply a resultant 'have' relationship. It is also clear that they differ in the kinds of things which may be denoted by the direct object noun phrase.

A further argument for the necessity of describing the conditions for a given rule's application in terms of the assumptions of speakers and beings presumed by them to be capable of thought is provided by another fact discussed in chapter 3. For several classes of verbs, the possibility of a dative-movement alternation depends on whether or not the speaker assumes, and assumes that the referent of the subject of the commanding world-creating verb (if any) assumes, that the referents of direct and indirect object noun phrases exist in the same world with each other and with the referent of the subject of the dative-movement verb.

A second kind of support for the hypothesis that the government of syntactic rules is semantic in nature is derived from the fact that in a number of cases there was evidence that particular classes were to be defined in semantic terms. These were cases where a particular non-obvious detail of the semantic description was necessary to exclude from class membership verbs which would be members if a cruder class description was given, but which did not behave at all like members, or like real exceptions. They were obviously ungrammatical in constructions where [other] class members were perfectly grammatical and acceptable. Judgments of acceptability did not fluctuate from speaker to speaker, and such verbs were not a source of difficulty for learners of the language. For instance, it is a relatively simple matter to observe that one large class of dative-movement verbs involves the notion of 'giving.' Previous writers who have observed this have never been able to account satisfactorily for the fact that *donate, contribute,* and *distribute* do not participate in dative-movement alternations. Phonological conditions were inadequate to predict correctly the verbs which would fail to participate in dative-movement alternations, and the claim that these words are simply exceptions to a rule of dative movement predicts incorrectly that children will have difficulty learning how to use them, and that they will be subject to analogic levelling among speakers who use them frequently, so that their exceptionality will fluctuate from speaker to speaker. Furthermore, neither of these putative accounts can explain the fact that *give away,* and *give out,* near-synonyms of *donate, contribute,* and *distribute,* likewise do not participate in dative-movement alternations, and there is no independently motivated reason for this failure. However, all five of these words differ from 'giving' words which do undergo dative movement, in that their meanings are differentiated from those of the dative-movement verbs. They involve presuppositions about the indirect object: the use of *donate, contribute,* and *give away* requires an assumption by the speaker that the indirect object will be receiving contributions from more than one source, and that he will use them "properly."[1] The use of *distribute* and *give out* requires an assumption that the indirect object is a set containing at least two members. The assumptions which differentiate from one another the 'giving' verbs which do participate in dative-movement alternations concern the pragmatic nature of the direct object, and conditions on the transfer of the direct object from the subject to the indirect object.

Similarly, the characterization of the performance verbs involved in dative-movement alternations is not at all obvious, but it appears to be the case that verbs denoting kinds of non-vocal performances which are characterized by special properties of the work performed or the instrument performed upon do not participate in alternations, while verbs that do participate may be differentiated from one another as describing different modes of production which are a function of the nature of the work performed or the "instrument" performed upon, if they describe vocal productions.

A further example of particular semantic criteria being necessary to exclude from a class verbs which lack the syntactic property under investigation may be found in the description of the *read*-class. Although means and manner adverbials function alike in many syntactic rules, including pre-lexical structure-reducing rules (cf. Appendix III), it is necessary to describe the *read*-class as restricted to verbs denoting a means of communication, because verbs denoting a manner of communicating, such as *mutter, mumble, mention,* etc. are never involved in dative-movement alternations.

In a third kind of case, the appearance of two non-synonymous sentences being related by a dative-movement rule was exposed in chapter 4, section B, as an illusion involving related homophonous verbs. The argument derived considerable support from the fact that there were syntactic properties which distinguished between the different senses, and that they were correlated with the semantic properties which distinguished between them.

A fourth way in which this study of dative movement has provided support for the hypothesis that syntactic properties are a function of

---

[1] This description of the assumptions required for the use of these verbs may not be exactly correct, but something like it will be necessary to account for the following facts: (1) these verbs may not be used if it is assumed that all the donations to the indirect object will come from a single source (cf. Dixon 1970), (2) they may be used of "gifts" to wealthy political parties and educational institutions, as well as to needy organizations and individuals, (3) they generally cannot be used of money or other gifts given to panhandlers.

semantic structure is found in the possibility of predicting from semantic analyses proposed to describe classes of dative-movement verbs whether certain ambiguities will occur, and whether certain syntactic alternations other than dative movement will be permitted. For example, the fact that the scope of time and place adverbs in final position is ambiguous with promise and permission verbs is predictable from the semantically justified representation of such verbs given as (179a–b), in which a time or place adverb could have as its scope either a clause whose main predicate was a predicate of saying or granting, or a clause whose main predicate expressed a relation of 'having,' to occur in the future relative to the time of saying, etc. Thus, in an expression in which the predicates of saying and having were represented by a single word, a following time or place adverb could be interpreted as referring to either of them. Likewise predicted by this kind of semantic representation for these verbs is the syntactic fact that time adverbs cannot be preposed to initial position if they must be interpreted as referring to the time of the having, as, for instance, adverbs which refer to the future, when the surface dative-movement verb is in the past tense. This syntactic fact follows from the proposed semantic representation because it is generally the case that adverbs may be preposed only to the head of the clause whose main predicate they modify.

Similarly predictable from the proposed semantic representation is a fact about *until*-clauses which specify the time of cessation of a 'having' relationship, namely that these may not appear in sentence-initial position in dative-movement sentences. Given the general constraint on the preposability of adverbs and adverbial clauses, this fact follows from an underlying structure in which the clause asserting the 'have' relationship occurs embedded as a complement of some higher verb, and precisely this sort of underlying structure was proposed for dative-movement verbs.

A semantic fact which is predicted only by the syntactic representation of such semantic structures as are proposed for dative-movement verbs is that when adverbs like *again* occur after these verbs they may refer to a repetition of the 'having' situation, without implying a repetition of the saying, arranging, causing, etc. denoted by the dative-movement verb. The fact that this reading is not found when the adverb precedes the dative-movement verb is again predicted by the proposed underlying structures, and the independent constraint on the preposability of adverbs.

2   *General residue*

Of course, my proposals regarding dative-movement verbs do not explain every conceivable aspect of their syntactic distribution. In particular, while they predict that certain ambiguities will occur, and that certain others will fail to occur, there are still other lacks of ambiguity which they do not account for. They do not explain, for instance, the lack of ambiguity of time adverbs with *owe*, or why *to*-class 1 verbs like *bring* do not have a reading with *until*-clauses in which only the time at which the 'having' relation will cease is specified. But I know of no other proposals which do explain these gaps, and indeed I know of no other proposals which predict the ambiguities which do occur, and the precise differential behavior with respect to the preposability of adverbs. I would speculate that we will eventually be able to show that these unpredicted gaps follow from structural and semantic details in the representation of the particular verbs which I have not focused on, according to general and independently motivated syntactic and semantic principles, just as certain facts about the syntax of promise and permission verbs followed from the underlying representations proposed in chapter 3.

Other unexplained distributions are found in the data concerning reflexives and types of co-reference. Some of the paradigm gaps followed from real-world constraints on what individuals can do to or with themselves. A few gaps appeared to be related to other gaps, but their probable origin remained an object of speculation. It was found necessary to distinguish among several kinds of co-reference expressed by reflexive pronouns (e.g. same world, across worlds, willful agent/ physical object, mind/body, etc.), but, even so, several gaps and kinds of differential behavior remained mysterious. I would hope and expect that these could eventually be explained as consequences of facts brought out by a more systematic study of the semantic and syntactic conditions under which reflexives occur, and by more detailed investigation of the semantics of the verbs involved. Is there something, for instance, about the semantics of the predicates involved which predicts that certain kinds of co-reference between arguments will not be permitted?

Ironically, as is evident from a glance at Appendix I, the passive data, the very data which forced Fillmore to the counter-intuitive argument that there must be more than one dative-movement rule, remain unexplained. The formation and semantics of passive sentences are, along with pronominalization, among the least understood of linguistic phenomena. Whether the possibility of various passive versions of an active sentence reflects some deep and subtle aspects of the semantics of such sentences or whether it reflects mere exceptional idiosyncracies of the verbs involved awaits further research. The possibility of an indirect object passive for dative-movement verbs appears not to correlate significantly with any other property I have investigated.

3   Particular residue

Despite all my efforts to show that dative movement was not an idiosyncratic rule which applied to an arbitrary subset of all the constructions which met its structural description, by finding classes of dative-movement verbs definable in terms of their semantic structure which were homogeneous with respect to certain syntactic properties involving dative movement, there remained a handful of verbs which appeared to be exceptional. They seemed to meet the semantic criteria for inclusion in the class, but they did not exhibit the syntactic behavior common to other members of the semantic class. It was argued in chapter 5, section B, that the interactions of these apparently exceptional verbs with various constraints on surface form differentiated them from syntactically restricted idioms on the one hand, and from semantically more systematic classes of restricted expressions on the other. It was not shown conclusively, however, that these putative exceptions were linguistically real exceptions rather than merely reflecting errors in the details of my analyses, or being counterexamples to my hypothesis that a verb's permitting the application of a given governed[1] rule is predictable from the semantic class it belongs to. To show that they were true exceptions it would be necessary to show that they are a source of difficulty in learning the language and that they are subject to variation across idiolects, but are distributionally consistent within each idiolect. If they are really exceptions to psychologically real rules (and I see no reason for linguists to be interested exclusively in any other kind), speakers will be consistent in their use of them, although the exact details of their exceptionality may, and probably will, vary from speaker to speaker.

If the use and number of these items turns out to be quite consistent not only within idiolects, but across them as well, and if learning their

---

[1] Governed in my sense. Cf. chapter 2, sec. D.5.

syntactic properties presents no particular difficulty, then the claim that they are members of a semantic class to which dative movement applies is suspect. Such a situation would indicate that the proposed semantic representations of the regular and exceptional items were in need of re-examination. I have already indicated that in my own speech the membership of the set of "exceptions" fluctuates more or less randomly from day to day, and I do not know of any cases of learners being corrected for wrongly applying dative movement to such items, but more research would be necessary to rule this out as a possibility.

If, however, it turned out that the use and number of "exceptional" items was not even consistent within the speech of individual speakers, and that individual speakers were inconsistent in making judgments of acceptability on perfectly understandable sentences using these items, then we might want to suppose that there is some sort of indeterminacy in the psychologically real linguistic rules specifying the semantic classes subject to dative-movement alternations, be they redundancy rules or the syntactic dative-movement rules themselves. Or there could be an indeterminacy in the semantic representation of certain lexical items or classes of lexical items, as suggested for independent reasons in chapter 4, section B.2, and Appendix III. This would be the most plausible explanation for the fact that speakers are often unable to make clear judgments about the applicability of certain sentences to certain situations. One such case was described in chapter 3, section c.6.c. If the hypothesis is correct that linguistic rules may be partly indeterminate and we can pinpoint the indeterminacies, then we can explain the fact that speakers are inconsistent in their use of certain items, and unable to make consistent judgments of acceptability regarding them, because this hypothesis implies that speakers competent in the ordinary sense would not know precisely how to use a few items. It implies that there are small gaps in the competence-in-the-technical-sense of flesh-and-blood speakers. This is a theoretical implication of considerable importance, and for that reason deserves careful investigation.

C Summary of theoretical implications

I do not think that there can be any doubt that I have demonstrated the utility of assuming the existence of systematic semantic explanations for syntactic properties which upon superficial examination appear to be idiosyncratic. With this assumption, and the empirically constrained

role for exceptions which it required, I was able to reduce the unpre-
dictability of verbs with respect to dative-movement alternations from
total, or nearly so, to almost nothing. This might have been expected.
But the investigations described in chapters 3 to 5 held some theoretical
surprises as well. In addition to the implications of the residual unpre-
dictabilities, discussed just above, this study has brought out several
facts of unforeseen theoretical significance.

For one thing, attempts to justify semantic representations for various
obviously causative verbs made it clear that distinctions among kinds of
causation of the sort that have concerned philosophers for centuries are
psychologically real, since the various kinds function differently from
each other in linguistic rules. Thus, as remarked in Appendix v, only
a relatively direct sort of causation may be referred to by *give* in expressions describing the genesis of some mental or physical condition such
as *give someone a cold*. For this reason, we may use *give* in such sentences
as (2a–d):

2a. John gave Mary a cold by breathing in her face.
2b. Mandrake the Magician gave Mary a cold by snapping his
    fingers.
2c. Standing in the rain gave Mary a cold.
2d. Having to stand out in the rain gave Mary a cold.

but not in such sentences as (3a–b), where the more general expression
cause to come to have must be used:

3a. *John gave Mary a cold by locking her out and making her
    stand out in the rain.
3b. *Being locked out gave Mary a cold.

4a. John caused Mary to come to have a cold by locking her out
    and making her stand out in the rain.
4b. Being locked out caused Mary to come to have a cold.

In contrast, the use of *teach*, as described in chapter 4, section B, is
limited to the initiation or causation of 'natural' processes of learning.
Teach, with abstract as well as animate subjects, may not be used if the
causation is indefinitely indirect or magically and immediately direct.
And *melt* with an abstract subject may be used for 'natural' causation of
indefinite directness, as shown in (5a–c), but *melt* may not be used for
mystically direct causation with this kind of subject, as shown by (5d):

5a. Heating ice to 40° F will melt it.

    5b. John's heating the metal melted the ice that was sitting on it.

    5c. A nuclear explosion in Tangiers will melt ice as far away as Juneau.

    5d. *John's heating the ice to 20° F melted it, just as the witch said it would.

although *cause to melt* could be used here. However, if *melt* has an animate subject, it may be used anywhere that *cause to melt* may be used, and covers cases of indefinitely indirect causation, as well as unnaturally direct causation.

Second, while these studies have not confronted the logical nature of linguistically relevant presuppositions in any technical sense of the word *presuppositions*, they have unearthed at least two kinds of assumptions which, though previously unnoticed, are required on the speaker's part for the use of lexical items in certain syntactic constructions. The question of the existence of referents for certain kinds of noun phrases in certain contexts (e.g. *the king of France* in *The king of France is bald*) has been a subject of study by philosophers and linguists for some time. The investigation of conditions on dative-movement alternation reported in chapter 3 indicates that not only do speakers have to assume the existence of referents for definite descriptions they use in "referring contexts" in order to use sentences felicitously, but in order to use certain datives without prepositions they must assume that referents of the subject, direct object, and indirect object noun phrases do, did, will, or can exist in the same world as each other, depending on the tense and mood of the verbs involved. An assumption of co-existence is not a requirement for felicitous use of language in general, as demonstrated by the fact that if the datives are preceded by prepositions, the sentences are perfectly felicitous, even when referents of indirect and direct object are not assumed to exist in the same world.

A second kind of assumption required for the felicitous use of dative-movement variants with prepositionless indirect objects was discussed in chapter 3, section c.3.*a*. Here it was claimed that the possibility of using such forms was contingent upon the speaker's assumption that the verb involved described an activity which was not unusual for the subject. If this is correct, it may provide an explanation for the fact that polysyllabic verbs are generally not subject to dative-movement alternations. Polysyllabic verbs usually describe relatively specialized activities and relations, which are statistically unlikely to be usual. If the activities come to be usual for a significant portion of the language community, the polysyllabic verbs describing them are likely to be shortened or replaced by shorter words.

The existence of conditions on syntactic rules like these is of considerable theoretical importance. These conditions refer to a *speaker's* assumptions (or his assumptions about a lower subject's assumptions), and do in a direct way what is done by the covert but nonetheless real distinctions among kinds of causation required or permitted for the use of lexical items in a more indirect way: they provide linguistic evidence for the psychological reality of linguistic rules. Neither the relation between dative-movement variants nor the principles required for determining the appropriateness of using certain lexical items can be accurately described without reference to the assumptions made by the users of such forms. A system of mathematical functions alone is insufficient for this task, as is even such a system hooked on to an omniscient observer of the real world. The fact that some rules which are required for the description of a speaker's linguistic competence must refer to assumptions which the speaker holds regarding the objects of his discourse means that there is no longer any point in pretending to write self-contained descriptions of a language which are independent of use of that language by flesh-and-blood speakers. It becomes all the more important then to investigate the nature of linguistic rules and other theoretical constructs which appear to be psychologically real, in order to ascertain the extent to which they may have the sort of indeterminacy discussed in section B.3 of this chapter. The extent to which the results of such investigations predict or follow from things we already know about linguistic rules should be one measure of the correctness of such an approach.

Appendix I Properties of dative-movement expressions

Explanation of tables 3 and 4

The first column refers to the verb's ability, in its dative-movement sense, to occur in the passive voice with the underlying indirect object as subject, e.g. in the frame **Indirect object** *was* *-ed* **direct object**. The second column charts the possibility that the verb may occur as a passive whose subject is the underlying direct object, e.g. in the frame **Direct object** *was* *-ed* (*to, for*) **indirect object**. The third, fourth, and fifth columns chart the ability of the verb to occur with no surface indirect object. They differ as to whether an indirect object may be reconstructed as indefinite (third column, verb fits in frames like *Your responsibility will be to* **direct object** [to anyone who might be interested]),[1] whether an indirect object need not be reconstructed at all (fourth column, verb fits in frames like *Go to your room and practice -ing* **direct object**), or whether the indirect object may be reconstructed as referring to some definite, previously mentioned being (fifth column, verb occurs in frames like **Indirect object** *wanted* **direct object**...*so we* *-ed* **direct object** [to, for indirect object]). The sixth column charts the verbs' occurrence with no surface direct object, e.g. in such frames as *We* *-ed* (*to, for*) **indirect object**. The seventh column records the possibility of preposing the indirect object phrase.

Verbs enclosed in parentheses are verbs which are not in my *active* vocabulary, and for the syntactic properties of which I am therefore unable to give reliable judgments. I have included them in the charts because they may be dative-movement verbs in other idiolects. Verbs marked with an asterisk are ones whose ability to occur in dative-movement alternations I am uncertain of.

---

[1] Among the *for*-class verbs, I am unable to distinguish clearly between cases where indefinite indirect objects have been deleted, and cases where there is no indirect object, or it is understood as referring to some definite person.

TABLE 3 *Some syntactic properties of classes of dative-movement expressions*

	I.o. psv.	D.o. psv.	I.o. deln.	No i.o.	Understood i.o.	D.o. deln.	Preceding i.o.
				To-classes			
1	Some	All	Few	Some	Some	None	All
2	Most	All	Most	Few	Few	Few [a,c] Some [a,d]	All
3	Some	All	Most	Most	Most	Few [d]	All
4a$_1$	Most	All	None	None	All	All [c]	All
4a$_2$	Some	All	Some	None	All	Some [d]	All
4b	All	All	All	All	All	. . . [b]	All
5	All	All	Most	Few	Some	Few [c]	All
				For-classes			
1	Some	All	All	?	Most [d]		All
2	Most	All	All	Most	Few [d]		All
3	Few	All	All	All	All [d]		All
4	None	All?	None	All	None		None
5	Some	All	All	All	Some [d]		All

[a] Not including *give*.
[b] Only *write, teach,*[c] and *show.*[c]
[c] Indirect object must not have a preposition.
[d] Indirect object must have a preposition.

TABLE 4   *Some syntactic properties of dative-movement expressions*

	I.o. psv.	D.o. psv.	I.o. deln.	No i.o.	Understood i.o.	D.o. deln.[a,b]	Preceding i.o.
To-class 1							
Bring	+	+	+		+		+
Carry		+	+	+			+
Drag	+	+		+			+
Hand	+	+					+
Haul		+		+			+
Pass	+	+			+		+
Pull		+		+			+
Push		+		+			+
Take		+					+
Bring down	+	+	+		+		+
Bring up		+	+		+		+
Bring over		+	+		+		+
Take down		+	+	+			+
Take over		+	+		+		+
Take up		+	+				+
Push, etc.		+					+
Non-alternating verbs apparently of this class							
Surrender		+	+		+		+
(Tug)							
Deliver		+	+		+	++	+
Administer [punishment]	+	+	+		+		+
To-class 2							
Advance	+	+					+
Award	+	+	+				+
Cede	+	+					+
Concede		+			+	++	+
Dish out	+	+	+	+			+
Entrust	+	+					+
Feed	+	+				+	+
Give	+	+	+	+	+		+
Lease	+	+	+			++	+
Lend	+	+	+			++	+
Loan	+	+	+				+
Pay	+	+	+			+	+
Rent		+	+			++	+
Sell	+	+	+			++	+
Serve	+	+	+	+		+	+
Non-alternating verbs apparently of this class							
Restore		+					+
Return		+	+		+		+
Submit		+	+		+		+

TABLE 4 – *continued*

	I.o. psv.	D.o. psv.	I.o. deln.	No i.o.	Under- stood i.o.	D.o. deln.	Pre- ceding i.o.
To-class 3							
(Bus)							+
(Cast)							+
Fling	+	+	+	+			+
Float		+		+			+
Forward	+	+	+		+		+
(Hurl)							+
Lower	+	+	+	+	+		+
Mail	+	+	+	+	+		+
Pitch		+	+	+		+	+
Push		+		+	+		+
Relay		+	+		+		+
Roll		+		+			+
Send	+	+	+	+	+		+
Shove	+	+		+	+		+
Slide		+		+	+		+
Ship	+	+	+		+	+	+
Throw	+	+	+	+	+	+	+
Toss	+	+		+	+	+	+
Non-alternating verbs apparently of this class							
Convey							+
Drift						+	+
Lift			+	+		+	+
Raise			+	+			+
Transport			+	+	+		+
To-class 4a$_1$							
Cable	+	+			+	+	+
Radio	+	+			+	+	+
Telephone		+				+	+
Phone	+	+			+	+	+
Telegraph		+			+	+	+
Wire	+	+			+	+	+
To-class 4a$_2$							
Mail	+	+			+		+
Relay		+	+		+		+
Shout		+	+		+	+ +	+
Whisper, etc.	+	+	+		+	+ +	+
To-class 4b							
Cite	+	+	+	+	+		?
Preach	+	+	+	+	+		?
Quote	+	+	+	+	+		+

TABLE 4 – *continued*

	I.o. psv.	D.o. psv.	I.o. deln.	No i.o.	Under- stood i.o.	D.o. deln.	Pre- ceding i.o.
Read	+	+	+	+	+		+
Show?	+	+				+	+
Tell	+	+	+	+	+	?	+
Teach?	+	+				+	+
Write	+	+	+	+		+	+

Some non-alternating verbs apparently of this class

	I.o. psv.	D.o. psv.	I.o. deln.	No i.o.	Under- stood i.o.	D.o. deln.	Pre- ceding i.o.
Admit			+		+		+
Announce		+			+		+
Articulate		+		+	+		+
Broadcast		+			+	++	+
Communicate		+	+		+	++	+
Confess		+	+		+	++	+
Declare					+		+
Demonstrate		+	+		+		+
Describe*	?	+	+		+		+
Display		+			+		+
Drawl			+	+	+		+
Elucidate			+		+		+
Exhibit		+		+	+		+
Explain*	+	+	+	+	+		+
Explicate		+	+	+	+		+
Illustrate		+	+	+	+		+
Indicate		+	+	+	+		+
Mention		+	+	+	+		+
Mutter		+	+		+	++	+
Narrate	?	+			+		+
Portray					+		+
Propose		+			+		+
Prove		+	+	+	+		+
Recommend*	?	+	+		+		+
Recite		+	+	+	+	++	+
Recount*	?	+	+		+		+
Refer		+					+
Repeat	?	+	+	+	+		+
Report		+	+		+	++	+
Reveal	?	+	+	+	+		+
Scream		+	+	+	+	++	+
State		+	+	+	+		+
Suggest		+		+	+		+
Utter							+
Voice					+		+
Yell*		+	+	+	+	++	+

To-class 5a

	I.o. psv.	D.o. psv.	I.o. deln.	No i.o.	Under- stood i.o.	D.o. deln.	Pre- ceding i.o.
Guarantee	+	+	+		+		+
Promise	+	+	+		+	+	+

To-class 5b

	I.o. psv.	D.o. psv.	I.o. deln.	No i.o.	Under- stood i.o.	D.o. deln.	Pre- ceding i.o.
Grant	+	+	+		+		+

TABLE 4 – *continued*

	I.o. psv.	D.o. psv.	I.o. deln.	No i.o.	Under- stood i.o.	D.o. deln.	Pre- ceding i.o.
Offer	+	+	+	+	+		+
Permit (Proffer)	+	+	+				+
To-class 5c							
Allot	+	+		+	+		+
Assign	+	+	+	+			+
Bequeath	+	+					+
Leave (Accord)	+	+	+				+
Some non-alternating verbs apparently of this class							
Deed over*		+			+		+
Delegate* [responsibility]	+	+	+				+
To-class 5d							
Owe	+	+	+		+	+	+
For-class 1[c,d]							
Bake	+	+		+		+	+
Boil		+		+		+	+
Build	+	+		+		+	+
Cook	+	+		+		+	+
Create		+		+		+	+
Crochet		+		+		+	+
Draw	+	+		+		+	+
Embroider		+		+		+	+
Fricassee		+		+		+	+
Fry		+		+		+	+
Knit		+		+		+	+
Make		+		+			+
Paint	+	+		+		+	+
Pour	+	+		+		+	+
Roast	+	+		+		+	·÷
Sew		+		+		+	+
For-class 2[e]							
Buy	+	+		+	+	+	+
Choose	+	+		+		+	+
Find	+	+		+	+		+
Get	+	+		+	+		+
Keep		+		+			+
Leave	+	+		+	+		+
Pick out		+		+			+

TABLE 4 – *continued*

	I.o. psv.	D.o. psv.	I.o. deln.	No i.o.	Under-stood i.o.	D.o. deln.	Pre-ceding i.o.
Save		+		+	+		+
[Spare]		+					+
Select		+		+		+	+
Steal	+	+		+	+	+	+

For-class 3

	I.o. psv.	D.o. psv.	I.o. deln.	No i.o.	Under-stood i.o.	D.o. deln.	Pre-ceding i.o.
Chant		+		+	+	+	+
Dance		+		+	+	+	+
Play		+		+	+	+	+
Recite	?	+		+	+	+	+
Sing	+	+		+	+	+	+
Whistle		+		+	+	+	+

For-class 4

	I.o. psv.	D.o. psv.	I.o. deln.	No i.o.	Under-stood i.o.	D.o. deln.	Pre-ceding i.o.
Earn		?			+		*f*
Gain		+			+		
Win		?			+		

For-class 5

	I.o. psv.	D.o. psv.	I.o. deln.	No i.o.	Under-stood i.o.	D.o. deln.	Pre-ceding i.o.
Capture		+		+	+		+
Crucify		+		+	+		+
Kill	+	+		+	+	+	+
Sacrifice	+	+		+	+	+	+
Slaughter	+	+		+	+	+	+
Take [a prisoner]		+		+	+		+

[a] + = No preposition allowed before indirect object.

[b] + + = Preposition must occur before indirect object.

[c] Membership in this class is dependent on assumptions that the activity is an artistic or creative one, and is relatively usual for the subject (cf. chapter 3, sec. c.3).

[d] The origin of expressions with absent but contextually reconstructible indirect objects has been impossible to determine.

[e] The acceptability of sentences with expressions of *for*-classes 2–5 with deleted indefinite indirect objects has been impossible to determine because it has been impossible to construct sentences where it is unambiguously an indefinite indirect object which has been deleted.

[f] Possibly, but only if the direct object is assumed to be an item of economic exchange (e.g. money).

Appendix II   The scope of adverbs and quantifiers with dative-movement constructions

Table 5 below summarizes the discussion in chapter 3, sec. C.7, concerning the scope and preposability of adverbials with dative-movement constructions. Some of the symbols in the chart require more explanation than the legend provides. The numerals at the left refer to semantic predicates. The numeral 1 refers to a predicate of causing, communicating, arranging, being obligated, making, selecting, performing, or doing, depending on the verb class under consideration. Where no slanted line occurs, the form or reading being considered occurs equally freely with internal or external indirect objects. If a mark occurs above a slanted line, the form or reading occurs only with an internal prepositionless indirect object. If a mark occurs below a slanted line, the form or reading occurs only with an external prepositional indirect object. A horizontal line distinguishes in a similar manner between two readings with *almost*.

215

TABLE 5   *The scope of adverbs and quantifiers with dative-movement constructions*

	1* Bring	2* Give	3* Send	4a* Radio	4b* Read	5† a. Promise b. Permit c. Assign d. Owe	1‡ Bake	2‡ Buy	3‡ Sing	4* Earn	5‡ Kill	
1	√P	√P				√P	√P	√P	√P		√P	**Time adverbs**
2										√P		
3												
1-(2)-3	√P	√P	√P	√P̄ / √P	√P	√ab						
1-2												
1	√P					√P	√P	√P	√P		√P	**Place adverbs**
2												
3										√P		
1-(2)-3	√P	√P	√P	√P	√P	√ab						
1-2		√P										
1		√P				√Pabc	√P	√P	√P		√P	**Source adverbs**
2	√											
3			√P									
1-(2)-3	√P		√P	√P	√P					√P		
1-2												
1	√P					√P	√P	√P	√P		√̄P̄	**Until-phrases**
2		√						√		√		
3		√	√							√P		
1-(2)-3	√P	√P	√P	√P	√P							
1-2												

						Almost
1		✓	✓	✓	✓	✓
2		✓	✓	✓	✓	
3	✓					
1-(2)-3	$\overline{\sqrt{M}{}^{a}}$				$\dfrac{\sqrt{}}{\sqrt{M}}$	ALMOST HAVE
1-2						HAVE ALMOST

						Again, another
1						
2						
3	√R	√R	√R	√R	√R	√R
1-(2)-3	✓	✓	✓	✓	✓	✓
1-2						

Legend: √ = occurs; √P = occurs and is preposable; *1 = CAUSE; †1 = COMMUNICATE, ARRANGE, or BE OBLIGATED; ‡1 = MAKE, SELECT, PERFORM, or DO; 2 = GO; 3 = HAVE; R = ANOTHER only; M = marginally.

Appendix III   Instrumental verb formation

The rule of instrumental verb formation has never to my knowledge been explicitly formulated, although some justification for it was given in Binnick 1968a, 1968c. Actually the term "instrumental" is a misnomer, for the relation in question involves actions related not only to instruments (hammer, file, etc.), as in (1):

    1a. Sheldon hammered the square peg into the round hole.
    1b. Wayne filed the metal smooth.

but also to other means (postal system, paint, etc.) as in (2):

    2a. Sheldon mailed the book from New York.
    2b. Wayne painted the MG purple.

and manners or modes of activity, as in (3):

    3a. Sheldon kicked Shirley into the river.
    3b. Wayne shot Marvin dead.

The argument in favor of a process forming so-called instrumental verbs from expressions with instrumental nouns, and/or from abstract representations of various actions which may be physically quite complex, but which are apparently rather simple cognitively, is as follows. Because these verbs take as complements directional phrases (as in 1a, 2a, and 3a) or resultative adjectives, as in (1b, 2b, and 3b), in addition to direct objects, and because they describe a change initiated by the subject in either (a) location, or (b) state, with respect to the direct object, they encode abstract notions which include predicates of causation, change, and location or state, as in (4):

    4a. Subject CAUSE direct object to $\begin{Bmatrix} \text{COME to BE} \\ \text{GO} \end{Bmatrix}$ Directional-Expression
        BY VERB-ing direct object.
    4b. Subject CAUSE direct object to COME to BE State BY VERB-ing direct object.

In almost every case, although there are exceptions, instrumental verbs occur also as simple transitive verbs, as in (5):

    5a. The blacksmith hammered the metal.
    5b. Wayne filed the metal.
    5c. Sheldon mailed the letter.
    5d. Sheldon painted the MG.
    5e. Sheldon kicked Shirley.
    5f. Sheldon shot Marvin.

which describe exactly the behavior used in bringing about the change in state or location in question. Some of the sentences (e.g. 5a–e) can be paraphrased with cognate nouns:

6a. The blacksmith worked (on) the metal with a hammer.
6b. Wayne worked on the metal with a file.
6c. Sheldon sent the book through the mails.
6d. Sheldon covered the MG with paint.
6e. Sheldon gave Shirley a kick.[1]

Others, such as (5f), describe a complex activity which has no suitable corresponding abstract or concrete noun. But this is really beside the point, since the relations I am concerned with are semantic in nature, not morphological. What is important for the claim that these verbs represent complex derived semantic structures is that the simple transitive verbs (as opposed to the homophonous instrumental verbs) do not take directional or state complements. To see this clearly, recall that transitive verbs may occur without direct objects in expressions referring to habitual or continuing activities, as in (7):

7a. We eat $\left\{\begin{array}{l}\text{dinner}\\ \text{food}\\ \text{whatever we have}\end{array}\right\}$ $\left\{\begin{array}{l}\text{at 7:00.}\\ \text{when we're hungry.}\\ \text{frequently.}\\ \text{quickly.}\end{array}\right\}$

7b. We eat $\left\{\begin{array}{l}\text{at 7:00.}\\ \text{when we're hungry.}\\ \text{frequently.}\\ \text{quickly.}\end{array}\right\}$

7c. The boys paint $\left\{\begin{array}{l}\text{cars}\\ \text{walls}\\ \text{pictures}\\ \text{whatever they can}\end{array}\right\}$ $\left\{\begin{array}{l}\text{on Saturday.}\\ \text{carefully.}\\ \text{whenever they're asked.}\end{array}\right\}$

7d. The boys paint $\left\{\begin{array}{l}\text{on Saturday.}\\ \text{carefully.}\\ \text{whenever they're asked.}\end{array}\right\}$

7e. The husbands clean $\left\{\begin{array}{l}\text{the houses}\\ \text{the kitchens}\\ \text{the cars}\\ \text{whatever needs it}\end{array}\right\}$ $\left\{\begin{array}{l}\text{on Fridays.}\\ \text{once a month.}\\ \text{only when they're told to.}\\ \text{very sloppily.}\end{array}\right\}$

7f. The husbands clean $\left\{\begin{array}{l}\text{on Fridays.}\\ \text{once a month.}\\ \text{only when they're told to.}\\ \text{very sloppily.}\end{array}\right\}$

---

[1] It is, of course, not clear whether the verb *kick* is derived from the noun, or vice versa, or whether neither is derived from the other.

In such constructions, where we can be sure it is the transitive sense, and not the "instrumental" sense we are dealing with, the verbs of (1–3) do not uniformly take directional or state complements:

8a. *Sheldon hammers into a hole very sloppily.
8b. *Wayne files smooth on Fridays.
8c. Sheldon mails from New York frequently.
8d. *Wayne paints purple whenever he is asked.
8e. ?Sheldon kicks into rivers carefully.
8f. *Wayne shoots dead when he is angry.

and, indeed, directional and state complements are characteristic of motion verbs and verbs of being, becoming, and changing, respectively, as in (9) and (10):

9a. The square peg went into the round hole.
9b. Sheldon sent the book from New York.
9c. Sheldon caused the book to go from New York.
9d. The ball went into the river.

10a. The metal became smooth.
10b. That is how the MG came to be purple.
10c. The vinegar turns the milk sour.

They do not occur indiscriminately with the verbs referred to as instrumental verbs, as (11) shows; directional complements are limited to verbs which describe changes in location effected by pragmatically restricted means or modes of activity, and state complements are limited to verbs which describe changes in state which are so caused.

11a. *Wayne painted the MG into the river.
11b. *Sheldon mailed the letter smooth.

It is assumed usually that transitive instrumental verb formation consists of jamming together into a single lexical item all the capitalized predicates in (4a) or (4b). The independently motivated rule of predicate-raising would account for the amalgamation of the predicates CAUSE, COME, BE (or GO), and sometimes the predicate describing the resultant state, as with *paint* and *clean*, into a single constituent, but I cannot say whether it could also put the verb of the instrumental-means-manner clause into this constituent, since I do not know what is the structure of sentences with such clauses, or what exactly is the structure of such clauses. Suffice it to say that there is evidence that instrumental verbs are complex semantically and syntactically, but that the precise formulation of an "instrumental verb"-formation rule depends crucially on knowledge of the structure of the "instrumental" clauses, and that knowledge is not now available to me.

What little I do know indicates that they are semantically more complex than is often thought. As is pointed out in chapter 4, sec. B, one can hammer something with a shoe, paint something with iodine, etc., so it would be wrong to say that the "instrumental" phrase consists of just (12).

12. 'BY USING NP (ON).'

Such a phrase would have to be qualified by an optional preceding 'as':

13. '(AS) BY USING NP (ON).'

Furthermore, instrumental verbs cannot be used to describe "non-standard" uses of instruments, methods, etc.; one cannot say, for example, *Joe radioed us the message* if he mailed us the message taped to a radio, or *Joe hammered the nail in* if he got it in by placing a hammer on it and leaning on the hammer to get it in, so an account of "instrumental" verbs must include or entail a disclaimer on the instrumental clause like (14):

14. 'in the usual manner, for the purpose for which it was designed'

or perhaps '...for which it was adopted' – cf. *We thumbed through the books* and *We thumbed to New York.*

One might imagine that the first-mentioned defect of (12) would be equally well remedied by something like (15):

15. 'BY USING (SOMETHING LIKE) NP (ON)'

But such a remedy would entail that (16)

16. He hammered the nail in with a shoe.

would mean 'by using something like a hammer on the nail, he caused the nail to go in with a shoe.' On the other hand, if it is claimed that the instrumental clauses are represented properly as (17):

17. 'BY USING NP$_{[actual\ object\ used]}$ AS NP$_{[instrument\ type]}$ (ON)'

one would not need to add a disclaimer like (14); a sentence like (18)

18. He hammered the nail in.

would be represented as something like 'by using a hammer as a hammer on the nail, he caused the nail to go in,' and a sentence like (16) would be 'by using a shoe as a hammer on the nail, he caused the nail to go in.' However, this analysis falsely predicts that sentences like (18) unambiguously indicate the use of the instrument lexically related to the "instrumental" verb; in chapter 4, sec. B, it is pointed out that such sentences are vague in regard to the actual instrument or means used. An optional 'as' constituent seems necessary to account for this vagueness, so a representation with the content of (19) is apparently indicated:

19. '(AS) BY USING NP (ON) in the usual manner, for the purpose for which it was designed'

Regarding the incorporation of the instrumental clause, there is some evidence that semantic information from the instrumental clause is copied into the causative verb, with the original clause then being deleted if it is identical to the instrumental constituent of the derived verb. This evidence is that when instrumental verbs occur with 'generic' or semantically predictable instrumental phrases, as in (20):

20. She painted the woodwork with paint.

they are unacceptably redundant, but when the instrumental phrases describe some noteworthy aspect of the instrument, means, manner, material, etc., as in (21):

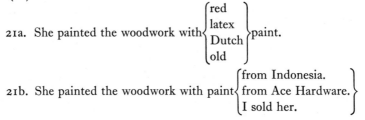

21a. She painted the woodwork with $\begin{Bmatrix} \text{red} \\ \text{latex} \\ \text{Dutch} \\ \text{old} \end{Bmatrix}$ paint.

21b. She painted the woodwork with paint $\begin{Bmatrix} \text{from Indonesia.} \\ \text{from Ace Hardware.} \\ \text{I sold her.} \end{Bmatrix}$

then they are not felt to be so redundant. It would be absurd to claim that the underlying representation of (21) was anything like the possibilities in (22):

22a. 'x CAUSED y to BECOME COATED BY USING PAINT ON y in the usual manner [etc.] BY USING RED [LATEX, . . . FROM INDONESIA, . . .] PAINT ON y.'

22b. 'x CAUSED y to BECOME COATED AS BY USING PAINT ON y in the usual manner [etc.] BY USING RED [LATEX, . . . FROM INDONESIA, . . .] PAINT ON y.'

and, in fact, the most plausible underlying semantic representation for (21) is (23):

23. 'x CAUSED y to BECOME COATED BY USING PAINT which was RED ON y in the usual manner [etc.].'

But if (23) is the underlying semantic representation for (21), then the token of 'USING PAINT' which is incorporated into the verb *paint* must be a copy of the token which occurs in the instrumental phrase, which is deleted when there is no qualifying phrase to distinguish it from the copied token. Thus in the derivation of (24):

24. She painted the woodwork.

there would be copying and then deletion of the original, while in the derivation of (21) there would be only copying.

If the conclusions I have drawn from the differences between (21) and (24) are correct, then both movement of semantic constituents (predicate-raising) and copying are involved in the derivation of "instrumental" verbs.[1]

---

[1] This argument was first put forth to my knowledge by Jerry Morgan, who distinguished between the "chopping rule" (predicate-raising) involved in the derivation of (1), and the copying and deletion rules required to derive (2):

It could be claimed that instrumental verbs are really nothing more than ordinary transitive verbs such as those cited in (5), and that *syntactic* rules of deletion and permutation transform *sentences* of the form of (25):

25a. NP_j cause+tense NP_i to come to be [Directional Expression] by verb+ing NP_i.

25b. NP_j cause+tense NP_i to go [Directional Expression] by verb+ing NP_i.

25c. NP_j cause+tense NP_i to come to be [State adjective] by verb+ing NP_i.

into sentences like (26):

26a. NP_j verb + tense NP_i [Directional Expression].

26b. NP_j verb + tense NP_i [State adjective].

It is doubtful, however, that such a rule could derive such instrumental causative verbs in English as *spirit*, as in (27):

27a. He spirited her away.

27b. He spirited her into the forest.

27c. He spirited her out of the room.

since English lacks a simple verb *spirit* (transitive or intransitive):

28a. *He spirited her.

28b. *He spirited.

At least one of the permutation and deletion rules would have to be normally optional but obligatory in exceptional cases, for a small closed class of "exceptional" verbs.

---

1. Ethelred decapitated Axelrod.

2. MacAdam asphalted the road.

on the basis of the difference in grammaticality between the sentences of (3) and those of (4):

3. *Ethelred decapitated Axelrod's $\begin{Bmatrix} \text{ugly} \\ \text{only} \\ \text{third} \\ \text{bloodied} \end{Bmatrix}$ head.

4. MacAdam asphalted the road with $\begin{Bmatrix} \text{hot} \\ \text{real} \\ \text{pure} \\ \text{O'Brien's} \\ \text{a ton of} \end{Bmatrix}$ asphalt.

Appendix IV   Properties of some idioms involving dative-movement expressions

TABLE 6   *Variation among idioms*

	Indirect object type				Is d.o. quantifiable?	If so, are there any NP which are OK as i.o.?	
	Internal		External			Internal	External
	Him	*It*	*Him*	*It*			
Give assistance	✓		✓		✓	✓	✓
Give attention					✓	✓	✓
Give birth			✓				
Give chase			✓				
(Give credence)							
Give substance		✓		✓	✓	✓	✓
Give support	✓	✓	✓	✓	✓	✓	✓
Give thought		✓			✓	✓	✓
Give voice				✓			
Give rein	✓				✓	✓	✓
Give rise				✓			
Give way			✓	✓			
Give a ring	✓						
Lend support	✓	✓	✓	✓	✓	✓	✓
Pay attention			✓	✓	✓	✓	✓
Pay heed			✓	✓			
Pay homage			✓				
Pay lip service				✓			
Bring word	✓		✓				
Send word	✓		✓				
Give a try		✓			✓	✓	

TABLE 7   *Variation within idioms*

Indirect object type	I.o. external only	I.o. internal only	Either position possible
Anaphoric pronoun		Give the ax Lend an ear Give a wide berth Give a ring[a] Drop a line Lend a hand[b]	Send word Bring word Read the riot act
Proper noun, name	Bring word	Give the ax Give a ring	Send word Lend a hand Read the riot act ?Lend an ear[c] Give a wide berth Drop a line
Article + noun	Bring word Read the riot act	Give the ax Give a ring	Send word ?Lend an ear Give a wide berth
Art. + adjective + noun	Bring word		Read the riot act Give the ax ?Lend an ear Give a wide berth Give a ring Send word

[a] *Give* here seems to be the same as in the third class of restricted *give*-expressions, but *ring* is used in a non-literal sense.

[b] This idiom appears to have the same constraints as the fourth class of *give*-expressions, although it is an idiom (neither *lend* nor *hand* have their usual meanings) whereas they are not.

[c] [?] indicates that both forms are equally bad.

Appendix V   Non-literal give-expressions

In order to approach the semantic representation of sentences with non-literal *give*-expressions, it is necessary to examine separately the groups mentioned in chapter 3, sec. c.2.*b*. Expressions of the first class, like *give someone a cold*, unlike other members of *to*-classes 1–3, do not denote the physical or legal transfer of an object, be it temporary or permanent. But, like the members of *to*-class 2, they do assert that the subject is the source of something described by the direct object, in this case a condition which the indirect object has come to have. In order to consider such expressions to have semantic representations similar to (165) it is necessary to understand HAVE as 'experience' rather than 'possess' or 'hold,' and CAUSE as being limited to being effected through relatively direct channels, since the expressions of this class are not appropriate to deviously indirect sorts of causation, as, for instance, if John caused Mary to come to have a cold by locking her out of the house and making her walk in the rain to the nearest phone a mile away, although they are appropriate to magically direct sorts of causation. We may say that a witch gave someone a cold, inferiority complex, black eye, sense of well-being, etc., even if we know that all she did was mutter a few magic words. We may then imagine that non-literal *give*-expressions of the first type have semantic representations on the order of (1):

1. Subject CAUSE$_{dir}$ indirect object to COME to HAVE$_{exp}$ direct object.

The subscripts on CAUSE and HAVE are not to be taken as serious proposals for semantic theory. They are *ad hoc* notations to describe the fact that the kinds of causation and having relevant here are restricted as specified, relative to the kinds of situations which the English words *cause* and *have* can sometimes refer to. For other examples of similar restrictions, cf. chapters 3, sec. c.6.*d*. and 4, sec. B. It may be the case that there are simply a small number of psychologically distinct and linguistically "prime" notions which describe causal relations, and whose distinctions are frequently neutralized in the causative morphemes and lexicons of most languages. Or, it may be the case that the notions of causation and having are psychologically "primes," and that these distinct notions are structurally complex in such a way that there is linguistic evidence for this complexity. This would imply a semantic representation in which the various HAVEs might be distinguished as, for example, HAVE the OBJECT, HAVE the CONDITION, HAVE the CONVICTION, etc. Investigating the psychological and linguistic evidence for such structures is unfortunately beyond the scope of the present endeavor.

Restricted *give*-expressions of the second class, such as *give someone a bath*, have been analyzed by Cattell (1970) as originating in dative constructions with "empty" non-stative verbs, as in (2):

2. John [+ V, −stative] a bath to the baby.

which must undergo a dative-movement rule before being subject to an optional rule which incorporates the "empty" verb and its no longer adjacent direct object into a single constituent, to produce ultimately sentences like (4) from structures which also underly sentences like (3):[1]

3a. John gave the baby a bath.
3b. John gave Harry a punch in the nose.
3c. John gave Harry a hearty handshake.

4a. John bathed the baby.
4b. John punched Harry in the nose.
4c. John shook Harry's hand heartily.

If this rule does not apply, *give* is inserted, Cattell claims, for the "empty" verb. He is correct in observing that the verb *give* does not add anything to the characterization of the action which is provided in such expressions by the direct object, but I think he is wrong in claiming that *give* is lexically empty. It identifies the subject as the agent or immediate source of the activity which is only vaguely referred to by the direct object noun phrase. The verb *give* specifies that the activity involves the subject and the indirect object, and not the indirect object and some unspecified person, or two unspecified entities. If there was really only an empty node underlying *give*, why couldn't *x gave y a bath* mean something like *x mentioned a bath to y*, rather than what it does mean? I am unprepared to propose a semantic representation for these expressions, or even to say whether or not forms like (4) resemble the semantic representation more closely than forms like (3), but I am certain that *give* here has *some* semantic content.

None of the members of the third class of restricted *give*-expressions has a paraphrase with a verb cognate to the direct object of the *give*-expression. Although the interpersonal behavior of the subject toward the indirect object which these expressions describe is often of a linguistic nature, strictly speaking, expressions of this class (e.g. *x gave y a piece of x's mind* and *x gave y some flak*) do not assert that x communicated something to y; they assert the occurrence of a particular kind of communication from x to y. Since expressions like *give someone some assistance*, *give someone a rough time*, *give someone a*

---

[1] Apparently this rule does not apply to some direct objects consisting of a noun and a modifier. For instance, while (3b,c) have counterparts in (4b,c) an expression like (1):

    1. John gave Harry a well-deserved punch in the nose.

has no such counterpart:

    2a. *John well-deservedly punched Harry in the nose.
    2b. *John punched Harry in the nose well-deservedly.
    2c. *John punched Harry well-deservedly in the nose.

dirty look exhibit similar syntactic properties, this class should probably be defined to include non-linguistic interpersonal directed behavior as well; one can give someone a rough time without ever saying or even hearing a word. The existence of a common English paraphrase with *have* or even *get* for these expressions is dubious, but in all cases they describe non-physical intentional behavior of the subject toward an indirect object which is assumed to be human, like the subject, or at least capable of being affected by the subject's production of whatever it is that the direct object denotes. It is true that in most cases, the direct object is not meant to be interpreted literally (e.g. flak, a piece of one's mind, rough time, dirty look), but I hesitate to call these *give*-expression idioms, since they seem to be definable as a class, and the class seems to be an open one.

Like the expressions of the third class, those of the fourth class (e.g. *give someone an idea*) must be such that the subject of *give* is represented as the source of the impression, idea, or whatever which the indirect object comes to have, and which is denoted by the direct object. Expressions of this class, however, have only non-volitional abstract subjects, while class 3 expressions as I have delimited them have only volitional animate subjects, so they cannot have the exact same semantic representation as class 3 expressions, if a distinction is to be drawn. Furthermore, these expressions describe an ultimate source, rather than an immediate one, and the effect that is described by the direct object, rather than being one which is imposed on the indirect object by the subject, is one that comes about through natural mental processes in the indirect object. I do not think it would be rash to suppose that expressions of this fourth class have semantic representations on the order of (5):

5. Subject CAUSE indirect object to COME$_{nat}$ to HAVE direct object.

The precise semantic representation of the fifth class of *give*-expressions poses a very interesting problem. If the semantic representation of, for example, (6a)

6a. Mary gave John a look at her etchings.

is something like (7), as suggested in Cattell 1970

7. $_s$[Mary [allow][$_s$John have a look at Mary's etchings]$_s$ to John]$_s$.

a curious paradox arises. *Give* as used in the expressions of this class is an *if*-verb; that is, if (6a) is true, then (6b) must also be, but even if (8a) is true, (8b) is not necessarily true.

6b. John had a look at Mary's etchings.

8a. Mary didn't give John a look at her etchings.
8b. John didn't have a look at Mary's etchings.

But the English verb *allow* is not at all implicative; (9a) doesn't imply (9b) any more than (10a) implies (10b);

9a. Mary allowed John to have a look at her etchings.
9b. John had a look at Mary's etchings.

10a. Mary didn't allow John to have a look at her etchings.
10b. John didn't have a look at Mary's etchings.

Sentence (9a) may be continued *but he declined,* and (10a) may be continued *so he broke into her apartment when she wasn't there in order to see them.* The English word *cause* is an *if*-verb like *give* in these expressions, but a sentence like (6a) simply doesn't mean what is asserted in (11):

11. Mary caused John to have a look at her etchings.

There is, however, a verb which like *cause* and *give* is an *if*-verb, and which, with *have, get,* or *take,* does come close to paraphrasing these expressions, namely *let,* as in (12):

12a. Mary let John have a look at her etchings.
12b. Subject LET indirect object HAVE direct object.

I should point out here that all I have done in proposing (12b) rather than something abstracted from (7) or (11) as a schema for semantic representations for sentences of this class is to reduce the present problem to a previously unsolved problem, for I am unable to specify precisely what *let* means as used in (12a), and how it is related to causing and allowing.

Works cited

Alexander, D. & Kunz, W. J. (1964). *Some classes of verbs in English*. Indiana University Linguistic Research Project Report. Reproduced as CFSTI document PB 166 561. Springfield, Virginia: Clearing-house for Federal Scientific and Technical Information.

Austin, J. L. (1956). 'A plea for excuses', *Proceedings of the Aristotelian Society*. Reprinted in his *Philosophical papers* (1961), edited by J. O. Urmson and G. J. Warnock, 123–52. London: Oxford University Press.

Bach, Emmon (1968). 'Nouns and noun phrases', in *Universals in linguistic theory*, edited by Emmon Bach and Robert T. Harms, 91–122. New York: Holt, Rinehart and Winston, Inc.

(1969). 'Anti-pronominalization'. Austin, Texas (mimeographed).

(Forthcoming). Binding.

Becker, A. L. & Arms, D. G. (1969). 'Prepositions as predicates', in *Papers from the Fifth Regional Meeting, Chicago Linguistic Society*, edited by Robert I. Binnick, *et al.*, 1–11. Chicago: Department of Linguistics, University of Chicago.

Binnick, Robert I. (1968a). 'On the nature of the "lexical item"' in *Papers from the Fourth Regional Meeting, Chicago Linguistic Society*, edited by Bill J. Darden, Charles-James N. Bailey, and Alice Davison, 1–13. Chicago: Department of Linguistics, University of Chicago.

(1968b). 'The characterization of abstract lexical items.' N.p. (duplicated).

(1968c). 'On transformationally derived verbs in a grammar of English.' N.p. (duplicated).

Bloch, Bernard (1941). 'Phonemic overlapping', *American speech* 16:278–84. Reprinted in *Readings in linguistics* 1, 4th ed. (1966), edited by Martin Joos, 93–6. Chicago: University of Chicago Press.

Cattell, Ray (1970). 'The role of *give* and some related verbs in English syntax'. Unpublished Ph.D. dissertation, University of Newcastle, Australia.

Chomsky, Noam (1957). *Syntactic structures* (Janua linguarum, 4). The Hague: Mouton and Co.

(1965). *Aspects of the theory of syntax*. Cambridge, Massachusetts: M.I.T. Press.

Chomsky, Noam & Halle, Morris (1968). *The sound pattern of English*. New York: Harper and Row.

Collingwood, R. G. (1940). *An essay on metaphysics*. London: Oxford University Press.

Dixon R. M. W. (1970). 'The semantics of giving'. Canberra (duplicated). (To appear in the *Proceedings of the International Colloquium on Formalization and models of linguistics*.)

Fillmore, Charles (1963). 'The position of embedding transformations in a grammar', *Word* 19:208–31.

(1965). *Indirect object constructions in English and the ordering of transformations* (Monographs on linguistic analysis, 1). The Hague: Mouton and Co.

(1966). 'Deictic categories in the semantics of "come"'. *Foundations of language* 2:219–27.

(1968). 'The case for case', in *Universals in linguistic theory*, edited by Emmon Bach and Robert T. Harms, 1–88. New York: Holt, Rinehart, and Winston, Inc.

(1969). 'Verbs of judging: an exercise in semantic description', *Papers in linguistics* 1:91–117.

Geis, Michael M. & Zwicky, Arnold M. (1971). 'On invited inferences', *Linguistic inquiry* 2:561–6.

Gildersleeve, B. L. & Lodge, Gonzalez (1895). *Latin grammar.* 3rd ed. London: Macmillan.

Green, Georgia M. (1969a). 'Some theoretical implications of the expression of emphatic conjunction'. Chicago (duplicated).

(1969b). 'On the notion "related lexical entry"', in *Papers from the Fifth Regional Meeting, Chicago Linguistic Society*, edited by Robert I. Binnick, et al., 76–88. Chicago: Department of Linguistics, University of Chicago.

(1970). 'How abstract is surface structure?' in *Papers from the Sixth Regional Meeting, Chicago Linguistic Society*, 270–81. Chicago: Chicago Linguistic Society.

(To appear). 'A syntactic syncretism in English and French', to appear in *Papers in linguistics in honor of Henry and Renée Kahane*, edited by Braj B. Kachru *et al.*, Urbana, Ill.: University of Illinois Press.

Gruber, Jeffrey S. (1965). 'Studies in lexical relations'. Unpublished Ph.D. dissertation, Massachusetts Institute of Technology.

(1967). *Functions of the lexicon in formal descriptive grammars.* Santa Monica, California: System Development Corporation.

Halliday, M. A. K. (1967–8). 'Notes on transitivity and theme', *Journal of linguistics* 3:37–81, 199–244; 4:179–216.

Hockett, Charles (1942). 'A system of descriptive phonology', *Language* 18:3–21. Reprinted in *Readings in linguistics* 1, 4th ed. (1966), edited by Martin Joos, 97–108. Chicago: University of Chicago Press.

Householder, Fred (1965). *Linguistic analysis of English.* Indiana University Linguistic Research Project Report. Reproduced as CFSTI document PB 167 950. Springfield, Virginia: Clearinghouse for Federal Scientific and Technical Information.

Joos, Martin (ed.) (1966). *Readings in linguistics* 1. 4th ed. Chicago: University of Chicago Press.

Karttunen, Lauri (1969). 'Migs and pilots'. Austin, Texas (duplicated).

(1970a). 'On the semantics of complement sentences', in *Papers from the Sixth Regional Meeting, Chicago Linguistic Society*, 328–39. Chicago: Chicago Linguistic Society.

(1970b). 'Implicative verbs', *Language* 47:340–58.

Katz, Jerrold & Fodor, Jerry (1963). 'The structure of a semantic theory', *Language* 39:170–210.

Keyser, S. J. (1968). Review of Sven Jakobson, 'Adverbial positions in English', *Language* 44:357–74.

Kim, Chin-Wu (1970). 'Two phonological notes: A# and B^b.' Urbana, Illinois (duplicated). To appear in *Contributions to generative phonology*, edited by M. Brame.

Kiparsky, Paul & Kiparsky, Carol (1970). 'Fact', in *Progress in linguistics*, edited by Manfred Bierwisch and K. E. Heidolph, 141–73. The Hague: Mouton and Co.

Kisseberth, Charles W. (1969). 'On the role of derivational constraints in phonology'. Urbana, Illinois (mimeographed).

(1970a). 'On the functional unity of phonological rules', *Linguistic inquiry* 1:291–306.

(1970b). 'The Tunica stress conspiracy'. To appear in *Linguistic inquiry*.

Klima, Edward S. (1964). 'Negation in English', in *The structure of English; readings in the philosophy of language*, edited by Jerry A. Fodor and Jerrold J. Katz, 246–323. Englewood Cliffs, New Jersey: Prentice-Hall, Inc.

Lakoff, George (1965). 'On the nature of syntactic irregularity'. Indiana University Ph.D. dissertation. Published as *Mathematical linguistics and automatic translation*, Report NSF-16 to the National Science Foundation. Cambridge, Massachusetts: Computation Laboratory of Harvard University. Reprinted (1970) as *Irregularity in syntax*. New York: Holt, Rinehart, and Winston, Inc.

(1966). 'Deep and surface grammar'. Cambridge, Massachusetts (mimeographed).

(1968). 'Pronouns and reference'. Cambridge, Massachusetts (mimeographed).

(1969a). 'Presuppositions and relative grammaticality', in *Studies in philosophical linguistics*, series 1, edited by William Todd, 103–16. Evanston, Illinois: Great Expectations.

(1969b). 'On derivational constraints', in *Papers from the Fifth Regional Meeting, Chicago Linguistic Society*, edited by Robert I. Binnick, et al., 117–39. Chicago: Department of Linguistics, University of Chicago.

(1970). 'Global rules', *Language* 46:627–39.

(1971). 'On generative semantics', in *Semantics: An interdisciplinary reader in philosophy, psychology, linguistics, and anthropology*, edited by Danny Steinberg and Leon Jakobovits. London: Cambridge University Press.

Lakoff, George & Ross, John R. (1966). *A criterion for verb phrase constituency. Mathematical linguistics and automatic translation*. Report NSF-17 to the National Science Foundation. Cambridge, Massachusetts: Computation Laboratory of Harvard University.

Lakoff, Robin (1968). *Abstract syntax and Latin complementation* (Research monograph series, 49). Cambridge, Massachusetts: M.I.T. Press.

   (1969). 'A syntactic argument for negative transportation', in *Papers from the Fifth Regional Meeting, Chicago Linguistic Society*, edited by Robert I. Binnick *et al.*, 140–7. Chicago: Department of Linguistics, University of Chicago.

Langacker, Ronald (1969). 'Pronominalization and the chain of command', in *Modern studies in English*, edited by David A. Reibel and Sanford A. Schane, 160–86. Englewood Cliffs, New Jersey: Prentice-Hall.

Lees, Robert B. (1963). *The grammar of English nominalizations* [3rd printing]. Bloomington, Indiana: Indiana University Research Center in Anthropology, Folklore, and Linguistics. Reissued (1968). The Hague: Mouton and Co.

Lehrer, Adrienne (1969). 'Semantic cuisine', *Journal of linguistics* 5:39–56.

Lindholm, James M. (1969). 'Negative-raising and sentence pronominalization', in *Papers from the Fifth Regional Meeting, Chicago Linguistic Society*, edited by Robert I. Binnick *et al.*, 148–58. Chicago: Department of Linguistics, University of Chicago.

Lyons, John (1968). *Introduction to theoretical linguistics*. London: Cambridge University Press.

McCawley, James D. (1967a). 'Meaning and the description of languages', *Kotoba no uchū* 2:10–18, 38–48, 51–7.

   (1967b). 'The annotated respective'. Chicago (mimeographed).

   (1968a). 'The role of semantics in a grammar', in *Universals in linguistic theory*, edited by Emmon Bach and Robert T. Harms, 124–69. New York: Holt, Rinehart and Winston, Inc.

   (1968b). 'Concerning the base component of a transformational grammar', *Foundations of language* 4:243–69.

   (1968c). 'Lexical insertion in a transformational grammar without deep structure', in *Papers from the Fourth Regional Meeting, Chicago Linguistic Society*, edited by Bill J. Darden, Charles-James N. Bailey, and Alice Davison, 71–80. Chicago: Department of Linguistics, University of Chicago.

   (1970a). 'Where do noun phrases come from?' in *Readings in English transformational grammar*, edited by Roderick A. Jacobs and Peter S. Rosenbaum, 166–83. Waltham, Massachusetts: Ginn and Co.

   (1970b). 'English as a VSO language', *Language* 46:286–99.

Makkai, Valerie Becker (1969). 'On the correlation of morphemes and lexemes', in *Papers from the Fifth Regional Meeting, Chicago Linguistic Society*, edited by Robert I. Binnick *et al.*, 159–66. Chicago: Department of Linguistics, University of Chicago.

Mathesius, Vilém (1928). 'On linguistic characterology, with illustrations from modern English', in *Actes du Premier Congrès International de Linguistes à la Haye*, 56–63. Reprinted (1964) in *A Prague School reader in linguistics*, compiled by Josef Vachek, 59–67. Bloomington, Indiana: Indiana University Press.

Morgan, Jerry L. (1968). 'Irving'. Urbana, Illinois (duplicated).

(1969a). 'On arguing about semantics', *Papers in linguistics* 1:49–70.

(1969b). 'On the treatment of presupposition in transformational grammar', in *Papers from the Fifth Regional Meeting, Chicago Linguistic Society*, edited by Robert I. Binnick *et al.*, 167–77. Chicago: Department of Linguistics, University of Chicago.

(1970). 'On the criterion of identity for noun phrase deletion', in *Papers from the Sixth Regional Meeting, Chicago Linguistic Society*, 380–9. Chicago: Chicago Linguistic Society.

(Forthcoming). 'Presuppositional structure'.

Pedersen, Holger (1931). *The discovery of language; linguistic science in the 19th century*, translated by John Webster Spargo. Reprinted (1962). Bloomington, Indiana: Indiana University Press.

Perlmutter, David M. (1968). *Deep and surface structure constraints in syntax*. Ph.D. dissertation, Massachusetts Institute of Technology. Published 1971. New York: Holt, Rinehart and Winston, Inc.

Postal, Paul M. (1968). *Cross-over phenomena* [published 1971]. New York: Holt, Rinehart and Winston, Inc.

(1969). 'Anaphoric islands', *Papers from the Fifth Regional Meeting, Chicago Linguistic Society*, edited by Robert I. Binnick *et al.*, 205–39. Chicago: Department of Linguistics, University of Chicago.

(1970). 'On coreferential complement subject deletion', *Linguistic inquiry* 1:439–500.

Quirk, Randolph (1965). 'Descriptive statement and serial relationship', *Language* 41:205–17.

Rosenbaum, Peter S. (1967). The grammar of English predicate complement constructions. (Research monograph series, 47). Cambridge, Massachusetts: M.I.T. Press.

Ross, John R. (1967). 'Constraints on variables in syntax'. Unpublished Ph.D. dissertation, Massachusetts Institute of Technology.

(1969). 'The noun phrase stress conspiracy'. Cambridge, Massachusetts (duplicated).

Searle, John R. (1969). 'Assertions and aberrations', *Symposium on J. L. Austin*, edited by K. T. Fann, 205–18. London: Routledge and Kegan Paul.

Vendler, Zeno (1967). 'Verbs and times', *Linguistics in philosophy*, 97–121. Ithaca, New York: Cornell University Press.

Zwicky, Arnold M. (1968). 'Naturalness arguments in syntax', *Papers from the Fourth Regional Meeting of the Chicago Linguistic Society*, edited by Bill J. Darden, Charles-James N. Bailey, and Alice Davison, 94–102. Chicago: Department of Linguistics, University of Chicago.

(1971). 'In a manner of speaking', *Linguistic inquiry* 2:223–32.

Index